Writing the Global City

Over the last three decades, our understanding of the city worldwide has been revolutionised by three innovative theoretical concepts – globalisation, post-colonialism and a radically contested notion of modernity. The idea and even the reality of the city has been extended out of the state and nation and re-positioned in the larger global world.

In this book Anthony King brings together key essays written over this period, much of it dominated by debates about the world or global city. Challenging assumptions and silences behind these debates, King provides largely ignored historical and cultural dimensions to the understanding of world city formation as well as decline. Interdisciplinary and comparative, the essays address new ways of framing contemporary themes: the imperial and colonial origin of the contemporary world and global cities, actually existing postcolonialisms, claims about urban and cultural homogenisation and the role of architecture and built environment in that process. Also addressed are arguments about indigenous and exogenous perspectives, Eurocentricism, ways of framing vernacular architecture, and the global historical sociology of building types. Wide-ranging and accessible, *Writing the Global City* provides essential historical contexts and theoretical frameworks for understanding contemporary urban and architectural debates. Extensive bibliographies make it essential for teaching, reference and research.

Anthony D. King is Emeritus Professor of Art History and of Sociology at Binghamton University, State University of New York, USA, and now lives in the UK. He has been Visiting Professor of Architecture at University of California, Berkeley, USA, and was, for five years, Professor of Humanities and Social Sciences at the Indian Institute of Technology, New Delhi, India.

THE ARCHI*TEXT* SERIES

Edited by Thomas A. Markus and Anthony D. King

Architectural discourse has traditionally represented buildings as art objects or technical objects. Yet buildings are also social objects in that they are invested with social meaning and shape social relations. Recognizing these assumptions, the Architext series aims to bring together recent debates in social and cultural theory and the study and practice of architecture and urban design. Critical, comparative and interdisciplinary, the books in the series, by theorizing architecture, bring the space of the built environment centrally into the social sciences and humanities, as well as bringing the theoretical insights of the latter into the discourses of architecture and urban design. Particular attention is paid to issues of gender, race, sexuality and the body, to questions of identity and place, to the cultural politics of representation and language, and to the global and postcolonial contexts in which these are addressed.

Framing Places
Mediating power in built form
Kim Dovey

Gender Space Architecture
An Interdisciplinary introduction
Edited by Jane Rendell, Barbara Penner and Iain Borden

Behind the Postcolonial
Architecture, urban space and political cultures in Indonesia
Abidin Kusno

The Architecture of Oppression
The SS, forced labor and the Nazi monumental building economy
Paul Jaskot

Words Between the Spaces
Buildings and language
Thomas A. Markus and Deborah Cameron

Embodied Utopias
Gender, social change and the modern metropolis
Rebeccah Zorach, Lise Sanders and Amy Bingaman

Writing Spaces
Discourses of architecture, urbanism and the built environment
C. Greig Crysler

Drifting – Migrancy and Architecture
Edited by Stephen Cairns

Beyond Description
Singapore, space, historicity
Edited by Ryan Bishop, John Phillips and Wei-Wei Yeo

Spaces of Global Cultures
Architecture urbanism identity
Anthony D. King

Indigenous Modernities
Negotiating architecture and urbanism
Jyoti Hosagrahar

Moderns Abroad
Architecture, cities and Italian imperialism
Mia Fuller

Anthony D. King

Writing the Global City

Globalisation, postcolonialism
and the urban

LONDON AND NEW YORK

First edition published 2016
by Routledge
2 Park Square, Milton Park, Abingdon, Oxon OX14 4RN

and by Routledge
711 Third Avenue, New York, NY 10017

Routledge is an imprint of the Taylor & Francis Group, an informa business

British Library Cataloguing in Publication Data
A catalogue record for this book is available from the British Library

Library of Congress Cataloging in Publication Data
Names: King, Anthony D., author.
Title: Writing the global city : globalisation, postcolonialism and the urban / Anthony D. King.
Description: Abingdon, Oxon ; New York, NY : Routledge, [2016] | Includes bibliographical references and index.
Identifiers: LCCN 2015041863 | ISBN 9781138949560 (hardback : alk. paper) | ISBN 9781138949584 (pbk. : alk. paper) | ISBN 9781315668970 (ebook)
Subjects: LCSH: Urbanization. | Urban economics. | Sociology, Urban. | Postcolonialism. | Globalization.
Classification: LCC HT361 .K5673 2016 | DDC 307.76--dc23
LC record available at http://lccn.loc.gov/2015041863

ISBN: 978-1-138-94956-0 (hbk)
ISBN: 978-1-138-94958-4 (pbk)
ISBN: 978-1-315-66897-0 (ebk)

Typeset in Frutiger
by Saxon Graphics Ltd, Derby

Printed and bound in Great Britain by
TJ International Ltd, Padstow, Cornwall

To Ursula, the family,
and
friends, colleagues and graduate students
at Binghamton University 1988–2005,
and remembering
Barbara Abou-El-Haj
(1943–2015)

Contents

Defining contemporary and historical cities

Illustrations

Preface

The origins of this book are to be found in some persuasive comments of my good friend and one-time Art History colleague at Binghamton University, Nancy Um, at a convivial celebration held there in October 2013. With the help of the library, Nancy had excavated various papers I'd published in some lesser known publications, which she thought would help make a useful book for teaching purposes.

In the event, what has emerged is a combination of some of these papers, plus various contributions to edited books, put together either from conferences or from themed collections. I also have to thank Nancy for the title, *Writing the Global City*, which helped give the book some additional direction. Three generous (and anonymous) reviewers also gave me some valuable suggestions, most of which I have taken on board.

The chapters address a number of themes, of which the most important is the imperial/colonial origin of world and global cities. Other topics include: colonial architecture and urbanism; cities and the world economy; imperial and global cities; the global sociology of building types; postcolonial criticism; the historical framing of vernacular architecture; imperialism, world cities and the grand hotel; and the connection of globalisation to the homogenisation of architecture worldwide. The different disciplinary vocabularies used to explore these themes include those of sociology, architectural, urban and planning history, geography and postcolonial studies. Putting together previously published papers almost certainly leads – despite all efforts – to some repetition. For this, I apologise and ask for the reader's patience.

Although the essays were written between 1989 – the year after I joined Binghamton University – and 2015, the period they cover is mainly from the 1950s until the present. The 15 essays are divided into three parts and are (largely) in the order in which they were written. Apart from Chapters 7 and 9, which are shorter versions of the original essays, and a few minute changes to some of the opening sentences, spelling, reference styles and citation format, all the papers are as originally written and published.

Acknowledgements

Most of the chapters in this book have come either from invitations to speak or write, or from papers written for conferences. As such I owe my thanks to a number of conference organisers and also hosts for their kindness and hospitality, in particular: for Chapter 1, John Archer, for his invitation to speak on the topic of 'Architecture, Capital and the Globalisation of Culture' at the University of Minnesota, Minneapolis, 1989; for Chapter 2, to Michael Harlowe, for the invitation to guest edit an issue of the *International Journal of Urban and Regional Research*, on the topic of 'Colonial Cities', 1989; for Chapter 3, to Nicholas Dirks, for his invitation to write a review article for *Comparative Studies in Society and History* on the theme of 'Writing Colonial Space', 1995; for Chapter 4, to Paul Knox and Peter Taylor, for their invitation to a conference on 'World Cities in a World-System', at the Center for Innovative Technology, near Washington, DC, 1993; for Chapter 5, to Gary Bridge and Sophie Watson for their invitation to write on 'Postcolonialism, Representation and the City' in an edited collection, *A Companion to the City*, 2000; for Chapter 6, to Jan Nederveen Pieterse for his invitation to a conference on 'Global Futures: Shaping Globalization' at the Institute of Social Studies, The Hague, 1997; for Chapter 7, to Ryan Bishop, John Phillips and Wei Wei Yeo, for their invitation to a conference on 'Perpetuating Cities' at the National University of Singapore, 2001; for Chapter 8, to Warren Hofstra and Camille Wells, for their invitation to the 25th Anniversary meeting of the Vernacular Architecture Forum, Tucson, Arizona, 2005; for Chapter 9, to Helmuth Berking, for his invitation to a conference at the Technical University of Darmstadt on the theme of 'Negotiating Urban Conflicts', 2005; for Chapter 10, to Michael Guggenheim and Ola Söderström for their invitation to a conference on 'Urban Artefacts: Types, Practices and Circulations', University of Neuchatel, 2007, and also to Rob Shields, for his invitation to speak on the same topic at the University of Alberta, Edmonton, March 2009; for Chapter 11, to Peter Taylor for his invitation to contribute to an edited collection on the *International Handbook of Globalisation and World Cities*, 2012; for Chapter 12, to Laura Kolbe, for her invitation to a workshop on 'Grand Hotels: Global Perspectives and Local

Experience', at the Centre for Metropolitan Studies, Technical University of Berlin, and to Dorothee Brantz, for her invitation to stay as a Visiting Scholar during August 2013; for Chapter 13, to Farrokh Derakhshani, for his invitation to the Aga Khan Award for Architecture workshop on the 'Homogeneity of Representations', University of British Columbia, Vancouver, 2009; for Chapter 14, to Rob Kitchin and Nigel Thrift, for their invitation to contribute to the *International Encyclopaedia of Human Geography*, 2009; and for Chapter 15, to Roland Robertson and Jan Aart Scholte, for their invitation to contribute to the *Encyclopedia of Globalisation*, 2006.

As always, I have greatly benefited from the comments of Abidin Kusno on many, if not all, of these papers; others have been improved by the suggestions of Ursula King, who has also helped in ways too numerous to mention. In the spring of 1991, not long after I moved to Binghamton, Nezar Alsayyad invited me to U.C. Berkeley to teach two courses to his graduate students; this was not only a rewarding and enjoyable experience at the time but, serendipitously, it enabled me to meet some of what were to become the next generation of colonial architecture and urbanism scholars. Other friends have, sometimes unknowingly, helped to keep the wheels turning, particularly Rob Home, Alex Bremner, Jiat-Hwee Chang, and especially Mike Safier. At Routledge, Fran Ford has given me excellent support and both Grace Harrison and Christina O'Brien have given excellent assistance. My many thanks to all. In the decade or more since leaving Binghamton in 2004, some dozen Archi*text* authors have kept co-editor Tom Markus and I in touch with leading-edge interdisciplinary scholarship. My many thanks to Tom for his valuable comments on this book as well as 20 years of rich and friendly exchanges in regard to the Archi*text* series. Frances King has provided excellent technical support. Without my graduate students, friends and colleagues at Binghamton University, and especially Nancy Um, the book wouldn't have happened.

Introduction

What is the point of re-publishing essays which, like some of those in Part I, were written 15 or even 25 years ago? First, they document changes that have taken place in urban and architectural studies over these three decades. Second, they can show us not only what has changed in these 30 years, but also what's remained the same. Third, they provide some background for the later essays and should be of historiographical interest.

How do we bring the issues discussed in these early (Part I) chapters up to date? Where are we now in terms of scholarship, beyond the first generation of 'colonial city' scholars whose work I discuss in Chapter 3? Initially I had envisaged producing a lengthy annotated bibliography providing the reader with a 'state of the art' account of research in this multifaceted field. However, so extensive is the amount of relevant literature today, especially given the number and variety of disciplinary fields drawn upon, that nothing short of a hefty monograph would suffice.

Instead, in this introductory section, I draw on four relatively recent books or journals (i.e. from c.2005 onwards), which are either collections of essays or review essays with extensive bibliographies, which, were I preparing a two-semester graduate seminar on the topic of colonial and postcolonial architecture and urbanism, would provide a wealth of relevant sources. From each collection, I have chosen one item (and author), representative of the whole and which I have discussed or, alternatively, have simply reproduced verbatim. These I regard as representative of current thinking in regard to particular topics.

The essays address four themes, the first of which concerns the origin of studying cities and the urban 'in global context'. When did urbanists start thinking globally? What circumstances brought this about? And what difference has it made to our scholarship?

CITIES IN GLOBAL CONTEXT

> It is only … since the early 1980s that urban scholars have begun to explore the question of how global forces and dynamics impact local and regional social space.
>
> (Brenner and Keil 2006:5)

> Studies of cities in global context have been around almost as long as scholars have been studying cities.
>
> (Davis 2005:92)

I first began research on colonial urbanism and architecture in New Delhi early in 1970. Finding an appropriate theoretical framework which enabled the spaces and built environment of both imperial and colonised societies to be considered as a single entity was a serious challenge. In the conceptual language of the day, India was part of the 'Third World', not, as today, the 'Global South'. As Davis points out in her comprehensive account (on which I draw extensively in the following), 'Third World' urban studies at this time were characterised by social, economic and urban problems – informal settlements, urban marginality, physical and economic polarisation, among others. There was a 'macroeconomic framework [but] … it did not extend to the global context' (Davis 2005:95). Patterns of urbanisation were to be explained by reference to *national* forces and conditions, not 'global' ones. Things changed in the 1980s with the adoption of ideas of 'dependency' and, reflecting Immanuel Wallerstein's influence, the 'world-systemic' context of 'Third World' cities and urbanisation. Ten years later, however, ideas about 'globalisation' had caught on and, by then, according to Davis, there were 'very few scholars who didn't take the global context as a key frame' (p.97), but for studying 'Third World' urbanisation rather than 'the world' as such. Architectural issues rarely came into this realm of urban theory, however theorised. Well down the agenda, they were subsumed under the vocabulary of the 'built environment' and 'physical and spatial urban form'.

With the fall of the Berlin Wall in 1989, the collapse of the Soviet Union (1991), the end of the Cold War and the worldwide popularity of neo-liberalism, the global context was to change dramatically. The breaking down of protectionist economic policies and acceleration of world trade were to bode well for the study of global cities. Most important, the collapse of the 'Second World' meant that the 'Three Worlds' metaphor was no longer valid. Added to this, the World Wide Web of Tim Berners Lee (1991) was to give a huge economic and also ideological boost to the global economy (Davis 2005:98). The nomenclature of 'global city' – a term that had been around for some time (see Chapter 15) – began to be applied to the world's major economic centres, New York, London and Tokyo, and was especially boosted by the circulation of Saskia Sassen's influential book, *The Global City* (1991). An alternative account of these developments is given in Adam's *The Globalisation of Modern Architecture*, where he refers to the years 1989–1993 as marking a 'New Global Era' (2013:75). The main argument of my own book,

Global Cities (1990a), however, was in the subtitle, Postimperialism and the Internationalisation of London, and also in that of its companion volume, Urbanism, Colonialism and the World Economy (1990b).

THE 'WEST' AND ALTERNATE URBAN VISIONS

> The 'West' remains the subject of urban theory, even when the putative object of discussion is a city 'beyond the West'. The un-namable region carries in its more typically used designation as 'non-West' the burden of difference, of being the 'reverse' of the namable subject: the prefix 'non' stands for an 'absence', a 'lack' of all that is 'important' and 'worthwhile' (Webster's Dictionary, 2001).
>
> (Chattopadhyay 2012:75).

Referring to the work of a second generation of historians of colonial architecture and urbanism, Chattopadhyay continues:

> Recent research has moved away from focusing solely on colonial domination and the Westernization paradigm to restore the power of imagination to the colonized and ex-colonized. There is a willingness to see in the historical record alternative voices and visions, often incommensurate with the authority of the colonizer (Yeoh 1996; Kusno 2000; Hosagrahar 2005; Chattopadhyay 2005; Glover 2007; Legg 2007; Kidambi 2007; Chopra 2011). For example, the 'colonial spatial imagination' (Glover 2007; 29–31) of British India was borrowed and built upon Indian buildings and urban traditions as much as it was imported. Further, it was liable to change because it was not operating in a socio-spatial vacuum.... The colonized population countered, replaced, modified and by-passed colonial intentions in innumerable ways.... The focus on indigenous actors in recent studies of colonial urbanism has thus made a convincing case for understanding these alternate urban visions.
>
> (Chattopadhyay 2012:86).

This extract is from an essay by Swati Chattopadhyay, one of 20 scholars from all over the world included in Urban Theory Beyond the West (2012). With almost 1,000 items listed in the bibliography, this makes an important contribution to recognising alternate urban visions.

POSTCOLONIALITY

> Postcolonial perspectives in architecture and urbanism offer ways of thinking about built form and space as cultural landscapes that are at once globally interconnected and precisely situated in space and time.... Some scholars define postcolonial studies as precisely focused on European colonization of the nineteenth and twentieth centuries. Others have a wider view that now includes the experiences of nations that have never been colonized, such as Turkey; the repercussions of earlier colonization in Latin America; recent imperialisms such as those by the US, Japan, or the USSR, as well as the multiple effects of colonial

experiences on Europe and the US. In its broadest definition, postcolonial perspectives give voice to all types and sites of struggle against hegemonic power. Its challenge is in legitimizing, enabling, and empowering alternative narratives and forms. Many critical readings about domination based on gender, race, caste, ethnic or religious groups, could thus be subsumed under postcolonial thought.

(Hosagrahar 2012:71)

In addition to addressing the key intellectual issues and concerns of postcolonial theory and four key areas of critical importance – historiography and repre-sentation, nationalism and nationhood, globalisation and preservation and cultural identity – Hosagrahar's contribution to our understanding of postcolonialism distinguishes itself from others by, among other things, addressing the important issues of design and practice.

IMPERIAL, COLONIAL AND GLOBAL CITIES

My argument about the imperial and colonial origin of many so-called world or global cities is not just a matter of 'getting things straight' or to add a missing history, even though these are legitimate tasks. The aim is rather to draw attention to the overly economistic nature of the criteria driving the 'world city' paradigm and its framing within a narrowly restrictive framework of urban political economy. It is also to highlight the ahistorical and analytically feeble nature of the category, 'global city'…. Though not sufficient in themselves, postcolonial histories are nonetheless central to any analysis of the multicultural nature of both suburbs as well as central areas of global cities in Canada, the USA, Australia, the Netherlands, France, Spain, Portugal and many other countries in Europe as well as elsewhere in the world (including Britain).

(King 2006:321, 323).

EPILOGUE

In conclusion, I should also say something of the theoretical and methodological assumptions behind this book, and also of the disciplinary fields to which they are related. If there is one assumption that has been undermined during the last half-century it is that the nation-state is not the most appropriate unit of social analysis to examine many phenomena in the modern world. Whether we adopt Immanuel Wallerstein's theorisation of the 'world system' or only borrow selected items from the vocabulary, that term has been too seductive for many writers to ignore, to be rivalled in the social sciences by notions of 'the global', 'glocal' and 'globalisation' made popular by Roland Robertson and his concept of 'the world as a single place'. My own stance is on the side of eclecticism.

In the last three decades, the growth of research and teaching in the history of colonial and postcolonial architecture and urbanism – including increasing nationalism and different versions of modernity – has enormously expanded. In the early years, scholars in this field were often from Europe (UK) and the United States; then, increasingly, indigenous postcolonial scholars were researching at home, in the one-time metropole, and especially in North America (not least, the University of California at Berkeley, where Nezar AlSayyad was an early influence in the field). Evidence for this growing academic postcolonial consciousness is to be found not only in the increasing number of scholars and graduate students working in the field, but also in the hundreds of titles in the recent bibliographies of Edensor and Jayne (2012), Home (2013), James-Chakraborty (2014), King (2004), Crinson (2003) and others. These more recent studies of colonial architecture and urbanism have, as the earlier quotation from Chattopadhyay (2012) suggests, given far more attention to the role and activities of indigenous actors, alternative voices and visions. The degree to which this knowledge has been used to transform, or reassert, the postcolonial built environment itself varies according to each individual case. As Rajagopalan and Desai (2012) point out, New Delhi's colonial past has (ironically) been recommissioned as the heritage of a contemporary nation – an outcome also to be found in other postcolonial cities.

As for methodology, it will be evident to the reader that, in comparison with my previous book (King 2004), I have made considerable use of the internet, not least in searching for 'grand hotels' worldwide. Ironically, considerable information comes from my collection of well-thumbed Baedeckers and similar guides. In the second half of this book, the empiricist in me has taken over from the theoretician. My interest in language as a tool for research covers everything from etymology to a more sophisticated interest in ethnosemantics and toponomy. For this kind of research it has considerable potential. My long-term interest in the history and sociology of building types (more precisely, the social production of building form, shared with Archi*text* co-editor Thomas Markus), informs much of my work; it offers an under-used route into understanding both large and also small-scale social, political and cultural change, from the local to the global. Mobility, between disciplines, institutions and countries, is good for research.

Limitations of space have prevented me from commenting on all of the essays that follow. However, it is evident that interest in particular themes (for example, investigating assumptions about the homogenisation of the built environment worldwide or the relation of the built environment to the globalisation of culture) have continued to be pursued (e.g. Adam 2013:100–2; Sadria 2012). Though some may think that 'post-colonial resentment' is 'fad(ing) into a distant memory' (Adam 2013:258), it is clear from the chapters that follow that not only is postcolonial *consciousness* alive and well, but is also a growing influence on the politics and attitudes of the present, not only in the scholarly world but also in the practices of architecture and planning. It would, for example, take a brave critic to assert that the historic colonial 'dual city', with its economic, social and spatial divide, has disappeared from the postcolony (Nightingale 2012). I would like to think that readers with similar interests will be encouraged, if not provoked, by these chapters.

BIBLIOGRAPHY

Adam, R. (2013) *The Globalisation of Modern Architecture: The Impact of Politics, Economics and Social Change on Architecture and Urban Design since 1900*, Cambridge: Cambridge Scholars Press.

Berking, H., Frank, S., Frers, L., Löw, M., Meier, L., Steets, S. and Stötzer, S., eds (2006) *Negotiating Urban Conflicts: Interaction, Space and Control*, Bielefeld: Transaction Publishers.

Bishop, R., Phillips, J. and Yeo, W.W., eds (2003) *Postcolonial Urbanism: Southeast Asian Cities and Global Processes*, New York and London.

Brenner, N. and Keil, R., eds (2006) *The Global Cities Reader*, London and New York: Routledge.

Bridge, G. and Watson, S. (2000) *A Companion to the City*, Oxford and Malden MA: Blackwell.

Chakrabarty, D. (2007) *Provincialising Europe: Postcolonial Thought and Historical Difference*, Princeton: Princeton University Press.

Chattopadhyay, S. (2005) *Representing Calcutta: Modernity, Nationalism, and the Colonial Uncanny*, London and New York: Routledge.

Chattopadhyay, S. (2012) 'Urbanism, colonialism and subalternity', in T. Edensor and M. Jayne, eds (2012) *Urban Theory beyond the West: A World of Cities*, London and New York: Routledge, pp.75–92.

Chopra, P. (2011) *A Joint Enterprise: Indian Elites and the Making of British Bombay*, Minneapolis: University of Minnesota Press.

Crinson, M. (2003) *Modern Architecture and the End of Empire*, Aldershot: Ashgate Press.

Davis, D.E. (2005) 'Cities in global context: a brief intellectual history', *International Journal of Urban and Regional Research*, 29, 1: 92–109.

Derudder, B., Hoyler, M., Taylor, P.J. and Witlox, F., eds (2012) *International Handbook of Globalisation and World Cities*, Cheltenham and Northampton, MA: Edward Elgar.

Dossal, M. (1991) *Imperial Designs and Indian Realities: The Planning of Bombay City 1855–1875*. Delhi: Oxford University Press.

Edensor, T. and Jayne, M. eds (2012) *Urban Theory Beyond the West*, London and New York: Routledge.

Evenson, N. (1989) *The Indian Metropolis: A View Towards the West*. New Haven: Yale University Press.

Friedmann, J. and Wolff, G. (1982) 'The world city hypothesis', *Development and Change*,17, 1: 69–84.

Glover, W. (2007) *Making Lahore Modern: Constructing and Imagining a Colonial City*, Minneapolis: University of Minnesota Press.

Guggenheim, M. and Söderström, O. (2010) *Re-shaping Cities: How Global Mobility Transforms Architecture and Urban Form*, London and New York: Routledge.

Home, R. (2013) *Of Planting and Planning: The Making of British Colonial Cities*, London and New York: Spon.

Hosagrahar, J. (2005) *Indigenous Modernities: Negotiating Architecture and Urbanism*, London and New York: Routledge.

Hosagrahar, J. (2012) 'Interrogating difference: postcolonial perspectives in architecture and urbanism', in G. Crysler, S. Cairns and H. Heynen, eds, *The Sage Handbook of Architectural Theory*, Los Angeles: Sage, pp.70–84.

James-Chakraborty, K. (2014) 'Beyond postcolonialism: new directions for the history of non-western architecture', *Frontiers of Architectural Research*, 3, 1: 1–9.

Kidambi, P. (2007) *The Making of an Indian Metropolis: Colonial Governance and Public Culture in Bombay 1890–1920*, Aldershot: Ashgate.

King, A.D. (1990a) *Global Cities: Post-Imperialism and the Internationalisation of London*, London and New York: Routledge.

King, A.D. (1990b) *Urbanism, Colonialism and the World-Economy: Cultural and Spatial Foundations of the World Urban System*, London and New York: Routledge.

King, A.D. (2004) *Spaces of Global Cultures, Architecture Urbanism Identity*, London and New York: Routledge.

King, A.D. (2006) 'World cities: global? Postcolonial? Postimperial? Or just the result of happenstance? Some cultural comments', in N. Brenner and R. Keil, eds, *The Global Cities Reader*, London and New York: Routledge, pp.319–24.

Kitchin, R. and Thrift, N. (2009) *International Encyclopaedia of Human Geography*, Amsterdam: Elsevier.

Knox, P. and Taylor, P.J. (1995) *World Cities in a World System*, Cambridge: Cambridge University Press.

Kusno, A. (2000) *Behind the Postcolonial: Architecture, Urban Space and Political Cultures in Indonesia*, London and New York: Routledge.

Legg, S. (2007) *Spaces of Colonialism: Delhi's Urban Governmentalities*, Oxford: Blackwell.

Metcalf, T.R. (1989) *An Imperial Vision: Indian Architecture and Britain's Raj*, Berkeley: University of California Press.

Nightingale, C.H. (2012) *Segregation: A Global History of Divided Cities*, Chicago: University of Chicago Press.

Pieterse, J.N., ed. (2000) *Global Futures: Shaping Globalisation*, London and New York: Zed Books.

Rabinow, P. (1989) *French Modern: Norms and Forms of the Social Environment*, Cambridge, MA: MIT Press.

Rajagopalan, M. and Desai, M.S. (2012) *Colonial Frames, Nationalist Histories, Imperial Legacies: Architecture and Modernity*, Farnham: Ashgate Press.

Robertson, R. (1992) *Globalisation: Social Theory and Global Culture*, London, Newbury Park, New Delhi: Sage.

Robertson, R. and Scholte, J.A., eds (2009) *Encyclopedia of Globalisation*, New Delhi: Sage.

Sadria, M., ed. (2012) *Homogenisation of Representations*. Geneva: Aga Khan Award for Architecture.

Sassen, S. ([1991] 2001) *The Global City: New York, London, Tokyo*, Princeton: Princeton University Press.

Tillotson, G.H.R. (1989) *The Tradition of Indian Architecture: Continuity, Controversy and Change since 1850*, New Haven: Yale University Press.

Wallerstein, I. (1974) *The Modern World-System: Capitalist Agriculture and the Origins of the European World-Economy in the Sixteenth Century*, New York and London: Academic Press.

Wright, G. (1991) *The Politics of Design in French Colonial Urbanism*, Chicago: University of Chicago Press.

Yeoh, B. (1996) *Contesting Space: Power Relations and the Urban Built Environment in Colonial Singapore*, Oxford: Oxford University Press.

FURTHER READING

Beverly, E.L. (2011) 'Colonial urbanism and South Asian cities', *Social History*, 36, 4: 482–97.

Bigon, L. (2008) 'Names, norms and forms: French and indigenous toponyms in early colonial Dakar, Senegal', *Planning Perspectives*, 23, 4: 479–501.

Bissel, W.C. (2005) 'Engaging colonial nostalgia', *Cultural Anthropology*, 20, 2: 215–48.

Bissel, W.C. (2011) *Urban Design and Colonial Power in Zanzibar*, Bloomington: Indiana University Press.

Celik, Z. (2008) *Empire, Architecture and the City: French–Ottoman Encounters, 1830–1914*, Seattle: University of Washington Press.

Duncan, M.J.S. (2012) *In the Shadows of the Tropics: Climate, Race and Biopower in 19th Century Ceylon*, London: Ashgate.

Fuller, M. (2006) *Moderns Abroad: Architecture, Cities and Italian Imperialism*, London and New York: Routledge.

Gillem, M. (2007) *American Town: Building the Outposts of Empire*, Minneapolis: University of Minnesota Press.

Haynes, D.E. (2013) 'Beyond the colonial city: re-evaluating the urban history of India, ca.1920–1970', *South Asia: Journal of South Asian Studies*, 36, 3: 317–35.

Immerwahr, D. (2007) 'The politics of architecture and urbanism in postcolonial Lagos 1960–1996', *Journal of African Cultural Studies*, 19, 2:165–86.

Kal, H. (2011) *Aesthetic Constructions of Korean Nationalism: Spectacle, Politics and History*, London and New York: Routledge.

Kincaid, A. (2006) *Postcolonial Dublin: Imperial Legacies and the Built Environment*, Minneapolis: University of Minnesota Press.

Kinsbrunner, J. (2005) *The Colonial Spanish–American City: Urban Life in the Age of Atlantic Capitalism*, Austin, TX: University of Texas Press.

Kusno, A. (2010) *The Appearances of Memory: Mnemonic Practices of Architecture and Urban Form in Indonesia*, Durham and London: Duke University Press.

Kusno, A. (2013) *After the New Order: Space, Politics and Jakarta*, Honolulu: University of Hawai'i Press.

Larsen, L. (2012) 'Replacing imperial landscapes: colonial monuments and the transition to independence in Kenya', *Journal of Historical Geography*, 38, 1: 45–56.

Lu, D., ed. (2010) *Third World Modernism: Architecture, Development and Identity*, London and New York: Routledge.

McFarland, C. (2010) 'The comparative city: knowledge, learning, urbanism', *International Journal of Urban and Regional Research*, 34, 4: 725–42.

Njoh, A.J. (2007) *Planning Power: Town Planning and Social Control in Colonial Africa*, London and New York: Routledge.

Osayimweise, I. (2013) 'Architecture and the myth of authenticity during the German colonial period', *Traditional Dwellings and Settlement Review*, 24, 11: 11–22.

Perera, N. (2002) 'Feminising the city: gender and space in colonial Colombo', in S. Sarker and E. Niyogi De, eds, *Trans-Status Subjects: Gender in the Globalisation of South and South East Asia*, Chapel Hill: Duke University Press: 67–87.

Pieris, A. (2009) *Hidden Hands and Divided Landscapes: A Penal History of Singapore's Plural Society*, Honolulu: University of Honolulu Press.

Robinson, J. (2010) 'Cities in a world of cities: the comparative gesture', *International Journal of Urban and Regional Research*, 35, 1: 1–23.

Robinson, J. (2013) 'The urban now: theorising cities beyond the new', *European Journal of Cultural Studies*, 16: 659–77.

Roy, A. and Ong, A. (2011) *Worlding Cities: Asian Experiments and the Art of Being Global*, Oxford: Wiley-Blackwell.

Scriver, P. and Prakash, V. (2007) *Colonial Modernities: Building, Dwelling and Architecture in British India and Ceylon*, London and New York: Routledge.

Shatkin, G. (2005) 'Colonial capital, modernist capital, global capital: the changing political symbolism of urban space in metropolitan Manila, the Philippines', *Pacific Affairs*, 78, 4: 577–600.

Silva, C.N. and Matos, M.C. (2014) 'Colonial and postcolonial urban planning in Africa', *Planning Perspectives*, 29, 3: 399–401.

Sklair, L. (2006) 'Iconic architecture and capitalist globalization', *City*, 10, 1: 21–47.

Sklair, L. (2011) 'Competing conceptions of globalisation', *Journal of World Systems Research*, 5, 2: 143–63.

Sklair, L. (2012) 'Towards an understanding of architectural iconicity in global perspective', in G. Bracken, ed., *Aspects of Urbanisation in China*, Amsterdam: Amsterdam University Press, pp. 27–46.

Ward, S. (2010) 'Transnational planners in a postcolonial world', in P. Healey and R. Upton, eds, *Crossing Borders: International Exchange and Planning Practices*, London and New York: Routledge, pp. 47–72.

Yoshikuni, T. (2007) *African Urban Experiences in Colonial Zimbabwe: A Social History of Harare before 1925*, Harare: Weaver Press.

Zandi-Sayek, S. (2012) *Ottoman Izmir: The Rise of a Cosmopolitan Port*, Minneapolis: University of Minnesota Press.

Re-theorising the city

Globalisation, colonialism, postcolonialism

Chapter 1: Architecture, capital and the globalisation of culture[1]

A topic as ambitious as that indicated in my title imposes both constraints as well as obligations: constraints in that if it addresses the concerns of practitioners in architecture and urban design as well as academics in sociology, geography and cultural theory,[2] it cannot be theoretically over-ambitious; obligations, in that it must, however, find a conceptual vocabulary which is available to all. Moreover, the projects of these different audiences do not necessarily coincide: architects and urban designers have to design buildings and cities (or parts of them) in a way that sociologists do not have to design societies; or not, at least, in the short term (one might say that Marx left a large number of design briefs around which, had he lived long enough to pick up the fees, would have earned him a small fortune).

But the task of developing a common conceptual framework and vocabulary is clearly an urgent and important task. Architects, planners, urban designers, indeed all those professions which deal with the realities of the built environment, need (and in many cases, also want) to understand questions concerning, for example, the long-term economic, social or political outcomes of particular design policies or decisions, or the meaning of different building forms in various cultures, or issues relating to the social organisation of space, whether at the level of the building or of the city. It is only quite recently, however, that social theories have begun to take a serious interest in such questions (at a theoretical, not an applied level) and many of the debates are still confined to questions of 'space', 'social relations and spatial structures' and do not address, as I shall discuss below, a more differentiated notion of the built environment and its relation to a vast array of social processes.

The larger problem I want to address can be put, in over-simplified terms, in the form of three questions:

1   What is the role of the multi-faceted forces of international capital (economic, political, technological, social), and the built environment which they help to produce, in contributing to the homogenisation of culture on a global scale?

This hypothetical question can be broken down into two more specific issues:

2   What is the role of the physical and spatial built environment in contributing
     to a globalisation of culture?

Here, I am suggesting that 'globalisation' can mean either the creation of
homogeneity (where everything becomes the same) or, following Robertson
(1987), the creation of heterogeneity (or difference) as *a response to* globalisation.
I am subsuming under the word 'culture' both the material culture of the built
environment itself as well as the systems of meaning, action and symbolic forms
with which this is connected.

3   What is the more specific role of architecture, urban planning and design,
     understood as distinctive, professional culture practices, in this process of
     globalisation?

Here, I am seeing architecture and urban design or planning as particular cultural
industries which might be compared, for example, with other major spheres of
cultural production such as the film, video or music industries, the realms of
television or advertising: the image-projecting and consciousness-transforming
industries, all those industries which, in short, in the conditions of contemporary
capitalism and along with a variety of other forms and processes, contribute to the
constitution, confirmation or reconstitution of human subjectivity and cultural
identity. I am suggesting, in brief, that architecture and planning, indeed all the
'design professions', are potentially major influences in contributing to the
transformation of culture on a global scale.

     However, in talking about the production of the built environment, I also
want to distinguish between the actions of individuals and organisations (maybe
individual architects, firms of developers of municipalities, agencies of one kind or
another) and the larger structures and conditions in which they operate: particular
modes of production or forms of socio-economic organisation and political control:
free market capitalism, state capitalism, socialism, welfare capitalism; or distinctive
regional or even national cultures. This is what we commonly accept as the
structure–agency question.

     It might be thought that to ask such questions is simultaneously irrelevant as
well as intellectually misconceived, an example of a 'totalising discourse' which
might be undermined from a variety of directions. I would suggest two very
practical reasons why I believe such questions to be legitimate.

     The immense acceleration in the processes of globalisation and 'global
compression' (to use Robertson's phrase) is most obviously seen in relation to the
economy: the three major players in the internationalisation of the economy since
the 1970s have been the banks, the global corporations and the state (Thrift 1986);
it has been accompanied by the internationalisation of production and of
consumption, of 24-hour global trading in securities, of revolutionary developments

in transport and telecommunications technology and the massive growth in international labour migration. These, in turn, have brought the deterritorialisation of cultures, the existence of cultures far from their places of origin.

Two particular aspects of the so-called new international division of labour which characterised these new developments in the capitalist world economy are of particular relevance to my theme. The first, drawing on the work of Friedmann and Wolff (1982), Friedmann (1986), Sassen-Koob (1984, 1986, 1990), Soja *et al.* (1983), Soja (1988) and others, concerns the shift of manufacturing industries from once-industrial cities to lower labour-cost countries and regions (or to their automation) and their replacement by higher level, producer service functions (international banking, financial services, insurance, real estate, design services, etc.). Because such activities rely on advanced information technology and are labour-intensive in terms of 'think work', in which core post-industrial states have a major competitive advantage on a global scale, these knowledge-intensive (and also ideology-producing) services, fed by the major centres of education and research, are largely concentrated in the major 'world cities' of the USA, Europe and the Far East, along with the headquarters offices of global corporations and international banks. Here, they provide, in Sassen-Koob's (1986) terms, the 'global control capability' in an increasingly global system of production. International contracts have become increasingly important for many architectural and engineering firms. In the mid-1970s already, one-third of US worldwide receipts on contracts for construction, consulting and design services were coming from OPEC countries (Sassen-Koob 1984) and this has increasingly been the case for UK companies (King 1990a). The 1980s has been the decade in which all companies, not least those in architecture and design services, have 'gone global'.

One of the best examples is that of Japanese construction contractors which have undergone a major process of internationalisation in the last decade. The lack of public works in Japan and declining profits prompted large corporations to 'go global' in the 1980s, helped of course by the surfeit of Japanese capital looking for profitable sites for investment. Between 1981 and 1988, Kumagai Gumi, once a small-scale Japanese contractor, moved from 135th to 6th place in the world's top international construction contractors. In the process they have had a massive effect on Australian urban and building development, leaving a string of luxury hotels, tourist resorts, condominiums and often unwanted developments around the Australian coast (Rimmer 1988). The spectre of capital combing the world looking for profitable sites for investment and, if necessary, tearing down existing environments to achieve it, if not the major feature of the 1980s, has nevertheless been a striking characteristic of urban development in that decade. It is now well known that 70 percent of downtown Los Angeles is foreign owned (Wald 1988:8). Other world cities have equally been the recipient of foreign capital investment. In New Delhi, the capital of India, a massive building boom has been underway since the mid-1980s, a considerable part of it fuelled by investment from 'NRIs' (non-resident Indians), often from capital generated in the Gulf but also from other international sources. The developments have had a significant and major effect on Indians' traditional investment practices as, over the last decade, they have moved accumulated and inherited wealth out of investment in (especially gold) jewellery to investment in property and land. The result has been the growth of a new 'South City' in Delhi, a spate of luxury building on a scale not seen since the establishment of colonial New Delhi in the early twentieth century, and the creation of 'designer housing' which apparently combines features from Riyadh, South Kensington and Bombay (*Cityscan*, 1989).

London, which was one of a number of cities targeted by oil surplus funds in the 1970s, has been especially transformed in the 1980s, largely in the run-up to and aftermath of the 'Big Bang'. Between 1985, when Japanese investment in British property was still rare, and 1987, Japanese banks' investment in UK property increased eightfold to around £250 million (King 1990a:108). Less well documented has been the laundering of drug profits and their investment in urban redevelopment round the world, including new developments in the London Docklands (King 1990a:148).

These are only some of the more obvious effects of the massive internationalisation of capital in the last decade and their impacts both on architectural production and on the profession itself. The decade also saw the first case of an architects' firm being listed on the London 'unlisted securities' market. Because of the creation of the single European market in 1992, consultants are being employed to buy up small architectural firms in preparation for what some see will be a boom in design work following the establishment of the single market, and where firms in England, say, will do design work cheaper than those in France.

Thus, even at this relatively elementary level of world economic forces and their effects on urban and building development, we need a framework for understanding the mechanisms, the institutions, the meanings and the economic, social and cultural consequences of these developments. How are we to understand this process of transnationalisation in this process of the transformation of space and form? What difference, if any, will it make to people's social, political or cultural consciousness? What kind of symbolic investment are they to make in these new environments, what meanings will they have and how will they mobilise these meanings for their own social or political purposes? More significantly, what are the prisms through which we should try to understand cultural resistance to these developments and the differences which are evident from one place to another? How relevant are the categories, for this purpose, of nation, locality, region, religion, class, gender, economy?

This, therefore, is what I would call the *external* justification for my theme: in a situation of 'global compression', I am concerned to find a framework for understanding transformations in space, building and urban form which extend well beyond the boundaries of the state. My *internal* justification comes from another, though related phenomenon: just as the new international division of labour is increasingly sending producer services in design outwards, to other countries in search of markets, so also is it bringing increasing numbers of protoprofessionals from so-called 'Third World' societies for professional education in countries at the core. As the quaternary sector of such countries expands, the educational component of that sector depends increasingly on this input of students from the global periphery. It is here where the totalising theories are constructed. So the experience (for a few) of flying round the world and needing schemata to make sense of what they see is increasingly complemented in the classroom back home by looking round the graduate seminar table and seeing students from all over the world. It is these conditions which are giving rise to the construction of global theories. We can address our larger questions through a series of different stages in which parts of the problem have been formulated. The first of these we can call:

THE SOCIAL PRODUCTION OF KNOWLEDGE

Much of academic work is concerned with filling in gaps, doing things which one thinks others have omitted; making visible what was previously invisible, creating discursive noise where there was previously silence. So, in the last 20 years, geographers have argued for the centrality of space and spatiality to the explanation of social process; in the urban field of sociology, transformed to urban political economy, capital became critically important in the 1970s and early 1980s, though later it emerged that politics had been neglected. My own experience, for what it is worth, of returning to Europe after living in India for five years, was to discover (in the early 1970s) that 'culture', in its old, 'anthropological' sense, was being neglected in the study of architecture and urban form. After some years working under the paradigmatic shadows cast by Harvey and Castells it wasn't in any way a sure thing that 'culture', in any sense, existed.

Over the same period meanwhile, feminists had made more than apparent the invisibility of women in history, architecture, anthropology; at another conjuncture, the state was discovered: it had to be brought back in. Decades before, social historians had discovered there was a (generally male) working class. Since the 1970s, in architectural history, scholars have pointed out that insufficient notice was being taken of 'the vernacular' and 'ethnic architecture'; ethnicity, of course, and ethnic difference, has been a major area of neglect and subsequent discovery across the spectrum of intellectual enquiry. For Foucault, the discovery was even greater: it was the appearance of man (and maybe woman) in the sphere of knowledge, not to mention discursive formations. In cultural studies and elsewhere, what has been neglected is the question of subjectivity, and the constitution of the class or gendered subject. And culture, 20 years ago thought to be about values, beliefs, world views, or alternatively about 'what you need to know to be accepted as one of them by any members of a cultural group', is now constituted through representation.

One could of course continue these examples, from discourses on language, religion, psychology, but what I want to ask is, what are the conditions under which these discourses are produced? Why does ethnicity, gender, class appear on the agenda? The answer of course is obvious enough but it raises questions not only in the sociology and geography of knowledge (who is producing it, who for and where is it being produced as well as sent to, and consumed) but also, in the history and political economy of knowledge (when is it being produced and who is paying for it; how is it being financed and for what purposes).

In one sense, knowledge is a very personal thing; it comes from personal experience, but personal experience which is situated and formed in particular social institutions and work contexts (like universities, departmental disciplines, professional organisations), in particular geographical locations (cities, regions, states, rich and poor parts of the world) and a product of particular temporal or historical periods, some of which are seen to be significantly formative (and in different states, according to different histories, acquire different labels, such as the 'Quit India' period, the 'Civil Rights' movement in the US or, in the UK, the apparently 'global 1980s'). So discourses, and the languages in which they're expressed, become fossilised, not only according to socially institutionalised disciplines (sociology, architectural history) and particular places (Chicago sociology, British architectural history) but also according to particular historical epochs (postwar Chicago sociology). And this brings me back to my own personal experience. For having discovered, after five years in India and returning to the UK, that it was 'culture' which was being left out, after a further few years working in London with students of building, planning, architecture and urban design from all over the world, it was obvious that two other massive realms were missing from the discourse about society and culture in the UK. One was the built environment, the other was the rest of the world.

THE BUILT ENVIRONMENT

Until quite recently, with its appropriation in the debate on postmodernism, one of the main silences in social theory has concerned the built environment. This is not the place to discuss this at length, nor to provide any theoretically coherent account, except to say that most of the work concerning, for example, the social production and organisation of space, of the built environment, of questions of meaning, or representation and cultural identity produced in the last 20 years has (with a few exceptions) been undertaken in anthropology, archaeology, geography, social history, or various hybrid fields such as man(sic)–environment studies, though very little in social theory.

Yet just as the feminist critique has exposed the folly of constructing totalising theoretical paradigms concerning class or employment without reference to gender, I would suggest it is equally fallacious to conceptualise society, culture, social organisation or process without reference to the physical and spatial material reality of the built environment. For the most part, social theory deals with a world of social relations, of discourses about culture, in which the built environment, understood as the physical and spatial contexts, the built forms, the socially constructed boundaries, material containers, the architectural representations, the socially specialised building types, not only do not exist but play no role whatsoever in the production and reproduction of society. It is as though it didn't matter whether all social life took place where it actually does or on a huge global beach, or if social subjects were somehow magically suspended in space. I am saying, in short, that the built environment, building and urban form in all their conceptualisations, do not just represent or reflect social order, they actually constitute much of social and cultural existence. Society, as Prior (1988) has pointed out, is to a large extent constituted as well as represented through the buildings and spaces that it creates.

Thus, if we are considering cultures in terms of the ways in which they are represented, either in a tangible, material sense such as in different kinds of texts and visual expression and in the production of different aspects of material culture, or in a non-material sense such as in music, oral culture and symbolic practices of different kinds, it can be argued that the demarcation and, subsequently, organisation of space is, in virtually all cases, a necessary prerequisite for all forms of cultural performance and representation. Second, many of these activities equally presuppose some form of socially and physically constructed space.

Moreover (and still speaking with reference to social theory), if built environments, in all their various conceptualisations, are as important as socially constituting mechanisms as I am arguing here, then they should (as indeed they do) provide us with some evidence, some data about the nature and organisation of society and culture as well as its spatial expression or constitution. They should tell us (as indeed they do) about its social and spatial division of labour (on the basis of gender, age or region), about its economic, social and political organisation as a whole.

The problem is of course that when you look at the built environment, at urban forms or hierarchies produced by a given economic and social formation, they do not fit into the politically or geographically defined nation-state, such as the UK or US, which has traditionally been taken as the unit of analysis in social theory. This is most obviously demonstrated, and illustrated, by examples of colonial societies. In the early twentieth century, Britain, South Africa, India, Australia, Kenya and many other places were, for the white British migrants who went there, in some sense, one single colonial society: not, in any way, a series of societal clones displaced round the world, but a single social and cultural system whose occupations, lifestyles and sub-cultures, as well of course as built environments, were determined by their participation in a colonial mode of production which was in turn part of a larger international division of labour.

Sociology, as both Robertson (1988) and Wallerstein (1987) have reminded us, has not been very good at coping with social and cultural systems which spill over the boundaries of nation-states. And it is to the alternative theorisations of these two scholars which I would like to turn. It is in attempting to cope with the problem of understanding the production and social meaning of built environments, of buildings and architecture on a scale that is outside and beyond the boundaries of individual states that I believe both of these scholars have contributions to make.

THE WORLD AS A SINGLE PLACE

Though the phrase of my sub-title is Robertson's, it would be generally agreed that the most widely accepted paradigm within which this phenomenon is discussed is the world-systems perspective of Immanuel Wallerstein. Though the focus of Wallerstein's work has shifted in recent years, the main features of the perspective remain: that since the sixteenth century there has been one principal mode of production and that is the capitalist world economy, and this is a single division of labour within which are multiple cultures. Other essential elements of this capitalist world economy are: production for profit in a world market; capital accumulation for expanded production as the key way of maximising profit in the long run; the emergence of three zones of economic activity (core, periphery and semi-periphery); the development over time of two principal world class formations (the bourgeoisie and the proletariat) whose concrete manifestations are complemented by a host of ethnonational groups. This historically unique combination of elements first crystallised in Europe in the sixteenth century and the boundaries slowly expanded to cover the entire world (Wallerstein 1979:159).

Readers familiar with Wallerstein's work, and the critiques made of it will know that until recently it has (as can be seen from these earlier sources) been principally concerned with the economic and political rather than the cultural (though see Wallerstein 1990).

Yet there are at least two features of Wallerstein's notion of the world-system which make sense when discussing the production and meaning of built environments, both historically and today. The first is the notion of the international division of labour nested in ideas of 'core' and 'periphery'; the second is the notion that the world-system is indeed 'systemic' in that economic, social and cultural processes in one part of the world are systematically related (if not mechanically or in a determinate fashion) to processes in other parts. Let me illustrate this by reference to economic, social and spatial divisions of labour and their relationship to the built environment.

To understand any built environment we need to understand the economic, social and political formations on which it is based; we need to understand both a social and spatial division of labour. There is no adequate explanation of, for example, the growth in the nineteenth century in northern England of industrial 'cotton towns' (sic) without reference to the transformation of Egyptian agriculture, the huge rise of cotton exports (under colonialism) and the creation of colonial Cairo from the 1880s. They are both part of the same mode of production and the built environment and architecture is one of the major clues. Not because it is 'the same' but because it is complementary: the Classical Revival banks are in the City of London, loaning money (at prohibitive rates) to the Egyptians to import manufactured goods; the Classical Revivalist mansions are in Cairo and Alexandria belonging to the Egyptian comprador bourgeoisie or the families of European officials or merchants.

The same holds true in the last decades of the twentieth century. No one can attempt to talk about New York and its buildings without reference to the world economy. The fact that New York has the largest number (56) of multinational headquarters buildings of any city in the world – only two of any of the huge Third World cities, many of which have larger populations than New York, have any multinational corporation headquarters at all (King 1990a) – also explains back-office functions located in the Caribbean and the low-rise factories which exist in Taiwan or the Philippines.

Yet whilst these notions, inherent in the world-systems perspective, do provide insights into especially economic processes and, by focusing on the level of the nation-state, on political processes as well, there are other dimensions which we need to take care of.

First, globalisation processes are only partial; they affect some regions of the world-economy more than others, and within regions, some social groups or sectors more or less than others, and this is important if we are trying to understand the production of particular built environments. Second, by focusing on what might be seen as the dominant economic processes (the international-isation of capital), we may seriously underestimate the processes of economic, social and cultural resistance, both in terms of scale (i.e. how large are they) and intensity (how strong are they). Finally, if we are interested in identifying and documenting cultural difference, distinctive cultures and the way they are represented in architecture and urban form, world-systems theory does not as yet have anything to say about this.

An alternative conceptualisation is that of Robertson's (1987) theory of globalisation, the term defined as 'the process by which the world becomes a single place'. What Robertson emphasises is that it is crucial to recognise that the contemporary concern with civilisational and societal (as well as ethnic) uniqueness, as expressed in such motifs as identity, tradition and indigenisation, largely rests on globally produced ideas. In an increasingly globalised world, 'characterised by historically exceptional degrees of societal and other modes of interdependence, as well as the widespread consciousness of their developments, there is an exacerbation of civilisational, societal and ethnic selfconsciousness' (1987). Robertson has suggested that globalisation theory turns world-systems theory on its head by focusing, first, on the cultural aspects of the 'world system' and, second, by the systematic study of internal societal attributes which shape orientations to the world as a whole (Robertson 1987).

Globalisation, according to Robertson, involves the development of something like a global culture, not as normatively binding but in the sense of a general mode of discourse about the world as a whole and its variety (1987).

Both Robertson's and Wallerstein's theorisations, therefore, in different ways, argue against the homogenisation of culture; that of Wallerstein, in a negative way, by implying the creation of processes which spark off cultural resistance and opposition; that of Robertson, by suggesting that the consciousness, or experience of globality will exacerbate, even provide new kinds of, cultural difference.

A third, and different, argument put forward by Stuart Hall (1990) suggests that it is precisely in the nature of capital, in its constant state of expansion, penetration and internationalisation, to work in and through difference, to celebrate, enhance and exaggerate cultural diversity.

To these propositions, other arguments might be added; first, that there is now no longer one core to the world-system but, rather, many cores exist, not least those located in Asia and Latin America, which are coming out with their own, alternative forms of cosmopolitanism (*Public Culture*, 1988). Cultural transformations are not just moving in one direction but many. If this is so, then my original hypothesis concerning a move towards a general, global cultural homogeneity is, theoretically at least, not likely to hold water.

So far, however, I have been speaking of these theories as theories: let me say something about them as empirical data.

All theories are themselves cultural products, produced under particular conditions, by particular people and in particular places. If the criticisms of Stuart Hall are taken seriously, then all globalising theories are 'the self-representation of the dominant particular'; they represent a 'certain configuration of local particularities which, in a hegemonic sweep, try to dominate the whole scene, to incorporate a variety of more localised identities into subordinate positions'.[3]

Other criticisms see these constructs – core/periphery, First World/Third World, centre/margin – as just that, social constructs with no real referents in social reality. They are all 'defined in difference' in terms of 'the Self and the Other' (Wolff 1990).

These criticisms I take less seriously; the fact that theories and conceptualisations are cultural products, social constructs, does not mean that they cannot take on their own reality. People do indeed take on identities and represent themselves as from the Third World, the periphery, as ethnic minorities or scheduled castes. The greater problem with these concepts is that they are generally binary constructs – black/white, male/female, self/other – as if there were no categories before, between and after. As Arjun Appadurai once pointed out, some others are more other than other others.

CONCLUSION

What suggestions do these various innovations from social and cultural theory offer for the understanding of architecture, built environments, societies and cultures on a global scale? I shall conclude by reaffirming some basic propositions and suggesting some more for further analysis.

First, that cultures, sub-cultures and economic, social and political formations are not only represented but also constituted in and through spatial and built form practices and today (as well as in the historic past) these are constituted on a global scale. The relationship is not necessarily 'one-to-one' and there may well be some cultural lag over time but this does not alter the basic proposition.

Second, there is indeed a world or global culture which is largely the product of a world political economy of capitalism, as well as being the outcome of its technological and communicative effects. However, while there may well be a globalising culture in relation to the built environment, it is not necessarily (and is as much likely to work against) a homogenising one.

Third, that changes in the construction of space, its organisation and physical containment and representation in building and urban form is a major factor in the transformation of (especially material) cultures on a global scale. However, form should not be confused with content nor should we fail to recognise that apparently similar forms can carry quite dissimilar meanings.

Fourth, and in regard to my propositions about the nature and organisation of societies, people belong to many different cultures and the cultural differences are as likely to be *within* states (i.e. between regions, classes, ethnic groups, the urban and rural) as *between* states. Architects and designers move more easily between New York, London and Bombay than between Bombay and the villages of Maharashtra.

Fifth, nation-states constantly aim to construct, define and monitor national cultures within the politically defined boundaries of the state (Wallerstein 1990). But these are constantly undermined, not only by cultural flows coming in from outside the state but increasingly from autonomous and hegemonic professional subcultures (such as architecture) which generally, though not necessarily, have their values and roots in institutions derived from capitalist social formations and practices which operate across national boundaries.

Sixth, that history is at least if not more useful than theory in charting the development of national, regional or international cultures and the way they get represented in the built environment. This can be more easily illustrated than explained; for example, societies and built environments in particular parts of the world can be understood better when conceptualised as 'postcolonial' or 'post-imperial' than as 'peripheral' or 'core'.

Finally, when it comes to the crunch, there's nothing like theoretically informed empirical and archival research on the history of the global production of building form (King 1990b). We need careful historical studies of the images, plans, ideas and symbols which are increasingly making the world's cities simultaneously similar to, and different from, each other.

NOTES

1 From Anthony D. King, 'Architecture, capital and the globalisation of culture', *Theory, Culture and Society*, 7, 1990 © Anthony D. King.

2 This paper is a slightly revised version of a lecture given at the University of Minnesota at Minneapolis in May 1989 and sponsored by the Program in Comparative Studies in Discourse and Society of the Department of Humanities, and Departments of Architecture, Urban Design, Sociology, Geography and International Studies. The paper also draws on contributions to a symposium on 'Culture, Globalisation and the World-System' by Roland Robertson, Immanuel Wallerstein, Ulf Hannerz, Janet Wolff and Stuart Hall held at the State University of New York at Binghamton in April 1989.

3 Comments by Stuart Hall in a discussion following a lecture on 'Globalization and Ethnicity', State University of New York at Binghamton, March 1989.

BIBLIOGRAPHY

Cityscan (1989) 'Land south of Delhi: Moneyscape' (November): 21–8.

Friedmann, J. (1986) 'The world city hypothesis', *Development and Change* 17, 1: 69–83.

Friedmann, J. and Wolff, G. (1982) 'World city formation: an agenda for research and action', *International Journal of Urban and Regional Research*, 6, 3: 309–44.

Hall, Stuart (1990) 'Globalization and ethnicity', in A.D. King, ed., *Culture, Globalisation and the World-System*, Binghamton: State University of New York at Binghamton and Macmillan.

King, A.D. (1990a) *Global Cities: Post-Imperialism and the Internationalisation of London*, London and New York: Routledge.

King, A.D. (1990b) *Urbanism, Colonialism and the World-Economy*, London and New York: Routledge.

Prior, L. (1988) 'The architecture of the hospital: a study of social organisation and medical knowledge', *British Journal of Sociology*, 39, 1: 86–113.

Public Culture (1988) 'Editorial', 1, 1: 1–6.

Rimmer, P. (1988) 'Japanese construction companies and the Australian states', *International Journal of Urban and Regional Research*, 12, 3: 404–24.

Robertson, R. (1987) 'Globalization: theory and civilisational analysis', *Comparative Civilisations Review*, 17: 20–30.

Robertson, R. (1988) 'The sociological significance of culture: some general considerations', *Theory, Culture & Society*, 5: 3–23.

Sassen-Koob, S. (1984) 'The new labour demand in global cities', in M.P. Smith, ed., *Cities in Transformation*, Beverly Hills and London: Sage, pp.139–72.

Sassen-Koob, S. (1986) 'New York City: economic restructuring and immigration', *Development and Change*, 17, 1: 85–119.

Sassen-Koob, S. (1990) *The Global City*, Princeton, NJ: Princeton University Press.

Soja, I., Morales, R. and Wolff, G. (1983) 'Urban restructuring: an analysis of social and spatial change in Los Angeles', *Economic Geography*, 59: 195–230.

Soja, E.W. (1988) *Postmodern Geographies: The Reassertion of Space in Critical Social Theory*, London: Verso.

Thrift, N. (1986) 'The geography of international economic disorder', in R.J. Johnson and P.J. Taylor, eds, *A World in Crisis? Geographical Perspectives*, Oxford: Blackwell, pp.12–67.

Wald, M.L. (1988) 'Foreign investors take more active roles', *New York Times*. Real Estate Report on Commercial Property (15 May): 5–12.

Wallerstein, I. (1979) *The Capitalist World-Economy*, Cambridge: Cambridge University Press.

Wallerstein, I. (1987) 'World-systems Analysis', in A. Giddens and J.H. Turner, eds, *Social Theory Today*, Binghamton: Department of Art and Art History, State University of New York at Binghamton, pp.309–24.

Wallerstein, I. (1991) 'The national and the universal: can there be such a thing as world culture?' in A.D. King, ed., *Culture, Globalization and the World-System*, Binghamton: State University of New York at Binghamton.

Wolff, J. (1990) 'The global and the specific: reconciling conflicting theories of culture', in A.D. King, ed., *Culture, Globalization and the World-System*. Binghamton: State University of New York at Binghamton and Macmillan.

Chapter 2: Colonialism, urbanism and the capitalist world economy[1]

INTRODUCTION

Considering its impact on contemporary urban political, economic and cultural life, the historical experience of colonialism and imperialism[2] is greatly under-researched. Despite the fact that virtually all one-time peripheral regions were controlled by European core powers for varying periods between 1500 and 1950, creating 'a world organised as one huge functional region of the core states' and which remains 'the dominant spatial organisation of the twentieth century' (Taylor 1985:67–68), the subject of imperialism is still largely neglected (Taylor 1985:67–68). This is particularly true in regard to its significance in structuring patterns of urbanisation and urbanism. Yet the majority of today's 'world cities' (Friedmann 1986), described by Feagin (1985) as 'the cotter pins of the world economy', were earlier either imperial metropolises (e.g. London, Paris, Brussels, Tokyo) or major cities of one-time colonial economies (e.g. New York, Sydney, São Paolo, Rio de Janeiro, Johannesburg, Toronto, Hong Kong, Singapore, Bombay), and the connection between these two phenomena is historical not accidental (King 1989b). Contemporary urban hierarchies and patterns of urbanisation have largely resulted from colonial rule (e.g. Brush 1970; Castells 1972a; Davis 1960; Kosambi 1985; Mabogunje 1980; Saueressig-Schreuder 1986; Southall 1971). Amongst the five major colonial powers (Spain, Portugal, the Netherlands, France, Britain) and within the larger secular movements of the capitalist world economy (in relation, for example, to international labour migration, or the internationalisation of capital) colonial histories have been crucial, if not determinant, in calling contemporary political tunes; the emergence of racism and the new right presupposes what were once 'colonial' populations 'at home' and nationalist policies abroad, whether in the Falklands or New Caledonia. The United States, the most obvious example of 'successful' colonialism, continues to confront the urban and racial heritage of slavery as it also benefits from massive immigration of labour from states in central and South America; these, while also 'successful' examples of colonialism, nonetheless remain comparatively impoverished as a result of informal recolonisation in the nineteenth and twentieth centuries. Whether in Fiji or Sri Lanka, Australia or the United Kingdom, problems of economy, polity and society all manifest ethnic, cultural and racial dimensions rooted in their colonial and imperial past. In South Africa, with its 'black townships' and apartheid, the questions of colonialism are still unresolved. For Becker and others (1987), international capitalism and development in the late twentieth century are best summarised as 'postimperialism'.

While the functional and spatial orientation of colonialism was originally rural, with the economic exploitation of mineral or agricultural products, its manifestation was equally urban: first, in the political, administrative and economic role of its cities and towns in their function of surplus extraction, and subsequently, in their increasingly significant role as markets, centres for consumption and 'theatres of accumulation' (Armstrong and McGee 1985). These were the colonial cities.

But where, in the first half of the twentieth century (and earlier), the urban site for the encounter between representatives of core industrial zones and those of ethnically, racially and culturally different less developed world regions was in the colonial cities of the periphery (from Casablanca to Lagos, Calcutta (now, Kolkata) to Kuala Lumpur), with independence, and world capitalist expansion in the second half of the twentieth century, the site of that encounter has been shifted to metropolitan cities at the core (King 1989b). The homogenisation of space, associated with the urban effects of the new international division of labour and the internationalisation of capital of the last two decades, has led to increasing convergence between the characteristics of so-called First and Third World cities (Armstrong and McGee 1985; Drakakis-Smith 1987): the one-time colonial city becomes like the metropole and the metropole takes on the characteristics of 'the colonial city' (King 1989b). As the 1980s have been characterised by increasing consciousness concerning the impact of world economic forces on cities, it is appropriate to look again at the phenomenon of colonialism and the colonial city. Why this is important is the subject of the section below.

COLONIAL CITIES AND THE WORLD ECONOMY

According to Friedmann (1986:6), it was the special achievement of Castells (1972b) and Harvey (1973) 'to link city forming processes to the larger historical movement of industrial capitalism'. However, it is only since 1980, in his view, that 'the study of cities has been directly linked to the world economy'.[3]

Whilst Friedmann's statement may be correct in terms of its precise wording and reference to world economy, the implication is misleading: fundamental to the development of the world economy (the term already in use in the 1880s: see Hobsbawm (1975)) and the world system in general, was the emergence of modern industrial colonialism, the cities which it created and also through which it operated. Hence, the study of cities as 'directly linked to colonialism' is the immediate and necessary prerequisite for understanding the development of cities as 'directly linked to the world economy'.

As indicated elsewhere, however (King 1985:9), the difficulties posed by the concept of the 'colonial city' arise from the radical transformations in the understanding of both the city and colonialism which have taken place since 1954 when the colonial city was first seriously considered.[4] On one hand, there is the shift in urban theory from a localised concern with urban ecology of the 1950s, to a pluralist urban political economy concerned with global economic, political and sociocultural processes of the late 1980s. The first phase of the radical transformation of urban social science on an international scale (variously described as 'structuralist' or 'urban political economy' approaches) occurred between 1970 and 1976 and is well described by Walton (1976:302–303). In terms of the discussion below, it is useful to mention the four characteristics of this work which he identified: (1) the search for theoretical perspectives that would explain the distinctive characteristics of urbanism and urbanisation in social processes; (2) the strong influence of Marxist theory and an endeavour to develop a materialist theory of urbanism; (3) an attempt to develop historical and economic foundations of urbanism and urbanisation and to account for urban forms by reference to changing modes of production; (4) the concern with, for example, urban social-spatial organisation, politics or social movements, as these grow out of particular forms of economic integration.

With some notable exceptions, however (including, for example, the work of Castells, Harvey, Walton and Roberts), the body of work which developed in the late 1970s and early 1980s was largely focused on European and North American urbanism, often with little reference to the 'world outside' (King 1983).[5] From about this time, however, urban social science has been increasingly characterised by two features: first, a rapidly growing awareness of the global context of urban growth, a concern with the world economy and various interpretations of the new international division of labour (e.g. Cohen 1981; Friedmann and Wolff 1982; Friedmann 1986; Drakakis-Smith 1986; Henderson 1986; Thrift 1986); second, a more diverse and politically pluralistic interpretation of urban research has developed, interested in the 'pre-economic' and concerned with a much wider range of issues, from questions of cultural consciousness, locality and difference, the constitution of the subject, to considerations of ethnicity and nationalism. And as Robertson (1987) has suggested, these latter issues are themselves to be understood within, and as part of a response to, an increased sense of globalisation, 'the rendering of the world as … a single place'.[6]

Similarly, the understanding of colonialism and its relationship to 'development', the globalisation of production and questions of consciousness and cultural change, has gone through a variety of paradigm shifts since the 1950s, understood through theories of diffusion, modernisation, dependency, world systems, modes of production and the internationalisation of capital (Chilcote 1984; Preston 1986); hence, each new shift in the understanding and conceptualisation of the macrostructures and processes in which cities are embedded ('society', in the 1970s, 'world economy' and 'globalisation' in the 1980s), has required a reformulation of the historical problem.

What this introduction proposes, therefore, is a consideration of two questions:

1   To what extent does earlier research on colonialism and colonial cities either anticipate or add to our understanding of the relationship between cities and the world economy which has emerged from publications in the 1980s?

2   To what extent does this earlier research either anticipate or add to current urban theoretical debates concerning, for example, questions of 'modernity', the 'relative autonomy' of culture as an explanatory variable (Robertson 1988:5), urban and regional restructuring, relations between the spatial and the social, or the role of built space and architectural form in changing consumption habits, patterns of accumulation, modifying consciousness or contributing to cultural change?

What the following section undertakes, therefore, is a brief and selective overview of theoretical writing on colonial cities from the 1950s.[7] It first looks at the macroeconomic, political, cultural, spatial or geographical (and implicitly, theoretical) conceptualisations within which colonial cities are discussed: for example, Europeanisation and westernisation (geographical-cultural in conception and diffusionist in terms of theory); industrialisation (economic-technological); modernisation; capitalist penetration, colonialism (political economy, or mode of production); etc. It then considers the main urban theoretical concerns and focus of the author(s) in question. The review, clearly, is not meant to be comprehensive but rather, its purpose is to draw attention to perspectives which have become increasingly relevant to current debates. To anticipate the conclusions, what it suggests is a consciousness, in regard to cities on the periphery, of their structural dependence on world economic forces a good deal prior to that identified for cities at the core. What is often missing, however, is an adequate theorisation of this connection.

THE COLONIAL CITY: A HISTORIOGRAPHICAL NOTE

The 1950s

The classic article of anthropologists Redfield and Singer on 'The cultural role of cities' (1954) has frequently been used as the base point for subsequent research on the colonial city. In the context of recent interest in the global context of metropolitan growth, this article is still of interest.

The macrocontext is essentially 'civilisational' and, theoretically, is based on a pre-neomarxist 'acculturation theory'; the objective, to analyse 'the role cities play in the formation, maintenance, spread, decline and transformation of civilisations with the authors emphasising change in the content and integration of ideas, institutions and ideals' (1954:56).

The main purpose of the paper was 'to set out a framework of ideas that may prove useful in research on the part played by cities in the development, decline or transformation of culture', the latter concept as used in anthropology. Ranging over large civilisational periods, their macrohistorical context is suggested by their illustrations: to examine, for example, an Asiatic city as:

> a link in the interaction of two distinct civilisations and see the problem of urbanisation in Asia as a problem of westernisation, or the problem of Spanish–Indian acculturation of Mexico after the conquest as a problem of deurbanisation and reurbanisation; or to show both western and eastern cities as variants of a single cultural and historical process.

In their classification of cities that follows, the basic division is twofold:

1) cities of the time *before the development of a world economy* (emphasis added),
2) cities of the modern era.

This division is expanded to (1) before and (2) after the industrial revolution and western expansion. In category (2) are 'metropolis-cities of the worldwide managerial and entrepreneurial class' (London, New York, Osaka, Yokohama, Shanghai, Singapore, Bombay),[8] as well as cities of modern administrations (Washington, DC, New Delhi, Canberra) and 'a thousand administrative towns, country seats of British and French colonial administration, etc.'.

The urban theoretical model which they develop is that for which the article is generally known, namely, their hypothesis of two basic types of city; the orthogenetic (the city of the moral order; the city of culture carried forward) and the heterogenetic (the city of the technical order), where 'local cultures are disintegrated and new integrations of mind and society are developed'. It is the heterogenetic transitions which have grown with '*the development of the modern industrial worldwide economy* together with the great movement of peoples and especially those incident to the expansion of the west' (emphasis added).

Amongst these heterogenetic cities were 'colonial cities ... the mixed cities on the periphery of an empire which carried the core culture to other peoples'. In modern times, such cities include 'the colonial cities of the European powers [which] admit native employees daily at the doors of their skyscraper banks'. In referring to such modern colonial cities (Jakarta, Manila, Saigon, Bangkok, Singapore, Calcutta), the authors ask whether they can reverse their heterogenetic to orthogenetic roles. Having developed as 'outposts of imperial civilisations ... will the cities change their cultural roles and contribute more to the formation of a civilisation indigenous to the area'? The major factor affecting what they term 'secondary urbanisation' (q.v.) is that 'the market, freed from controls of tradition, status and moral rule, becomes the worldwide heterogenetic institution' (p.63). Hence, their reference, not simply to an undifferentiated concept of 'world economy' but to the market as 'the worldwide heterogenetic economic institution' freed from the forces they indicate, suggests a subtle acknowledgement of the local historical and cultural constraints which act upon it.

The 1960s

In the 1960s, interest in the colonial city was primarily theoretical, concerned with questioning western and industrial urban models and privileging what today would be seen as a static concept of culture as an explanatory variable. Abu-Lughod (1965:429), who uses the term '"colonial" city' to refer to the European part of Cairo, regrets that 'no case studies had been made of the introduction of *western* urban forms into *non-western* countries' (emphasis added). Using a modernisation paradigm (though without the ideological trimmings this implies), Wheatley (1969:31) referred to the '*cultural hybrid* of the colonial city which typically subsumes elements of both the *traditional* and *modern* world' (emphasis added).

By 1967, however, McGee's substantial chapter on the colonial city in *The South East Asian City* had added a critical new dimension. Whilst the macrocontext was still apparently provided by a diffusionist geographical and cultural paradigm of 'The impact of the west' and Europeanisation, it is his specific reference to a given mode of production (though this phrase is not used), namely, capitalism, which distinguishes his account from earlier writings, i.e.:

> The most prominent function of these cities was economic; the colonial city was the 'nerve centre' of colonial exploitation. Concentrated there were the institutions through which capitalism extended its control over the colonial economy – the banks, agency houses, trading companies, shipping companies. These banks ... were, of course, largely European owned.
>
> (pp.56–57)

Or again:

> A situation was created in which the countryside, with the exception of the enclaves of foreign capitalism – mines and plantations – became increasingly impoverished in comparison to the towns.
>
> (p.72)

Whilst McGee elsewhere refers to the introduction of western-type suburbs and western city models into southeast Asia (p.139), not yet specifying that these themselves were products of capitalist forms of development in the core, the attention given to capitalism in the colonial transformation of south Asian cities, though not developed at length, predates the contributions of both Castells (1972a) and Harvey (1973) cited by Friedmann above.

Other than McGee, the most developed discussion in this period is that of Horvath (1969) whose theoretical focus, whilst also concerned with developing a more adequate crosscultural theory of urbanisation, moved the conceptual debate a stage further, beyond the economic-technological paradigm of Sjoberg (1960) towards a more political-economic and social focus, identifying *domination* as the 'key independent variable' in explaining the colonial city. And in viewing that city as a subsystem of a colonial society, Horvath states (significantly, in the late 1960s) that 'the basic characteristic of a colonial society is that it is *heterogeneous*, unlike the models of industrial or preindustrial societies which are basically or relatively more homogeneous' (p.74); (he refers particularly to their ethnic, racial, cultural, religious, economic and social composition, see page 77).

The 1970s

Rayfield's (1974) focus is similarly on theories of urbanisation and the problems posed for them by colonialism, which is taken as the macrohistorical context in which the topic is discussed. Writing on the basis of African urbanisation studies published between 1959 and 1971, and prior to insights from 'the new urban studies', Rayfield assesses 36 significant books and articles to show how the study of urbanisation in Africa compels a rethinking 'of theories of urbanisation in general' (p.163). Of the five themes identified in this pre-Castells (1968; 1972b) conception of 'the urban', I focus here on the structure of the city. All the accounts quoted by Rayfield agree that 'the modern colonial city, usually founded early in the twentieth century, was developed by foreigners to promote their own interests'. Drawing on Gordon Childe, Polanyi, Seward and Marx, Rayfield develops his own theory of urbanisation, identifying three phases in Africa. Though referred to only in his conclusion, it is evident that Rayfield's analysis is grounded in assumptions about the world economy. In the first phase, he discusses how the European discovery of the new world influenced the decline of urban civilisations of medieval Africa, first, by exploiting rival sources of luxury goods, next, by creating a profitable slave trade. In phase two, the cities of the Guinea coast were developed out of the transatlantic slave trade. In phase three, as the western world needed more and more raw materials and markets for manufactured goods, Europeans and Americans established cities, mainly on the Guinea coast, though others developed from mining activities in the western Sudan.

Rayfield concludes by referring to the way in which cities and national economies:

> depend on relationships with world economic and political powers....
> Urbanisation is seen as a concomitant of the chain reaction in which world
> economy penetrates even the remotest peasant farmers.
>
> (p.182)

By the early 1970s, dependency and dominance-dependent paradigms of Frank (1969), and notions of interdependence (Brookfield 1975), which gave explicit recognition to colonialism in creating these conditions, had become dominant paradigms. Whilst these assumptions provided the context for my own study (King 1976), with the macrohistorical context being colonialism *per se*, a key theme of the book is expressed by the title of the paper (1970) from which it developed: 'Colonial urbanisation: a crosscultural inquiry into the social use of space', i.e. space produced under the dominant-dependent conditions of colonialism. Whilst the larger framework made use of Castell's (1972a) concept of dependent urbanisation, the theoretical emphasis was not on the political economy of colonialism *per se*,[9] but on its spatial, and especially physical, and built form manifestations. Implicit in this discussion is the assumption that these built form and spatial dimensions are intrinsic to the process of economic, social and cultural transformation, with the added implication of cultural dependence. The 'dependent urbanisation' concept is extended to comprehend the incorporation of distinctive forms of built environment (including architecture and urban form), in both the metropole and the colony, as part of a single, interdependent system.

As with earlier accounts, however (see McGee 1967 above), the use of 'western', 'European' or even 'modern industrial' to describe the social, cultural, institutional and spatial forms introduced into the colonial society elided the problem of how these institutions and forms had *themselves* developed as part of the transition to a capitalist and industrial mode of production in Europe.[10]

Basu's volume on *The rise of colonial port cities in Asia* (1979) contains the papers and discussions of a conference on this topic held in 1976 and subsequently republished (1985). Whilst none of the essays develops a theoretical model of the colonial, or colonial port city, they provide various empirical case studies relevant to this task. Though impossible to summarise the theoretical or pretheoretical assumptions of the 28 participants and 20 papers (largely from economic and social history, geography, anthropology), the overriding paradigm seems to be provided by notions of the development of world trade, though there is also reference to 'European expansion', 'expansion of the capitalist world economy' and 'the remaking of Asia on western lines'. In the preface to the new edition (1985), Reed, a geographer, writing in 1983–84, refers to the increasing interest in colonial urbanism and the need for comparative study of the phenomenon 'before the more vivid imprints of imperialism on society and landscape become blurred by the relentless forces of modernisation and nationalism'.

As with Lowder (1986) or Drakakis-Smith (1987), Reed sees the object of interest as being 'the modern urban history of the third world' (p.ix) rather than that of the 'world economy' or 'world system' as such, though he refers to scholars interested in colonial towns and cities having become interested in the writings of Frank, Wallerstein and Amin in regard to 'the crystallisation of an interconnected world economic system' in recent times and 'the persistent dependency relationships that bind dominant industrial nations of the western core to subordinate states of a less developed periphery'. Such scholars, according to Reed, are concerned with the 'role of embryonic primate cities ... as essential instruments of exploitation and spatial integration through which metropolitan authorities in Europe projected decisive political-economic power into distant territories'. Others, '*who avoid a global perspective*' (emphasis added) 'focus on regional processes and accounts of particular towns and cities'.

The essays cover three broad themes: the relationship between the city and its hinterland (Melaka, Goa, Calcutta (today, Kolkata), Colombo); the development and character of mercantile elites (Bombay, Karachi); the rise, growth and morphology of colonial port cities (Madras, Bombay, Calcutta, Manila, Surat). In terms of a 'world economy' model and the role of particular cities within this, including questions of economic, political, social, cultural as well as physical and spatial transformation, there are various insights; e.g. on the development of 'modern' retailing and the ethnic groups and changing practices involved; on the formation of new social structures through recruitment to mercantile elites; on merchant lifestyles; on the constitution of real estate in Colombo or, through the process of colonial government and administration, the development of 'entitled' housing and its subsequent transformation into state housing for government employees. Because of its wide authorship (some of whom originally emanate from the countries discussed), more attention is given to the indigenous and local nature of the cases discussed, as opposed to much of the earlier work on colonial urbanism which has arisen from postcolonial European scholarship. This is discussed below. Basu's introduction refers to the persistence of precolonial traditions and the resurfacing of precolonial structures in ethnic recruitment, roles and merchant lifestyles.

The 1980s

The 14 essays in Ross and Telkamp's collection on *Colonial Cities* (1985) result from a one-day workshop held in 1980. Although the host was the Centre for the Study of 'European Expansion', University of Leiden, this theme was not necessarily the dominant paradigm for the papers. Again, whilst the aim was not to develop theoretical models, the urban theoretical input was represented by three themes suggested by the editors (though, unfortunately, infrequently followed in the case studies): city function, as a link between the outside world, world economy hinterland; organisation, in terms of governance and social control; spatial layout, and the way this encoded and determined social stratification and categorisation. However, the cities selected in the collection (located either in Latin America, Africa, south and southeast Asia) represent a conceptualisation of colonialism constrained by 'developmentalist' assumptions. They are, with two exceptions, cities: (1) where the dominant colonial minority is culturally European, racially Caucasoid and (in contrast to the belief systems of the areas where they were established) nominally or actually Christian; (2) created or influenced by a world system of capitalism; and (3) of what are now independent states where the earlier colonised peoples have subsequently re-established at least formal sovereignty over their own territory. They are cases of 'limited' or 'unsuccessful' colonialism (i.e. they do not include one-time colonial cities in North America or Australasia) (King 1985:9).

From the 1980s, however, work on colonial cities has incorporated insights from the political economy of urbanisation, world system, urban social spatial theory, work on the internationalisation of capital, and increasing attention to the significance of physical and spatial as well as representational and symbolic dimensions of the built environment both in regard to new forms of consumption and the culturally localised processes of a global transformation; the creation of markets in land, the constitution, and reconstitution of social categories and relationships, both in spatial and symbolic terms, and increased attention to the role of the built environment in questions of consumption (Armstrong and McGee 1985; King 1985; Smith and Nemeth 1986).

However, whilst there is wide acceptance of paradigms of 'the capitalist world economy', 'the new international division of labour' (Drakakis-Smith 1987), 'international capitalist system', 'dependent capitalism' and 'neocolonialism' (Lowder 1986), and 'global economy' (Simon 1984), the postcolonial city in these accounts is still ultimately located in the third world rather than the world economy as such. This is surprising when, seen in the context of changes over the last three decades, cities in both one-time metropoles and one-time colonies have increasingly developed similar characteristics: extensive international labour migration; ethnic, racial and cultural heterogeneity; economic, social and spatial polarisation; an 'informal sector' and, in regard to the built environment, investment-based high-rise office towers and consumption-oriented suburbs (King 1984b; 1986b), to mention these in their most general terms. That there is a Third World in major First World cities as well as a First World in major Third World ones has become commonplace since 1980. Likewise, reference by Massey (1988) or others to the 'Brazilianisation' of Britain echoes the use by McGee and others, 20 years earlier, of 'Europeanisation' to describe colonial cities in south Asia; both terms inadequately distinguish the geographical from the political, the material (or economic) from the cultural.

Other historical case studies (e.g. Bayly 1983; Oldenburg 1985; King 1984a, 1989a; Metcalf 1984; Rabinow 1989; Wright 1987, 1989 and the papers here) chart transformations in the built environment, including discussion on changes in taste and consumption habits and their relation to spatial and architectural forms, new forms of consciousness and subjectivity and cultural politics of the colonial state. These are areas about which much less is known and where new directions in critical and cultural theory offer many insights.

Three comments conclude this section: that virtually all of the studies cited above emanate from western scholars, often working in postcolonial situations, is sufficient warning about their authenticity, despite disclaimers (e.g. Rayfield 1974; King 1976). More studies, by scholars indigenous to the places discussed, are needed to defray charges of an orientalist 'occidentalism' (Said 1978; Clifford 1988).[11]

Secondly, despite mounting evidence on the role of colonial urbanism and urbanisation in the formation of the world urban system (colonial urbanisation is not discussed here but see, for example, accounts by Saueressig-Schreuder 1986, and Chaichan 1988), the most significant gap in our knowledge is of the impact of colonialism on urbanism and urbanisation in the metropoles themselves (King 1989b).

Thirdly, increasing commitment to, and salience of, different 'global' perspectives should encourage the more widespread development of conceptual and analytical categories which are applicable to urban phenomena in *all* parts of the world, an approach often absent in the past (Robertson 1989; Wallerstein 1987).

NOTES

1 From Anthony D. King, 'Colonialism, Urbanism and the Capitalist World-Economy', *International Journal of Urban and Regional Research*, 13, 1, 1989 © Edward Arnold, © Wiley.

2 'Colonialism' and 'imperialism' are used here as two sides of the same coin: colonialism referring to the society where exploitation by the imperial power takes place.

3 Friedmann refers to Browning and Roberts (1980); Cohen (1981); Portes and Walton (1981); Soja *et al.* (1983); and papers subsequently included in Smith and Feagin (1987) and Thrift and Taylor (1986).

4 See Redfield and Singer (1954). In a footnote, McGee (1967) refers to the use of the term 'colonial city' in 1907 to refer to Bangkok which was 'unique among colonial cities at that time because it had no clearly demarcated areas for Europeans'. See Young (1907).

5 The works cited by Friedmann in footnote 3 above are largely concerned with the negative impact of developments in the periphery on the urban economies of the core (especially the USA) rather than vice versa.

6 Robertson (1988) provides a valuable insight into the increasing significance given to culture and the different orientations towards it from sociology and social anthropology, the initial separation between the two disciplines attributable to 'a particular conjuncture in the long-term process of globalisation': 'On the face of it, a strict devotion to the social domain would seem to allow culture (as frequently conceived as a realm of values, beliefs and symbols) into the analytical picture only as a way of *explaining* social phenomena or as *explainable* by the latter' (1988:9–10). See also Robertson (1989).

7 The account does not consider the substantive issue of colonialism itself, nor does it take account of literature on North or South America, or in languages other than English. It is a selection of monographs and articles on theoretical discussions on colonial cities, largely relating to the British colonial experience. Studies of individual colonial cities, which no doubt would widen the terms of discussion, are not included.

8 Redfield and Singer make no reference here to the fact that some of these are colonial cities.

9 Gutkind draws attention to the absence of an economic analysis in his review in *International Journal of Urban and Regional Research* 5, 290–1.

10 This is revised in King (1984b).

11 Or studies by scholars from Brazil, India or China of postcolonial urbanism in Britain.

BIBLIOGRAPHY

Abu-Lughod, J. (1965) A tale of two cities: the origins of modern Cairo, *Comparative Studies in Society and History*, 7: 429–57.

Abu-Lughod, J. (1980) *Rabat, Urban Apartheid in Morocco*, Princeton: Princeton University Press.

Ardener, E. (1985) 'Social anthropology and the decline of modernism', in J. Overing, ed., *Reason and Morality*, London: Tavistock.

Armstrong, W. and McGee, T.G. (1985) *Theatres of Accumulation: Studies in Asian and Latin American Urbanisation*, London: Methuen.

Asad, T. (1983) *Anthropology and the Colonial Encounter*, New York: Humanities Press.

Basu, D., ed. (1979) *The Rise and Growth of Colonial Port Cities in Asia*, Lanham, MD: University Press of America (second edition, 1985).

Bayly, C. (1983) *Rulers, Townsmen and Bazaars: North Indian Society in the Age of British Rule, 1770–1870*, Cambridge: Cambridge University Press.

Becker, P.G., Frieden, J., Schatz, S.P. and Sklar, R.L. (1987) *Post-imperialism: International Capitalism and Development in the Late Twentieth Century*, Boulder, CO: Rienner.

Brookfield, H. (1975) *Interdependent Development*, London: Methuen.

Browning, H.L. and Roberts, B.R. (1980) 'Urbanisation, sectoral transformation and the utilisation of labour in Latin America', *Comparative Urban Research* 8: 86–104.

Brush, J.E. (1970) 'The growth of the Presidency towns' in R.G. Fox, ed., *Urban India: Society, Space and Image*, Chapel Hill, NC: Duke University Press.

Castells, M. (1968) 'Is there an urban sociology?' (translated by C.G. Pickvance, ed.) in M. Castells (1976), *Urban Sociology: Critical essays*, London: Methuen.

Castells, M., ed. (1972a) *Imperialismo y Urbanisation en America Latina*, Barcelona: Editorial Gustava Gili.

Castells, M. (1972b) *La Question Urbaine*, Paris: Maspero.

Chaichian, Mohammed A. (1988) 'The effects of world capitalist economy on urbanisation in Egypt', *International Journal of Middle Eastern Studies*, 20: 23–4.

Chilcote, R.H. (1984) *Theories of Development and Underdevelopment*, Boulder, CO: Westview Press.

Christopher, A.J. (1988) *The British Empire at its Zenith*, Beckenham: Croom Helm.

Clifford, J. (1988) *The Predicament of Culture: Twentieth Century Ethnography, Literature and Art*, Cambridge, MA: Harvard University Press.

Cohen, R.B. (1981) 'The new international division of labour, multinational corporations and urban hierarchy', in M. Dear and A.J. Scott, eds, *Urbanisation and Urban Planning in Capitalist Society*, London and New York: Methuen.

Davis, K. (1960) 'Colonial expansion and urban diffusion in the Americas', *International Journal of Comparative Sociology*, 1: 43–66.

Drakakis-Smith, D., ed. (1986) *Urbanisation in the Developing World*, Beckenham: Croom Helm.

Drakakis-Smith, D. (1987) *The Third World City*, London: Methuen.

Feagin, J. (1985) 'The global context of metropolitan growth: Houston and the oil industry', *American Sociological Review*, 90: 1204–30.

Frank, A.G. (1969) *Latin America: Underdevelopment or Revolution. Essays on the Development of Underdevelopment*, New York: Monthly Review Press.

Frank, A.G. (1971) *Sociology of Development and Underdevelopment of Sociology*, London: Pluto.

Friedmann, J. (1986) 'The world city hypothesis', *Development and Change*, 17: 69–84.

Friedmann, J. and Wolff, G. (1982) 'World city formation: an agenda for research', *International Journal of Urban and Regional Research*, 6: 309–43.

Harvey, D. (1973) *Social Justice and the City*, London: Edward Arnold.

Henderson, J. (1986) 'The new international division of labour and urban development in the world system' in D. Drakakis-Smith, ed., *Urbanisation in the Developing World*, Beckenham: Croom Helm, pp.63–82.

Henderson, J. and Castells, M., eds (1987) *Global Restructuring and Territorial Development*, London and Beverly Hills: Sage.

Hobsbawm, E.J. (1975) *The Age of Capital*, London: Weidenfeld and Nicolson.

Horvath, R.J. (1969) 'In search of a theory of urbanisation: notes on the colonial city', *East Lakes Geographer* 5: 69–82.

King, A.D. (1976) *Colonial Urban Development: Culture, Social Power and Environment*, London: Routledge and Kegan Paul.

King, A.D. (1983) 'The world economy is everywhere: urban history and the world system', in *Urban History Yearbook 1983*, Leicester: Leicester University Press.

King, A.D. (1984a) *The Bungalow: The Production of a Global Culture*, London: Routledge and Kegan Paul.

King, A.D. (1984b) 'The social production of building form: theory and research', *Society and Space*, 2: 429–46.

King, A.D. (1985) 'Colonial cities: global pivots of change', in R. Ross and G. Telkamp, eds, *Colonial Cities*, Dordrecht, Boston and Lancaster: Martinus Nijhoff for the University of Leiden, pp.7–32.

King, A.D. (1989a) *Urbanism, Colonialism and the World-Economy*, London: Routledge.

King, A.D. (1989b) *Global Cities: Post-imperialism and the Internationalisation of London*, London: Routledge.

Kosambi, M. (1985) 'Commerce, conquest and the colonial city: the role of locational factors in the rise of Bombay', *Economic and Political Weekly*, January 5: 32–7.

Lowder, S. (1986) *Inside Third World Cities*, Beckenham: Croom Helm.

Mabogunje, A.L. (1980) *The Development Process: A Spatial Perspective*, London: Hutchinson.

McGee, T.G. (1967) *The Southeast Asian City*, London: Bell.

Massey, D. (1988) 'A new class of geography', *Marxism Today*, May: 12–15.

Metcalf, T.R. (1984) 'Architecture and the representation of Empire: India, 1860–1910', *Representations*, 5: 37–65.

Metcalf, T.R. (1988) *An Imperial Vision: Indian Architecture and Britain's Raj*, Berkeley: University of California Press.

Oldenburg, V.T. (1985) *The Making of Colonial Lucknow, 1857–1870*, Princeton, NJ: Princeton University Press.

Portes, A.J. and Walton, J. (1981) *Labour, Class and the International System*, London: Academic Press.

Preston, P.W. (1986) *Making Sense of Development*, London: Routledge and Kegan Paul.

Rabinow, P. (1989) *French Modern: Norms and Forms of Missionary and Didactic Pathos*, Cambridge, MA: MIT Press.

Rayfield, J.R. (1974) 'Theories of urbanisation and the colonial city in West Africa', *Africa, the Journal of the International African Institute*, 44: 163–85.

Redfield, R. and Singer, M.S. (1954) 'The cultural role of cities', *Economic Development and Cultural Change*, 3: 53–73.

Roberts, B. (1978) *Cities of Peasants*, London: Arnold.

Robertson, R. (1987) 'Globalisation theory and civilisational analysis', *Comparative Civilisations Review*, 17: 20–30.

Robertson, R. (1988) 'The sociological significance of culture: some general considerations', *Theory, Culture and Society*, 5: 3–24.

Robertson, R. (1989) 'Globality, global culture and images of world order', in H. Haverkamp and N. Smelser, eds, *Social Change and Modernity*, Berkeley: University of California Press.

Ross, R. and Telkamp, G., eds (1985) *Colonial Cities*, Dordrecht, Boston and Lancaster: Martinus Nijhoff for the University of Leiden.

Said, E. (1978) *Orientalism*, New York: Pantheon.

Salinas, P.W. (1983) 'Mode of production and spatial organisation in Peru', in F.G. Moulaert and P.W. Salinas, eds, *Regional Analysis and the New International Division of Labour*, The Hague and London: Kluwer-Nijhoff.

Saueressig-Schreuder, Y. (1986) 'The impact of British colonial rule on the urban hierarchy of Burma', *Review*, 10: 245–77.

Simon, D. (1984) 'Third world colonial cities in context: conceptual and theoretical approaches with particular reference to Africa', *Progress in Human Geography*, 8: 493–514.

Sjoberg, G. (1960) *The Pre-industrial City*, Glencoe: Free Press.

Smith, D.A. and Nemeth, R.J. (1986) 'Urban development in south east Asia: a historical structural analysis' in D. Drakakis-Smith, ed., *Urbanisation in the Developing World*, Beckenham: Croom Helm, pp.121–40.

Smith, M.P. and Feagin, J.R., eds (1987) *The Capitalist City*, Oxford: Basil Blackwell.

Soja, E., *et al.* (1983) 'Urban restructuring: an analysis of social and spatial change in Los Angeles', *Economic Geography*, 59: 195–230.

Southall, A. (1971) 'The impact of imperialism on urban development in Africa', in V. Turner, *Colonialism in Africa, 1870–1960*, Cambridge: Cambridge University Press, vol. 3.

Taylor, P.J. (1985) *Political Geography: World-economy, Nation-state and Locality*, London: Longman.

Thrift, N. (1986) 'The geography of international economic disorder', in R.J. Johnston and P.J. Taylor, eds, *The World in Crisis? Geographical Perspectives*, Oxford: Basil Blackwell, pp.12–67.

Thrift, N. and Taylor, P.J., eds (1986) *Multinationals and the World Economy*, Beckenham: Croom Helm.

Wallerstein, I. (1987) 'World-systems analysis', in A. Giddens and J.H. Turner, eds, *Social Theory Today*, Cambridge: Polity Press, pp.309–24.

Walton, J. (1976) 'The political economy of world urban systems: directions for comparative research', in J. Walton and L. Masotti, eds, *The City in Comparative Perspective*, London: Sage.

Wheatley, P. (1969) *City as Symbol*, London: University College.

Wright, G. (1987) 'Tradition in the service of modernity: architecture and urbanism in French colonial policy, 1900–1930', *Journal of Modern History*, 59: 291–316.

Wright, G. (1989) *At Home and Abroad: French Colonial Urbanism, 1880–1930*, Chicago: Chicago University Press.

Young, E. (1907) *The Kingdom of the Yellow Robe*, third edition, London: Constable.

Chapter 3: Writing colonial space: a review article[1]

It would be tempting to suggest that it all started with Janet Abu-Lughod's seminal article on the origins of modern Cairo, published in this very journal 50 years ago:

> The major metropolis in almost every newly-industrialising country is not a single unified city but, in fact, two quite different cities, physically juxtaposed but architecturally and socially distinct.... These dual cities have usually been a legacy from the colonial past. It is remarkable that so common a phenomenon has remained almost unstudied.[2]

No longer. There are now enough monographs and articles in print on different aspects of colonial architecture and urbanism to put together a two-semester graduate seminar on the topic. The principal outcome, I suspect, would be to demonstrate the power of particular dominant theoretical paradigms circulating in the Western academy in the last two decades.

However, the academic historiography of colonial urbanism begins at least ten years before this with the equally classic article of anthropologists Redfield and Singer on 'The Cultural Role of Cities', in which they distinguish two types of city, the orthogenetic ('the city of the moral order; the city of culture carried forward') and the heterogenetic ('the city of the technical order'), and included among the latter 'colonial cities ... the mixed cities on the periphery of an empire which carried the core culture to other peoples. In modern times such cities include the colonial cities of the European powers' (such as Jakarta, Manila, Saigon, Singapore, Calcutta) 'which admit native employees daily at the doors of their skyscraper banks'.[3] After 15 years of Marxist political economy in the study of the city, the reversion to cultural paradigms (though perhaps throwing the baby out with the bathwater) makes Redfield and Singer's article still worth reading.

Yet these two more theorised accounts are only the modern instances of a much longer history of representations, always by Western travellers, usually representatives of imperial powers, of the colonial urban and architectural phenomenon. Thus, in 1860, *The Times* correspondent in India, W.H. Russell, wrote:

> The European station is laid out in large rectangles formed by wide roads. The native city is an aggregate of houses perforated by tortuous paths.... The natives live packed in squeezed up tenements.... The handful of Europeans occupy four times the space of the city which contains tens of thousands of Hindoos and Mussulmen.[4]

Russell's text can stand for many similar representations from Africa, Asia and, in reference to Iberian colonisation, South American experience. There are a number of issues here.

In considering colonial architecture and urbanism we are dealing with at least three levels of representation. The first is the physical, spatial, institutional and symbolic representation of the colonisers themselves and their relation, along similar dimensions, to the indigenous occupants of a country, where such exist. The next level is the discursive textual representation of the first level (as with Russell's account). The third level includes the increasingly self-reflexive, analytical or critically discursive accounts (such as the monographs under review) which take as their texts, in addition to levels one and two above, other representational texts such as graphic, photographic and cartographic archives which are then read through the infinite intertextualities of contemporary theory.

Irrespective of the nature and degree of theoretical investment in these accounts or of the moral, political or cultural positionality adopted towards the subject of colonisation, the constitution of the discourse on colonial urbanism is in the language of the coloniser, English (generally) or French and Spanish. With a handful of exceptions (to which I refer below) this is a discourse principally constructed through a postimperial[5] subjectivity and under the particular political economic conditions of academic production[6] which I have discussed elsewhere. The unequal development of global capitalism combines with continuing post- and neo-colonial connections to permit postimperial (usually) British and American scholars to do research in the one-time colonies; the peculiar cultural competence of these scholars that permits them to identify and culturally appraise historical traces of European or Western colonial landscapes; and finally, the availability of American or British publishing outlets to disseminate their views.[7] The fact that indigenous postcolonial scholars, for example Mariam Dossal, Nezar AlSayyad, Meera Kosambi,[8] have entered and contested the dominant discourse does not detract from my basic premise: despite its liberal intentions, the discourse still emanates from the West.

In this context, my earlier suggestion that contemporary writing on postcolonial cities would better come from representatives of those cities themselves,[9] serves only to confirm the duality of a Western epistemic positionality that then requires the construction of a non-Western, postcolonial subjectivity to occupy. Yet the adoption of such a subjectivity is also a choice. To expect an indigenous, non-postcolonial representation of what the Western postimperial scholar (and his or her indigenous postcolonial contestants) refers to as 'the postcolonial city' is a contradiction in terms.[10]

In short, for writers on colonial cities, the issue is one of a positionality defined in terms of the times and spaces they choose to inhabit and the authorial subjectivity they adopt. At one extreme, it is based on assumptions about what is seen as the cataclysmic disappearance of cultural difference, of the cultural homogenisation of the world. It is a position with analogies to another present-day situation in which, with the end of the Cold War, the West is left without an Other against which to define itself. Likewise, the disappearance of 'tradition' against which the 'modern', as Other, was constituted (and in the process, constructed both),[11] leaves the 'modern' with no direction to go.

The other point to address is how far the discourse on colonial architecture and urbanism has engaged with the rapidly expanding theoretical literature in postcolonial criticism.[12] Until 1994, the encounters were few,[13] though increasing in 1995.[14] What might be called the modern history of postcolonial (literary) criticism, informed by poststructuralism, began seriously in the early 1980s.[15] Its early exponents (Homi Bhabha, Edward Said, Gayatri Spivak) focused on a critique of literary and historical writing and, more important for my argument, were located in the humanities of the Western academy. The critique was directed especially at Eurocentricism and the cultural racism of the West. Subsequently, the objects of the deconstructive postcolonial critique expanded to include film, video, television, photography, all examples of cultural praxis that are mobile, portable, and circulating in the West. Yet given that such literature, photography or museum displays have existed for decades, why did this postcolonial critique only get established in the 1980s? And why has it not addressed the design and spatial disciplines of architecture and planning? The answer is apparently simple. Postcolonial criticism in the West had to wait until a sufficient number of postcolonial intellectuals, and an audience for them, was established in the Western academy; as for the second question, the critique has not addressed issues in architecture and space, not only because they belong to different disciplines (and are difficult to handle) but because the cultural products on which imperial discourses are inscribed – cities, landscapes and buildings – unlike literary texts, films and photography are, for these postcolonial critics and their Western audiences, static, not mobile; absent, not present; distant, not near. Critics have to take their own postcolonial subjectivity (developed from a dialectic between East and West, to use some shorthand) halfway round the world to experience them.[16]

With perhaps the single exception of France,[17] critical discourses on colonial urban culture, positioned from a white, male, Western viewpoint, and from different theoretical perspectives, began in the 1950s and were the result of social science scholars, often working in 'aid' or 'development' roles in the colony or postcolony.[18] It was a discourse which spoke especially to the cultural politics of urban planning. Yet the resuscitation of interest in these issues in the American and British academy in the late 1980s has more to do with issues of theory, cultural politics and racism in the West than those of urban policy and practice in the postcolony. Only recently has the colonial city concept been mobilised as a metaphor to represent the increasingly colonial, ethnically and spatially segregated situation of Western cities.[19]

In this context, reviewing these books four or five years after publication and many years after their authors settled on the narrative within which they were written is problematic. Though recent work in postcolonial criticism[20] or the cultural politics of landscape representation[21] might provide some protective footwear for authors now stepping cautiously into this epistemological minefield, most scholars exposed to the cultural and political shocks of colonialism, and with their authorial authority questioned by it, have long been aware of the necessities of deconstruction (if by other names) and the problems of representation prior to the emergence of today's more sophisticated theorising. As Paul Rabinow states in his preface, anthropologist Bernard Cohn was addressing questions of knowledge and power, colonies and space, long before he (Rabinow) had heard of Foucault.

In this context, Norma Evenson's *The Indian Metropolis: A View Towards the West* agonises least with the problematic of writing colonial space. Rather, as an architectural historian, Evenson makes a perceptive reading of more or less everything written in English on these cities to the time of writing, without specific reference to particular theoretical texts. Her aim, to produce 'a broad survey of the architecture and planning of Bombay, Calcutta, Madras and New Delhi from their inception until the present time' (p.vii), examining these British-created cities which 'served in themselves as instruments of cultural change in India, providing a theatre for the demonstration of European architectural and planning concepts' (p.vii).

Moreover, as Evenson states that 'in some respects, this study forms part of the history of Western architecture and urbanism' (p.vii), the strictures about positionality coming, for example, from Young, or Chakrabarty, that the space of 'Europe' invariably remains the 'sovereign theoretical subject of all histories,' a 'silent referent for all historical knowledge'[22] are not really allowed to surface. Similarly, the time of (a Western) modern – the subtext of Evenson's narrative – becomes the silent referent for geographical knowledge. Indeed, this is the case for all the books under review, and it is difficult to see how things could be otherwise, except by specifically acknowledging this position. The more searching question is what exactly is this Europe or, in the case of Evenson's narrative, the West, and the modern which, in writing about the 'Indian metropolis', constantly become 'Othered' because of the references to it.[23] Because Evenson's theme is the social, urban, cultural and especially spatial and architectural history of each of the four cities in relation to the West, her seven chapters speak from this position. The three cities are therefore 'hybrid': the 'Architecture of Europe' leads on to 'The Long Debate' about the appropriate architectural style for the British to adopt, followed by chapters on 'Modern (*sic*) Planning and the Colonial City', 'The Modern (*sic*) Movement' (with interesting comments on the absence of its social basis), concluding with the 'Post Independence City' and 'the Architecture of Independence'. Having said this, however, what is commendable in Evenson's account is precisely the care she takes to ferret out fascinating material and quotations that illustrate different Indian positions and meanings, not the least of which are those on recent views of urban development. Capitalism, however, is not part of the narrative.

There is much new historical material in this book, including attention to questions of gender; the reader gets a sense of the varying historical social, economic and cultural conditions responsible for producing the characteristics of these very different cities. Attention is paid to the way in which British institutions (like municipal organisations or the Royal Institute of British Architects) are extended to, and transformed in, India and the particular individuals involved in the process (though this comes out in all these books). Evenson is especially concerned to see architecture and space as a socialising, acculturating influence on Indian life, noting that the adoption of Western architecture brought Western interiors and Western lifestyle. However, as there is no specific discussion of consumption, this category again remains problematic. The author does use well-chosen quotations to raise questions of real and controversial interest to postcolonial theorists concerning the production of different subjectivities, such as the observation that 'in some ways, the cultural cross-currents of colonial India produced remarkable individuals. The cosmopolitan Indian might be seen as a genuine citizen of the world, multilingual, open-minded, flexible and tolerant. At the same time, the anglicised Indian might be viewed as a cultural traitor.... Was adaptability a form of duplicity?' (p.81). The same processes of cultural and political confrontation were also forming British identities, of course. As for Lutyens, the author might have been reading a milder version of Foucault: 'Architecture, more than any other art, represents the intellectual progress of those that are in authority' (p.105). Overall, this is a very readable account; yet, from a position of both practice and theory, various issues raised cry out for a more critical conceptualisation, not least the unproblematised notion of 'slums'.

Though also dealing with British India, Metcalf's agenda is quite different. Where Evenson engages with a realist present, both as commentator and critic, Metcalf's account is not only more selfconsciously theorised (rather than theoretical) but also more interpretative and textual. And where Evenson's main narrative is an unproblematised Westernisation, Metcalf's is 'architecture as representation', particularly under the cultural and political conditions of colonial power. The work of Foucault, both directly and via Paul Rabinow, on the relationships between knowledge and power, plus the critical use of Said's account of knowledge creation in the colonial enterprise, are Metcalf's main theoretical sources (these themes also inform Wright's account). Hence, his clearly expressed focus on 'how political authority took shape in architecture and how these colonial buildings helped shape the discourse on Empire' is not meant as a comprehensive architectural history. The book is, rather, a carefully researched documentation of these issues. Metcalf's objective is 'to make clear that colonial building in India is not unique but expressive of broader currents that set off the colonial world from that of Europe' sharpening 'those contrasts that do exist between the nature of colonialism in India and that in colonial territories elsewhere' (p.xii). On this, there are intriguing insights into the work of Lutyens' partner, Herbert Baker, in Pretoria.

Throughout Metcalf argues that architecture 'actively informs and gives meaning to the nature of Britain's Raj' (p.xii) (presumably for at least some of the British, as the issue of polysemicity is not dealt with).

Metcalf's gaze is mainly on the architectural hermeneutics of the Raj, on questions of style and meaning. His historian's skills are used to excavate the archive and buttress his interpretations. In 'The Mastery of the Past' he discusses how India's architecture was constructed to portray a 'traditional' society as a necessary complement to Europe's progress: the British cobbled together elements of India's architectural past to form the Indo-Saracenic style, which they then used to represent the Raj as legitimately Indian but also socially and culturally modern. In discussing the Native Princes' palaces, Metcalf departs from the hermeneutic task concerning architecture as symbol and treats it more as a social process, concerned with the social spaces of billiard rooms, dining rooms, libraries, as well as their gendered use, and supposed disciplinary function in processes of modernisation. Architecture and spatial organisation were used to back up English education and modernise the princely elite.

In an excellent chapter on 'Arts, Crafts and Empire', Metcalf argues how Britain, represented as the paradigmatic industrial society, came to regard India as the equally paradigmatic Other, a traditional society whose craft tradition could be used to critique industrialisation. As with Rabinow's and Wright's accounts, what is placed in the foreground here is the immensely important function of colonies, not only in the formation of British and French national and imperial identities but also, in the realm of culture, in the metropole, whether in relation to craftwork, architecture or community. These dimensions are generally absent from standard design histories, which are invariably treated within an autonomous national frame. The discovery in postcolonial and poststructural literary criticism of what is taken for granted in the writing of a text has so far not been extended to the recognition of colonialism in the construction of metropolitan tradition. Metcalf also has valuable things to say on classicism as the paradigmatic imperial architecture.

Metcalf implicitly prompts insights that Wright addresses more directly, namely, that many of the conditions and cultural contradictions subsequently arising in the West from the 1960s, and Eurocentrically labelled postmodern, were prefigured in European colonies at least a century before. Indeed, a major contribution of these books is to destabilise both the notion of the postmodern as well as the modern on which it rests.

In *The Tradition of Indian Architecture*, Giles Tillotson, the architectural historian, aims to study 'the changes in India's architectural tradition and in Indian taste that occurred in response to the influence of British architecture in India and the policies of British imperial rule' (p.vii). However, given the reflexive approach of Metcalf (or Rabinow), this self-evidential stance, which takes the concept of tradition as unproblematic, results in a '*wie es eigentlich gewesen war*' sort of narrative, lending support to the comments at the start concerning the conditions producing the colonial urban discourse. The book 'is not a critique of colonialism.

Its concern is to describe events in architectural history, not to evaluate political systems' (p.viii), presumably, in the opinion of the author, because each can be kept apart. Apart from Said's *Orientalism*, which, though mentioned in the bibliography, seems not to have influenced the text, there is no other theoretical source. Tillotson's relationship with his sources is therefore direct and unmediated, questions of taste in architecture being assessed 'according to an appropriate aesthetic canon' with which (we) 'must be acquainted'. There is, nonetheless, interesting historical material in Tillotson's account which complements that of the two previous texts, especially on the craft revival in England and India.

The questions prompted by this, but also by all of these books, are much more about the economic, social, cultural, and especially institutional conditions which sustain particular intellectual traditions and discursive forms, providing opportunities for publication and circulation. In all cases, India continues to provide the space on which different theoretical debates (and Western academic careers) are written.[24]

Such questions are equally pertinent for the last book on Indian colonial urbanism considered in the essay, as Dossal's study of the planning of Bombay city is one of the few studies emerging from the postcolony rather than the metropole. Though such dualistic categories may be suspect, space, academic networks, and questions of access to recent published scholarship are all powerful constraints on the production of knowledge. Rather than dealing with issues of tradition, representation, or cultural identity, Dossal, while hinting at various theoretical paradigms in her first chapter, in fact writes a conventional urban history of Bombay. Although the main focus on the British, 'among them … modern India's first urban planners, men who dreamt civic as well as imperial dreams, (men who) attempted to introduce the latest ideas in civil engineering and public health current in Europe', the author also aims to address 'Indian responses to British plans … [which were] frequently critical and sometimes even violently so.'

However, as virtually all sources used are British and few, if any, records exist of Indian views, the British set the agenda. It is their 'definition of the situation', as well as their definition of states of health which the author accepts. Various postcolonial critics have remarked that the West is always searching for an 'authentic voice': my own hope that the author would include some essentialist or (from my viewpoint) 'ethnomedical' discussion of Indian health states, or culturally or religiously different attitudes to water, for example, or some other essential Indian view is doubtlessly the result of my own post(?) imperial subjectivity. Instead, the narrative positionality adopted is more in keeping with the debates on public health and 'urban improvement' in Dyos and Wolff's *The Victorian City* of 1973.[25] From this stance, however, this extremely well-documented account (the first of a two-volume study on spatial restructuring and urban growth in Bombay) provides many insights into the (British) making of Bombay and its place in the British colonial urban system: the way in which, to use Rabinow's terms, the norms of London, Manchester and Leeds (such as 'the Sanitary Idea', health and density statistics) were used to shape the forms of Bombay (such as sewerage systems, urban layouts and civic space). The Europeans who formed 1 per cent of Bombay's population dominated the spatial development of the city, establishing its typical Victorian institutions. Driven by the demand for cotton from Britain and opium shipments to China, docks and warehousing were restructured in the mid-century. There is much in this book (and the others) to demonstrate the existence of a massive cross-cultural, worldwide practice of urban engineering and of ideas of civic culture based on the sanitary ideas of Britain and France in the mid-century. The fascinating study of dockland reclamation, railroads and Bombay's stock exchange, belongs as much to a history of nineteenth-century imperial space economies and the development of global capitalism as it does to India's.

Rabinow's *French Modern* is quite a different story (a kind of Arabian Nights set of tales, in fact, if the Orientalist metaphor can be forgiven). Methodologically, it is in a class by itself. It attempts, in a word, to form an answer to that old conundrum: How is society possible? The most ambitious in scope of the books here, it addresses the construction of modernity in France, though more especially the 'diverse construction of norms and forms adequate to understand and to regulate what came to be known as modern society' (p.9). A critical anthropologist who long ago absorbed what Foucault had to say, Rabinow provides the kind of defamiliarisation and relativisation of both society and the city which scholars in historical urban studies, while often looking for, have not managed to achieve since that field became a serious specialty in the 1960s. Because spatial organisation and, eventually, urban planning is so foundational to the disciplinary and formative nature of modern societies, Rabinow's detailed historical ethnography of developments in architecture, hygiene, politics, social statistics and planning, as well as biology, geography and social theory in France, is extremely valuable; his aim is to continue 'the exploration … of some of the contours of modern power and knowledge Foucault had begun to map', specifically the development of welfare to complement Marx's capitalism and Weber's bureaucracy. Rabinow traces 'the emergence of certain practices of reason' in France (and its colonies), fields of knowledge and the forms they take, and the 'technicians of general ideas', effectively, the development of the professional class who construct both the intellectual and physical space within which (form) social life operates, distinguishing between a 'middling modernism' of a more universal social and spatial environment and the 'techno-cosmopolitanism' of a more culturally differentiated one. Along with Markus' *Buildings and Power*,[26] Rabinow's discussion of the development of architectural typologies is a valuable contribution to understanding the socially constitutive nature of architectural space.

Colonialism is not told as any grand theory or metanarrative here but, rather, in terms of the careers and practices of individuals, especially the neo-conservative aristocrat Hubert Lyautey and the military technocrat Joseph-Simon Gallieni, whose administrative and urbanistic exploits in Morocco, Indochina and Madagascar are discussed by Rabinow in detail and at length, though there is insufficient space to do justice to his comments here.

The narrative of Rabinow's admittedly experimental text, punctuated throughout by terse theoretical subheads and ending with a highly structured index which, contradictorily, omits all proper names, is exactly represented by the title and sub-title. It is here that I have two related comments. The first is that, despite the revolutionary stimulus to rethink the nature of the social in France, the space of the nation, as implied by the title, is too constraining a space to capture the notion of the modern;[27] moreover, this national space depends not only on its imperial connections but, in another sense, on imperialism existing worldwide. It would have been good to see more of this, though perhaps that is another book.

Gwen Wright's *The Politics of Design in French Colonial Urbanism*, as befits the author's background in architecture as well as architectural history, is the most architecturally and design-oriented text of the group, as is demonstrated by the very well-chosen selection of plans and illustrations. Though sharing certain themes with Metcalf and some history with Rabinow, Wright's monograph contains excellent research that is, again, very different in terms of focus, narrative and methodology. In a study of the relation between history, power and architecture, her stated aim lies in 'a concern to analyse the relations between culture and politics, specifically efforts to use architecture and urban design, ranging from ornamental details to municipal regulations, as part of a complex political agenda' (pp.7–8). The space and time in which she operates is nineteenth- and early twentieth-century France (especially Paris) and the French colonies of Morocco, Indochina and Madagascar.

Wright pays more attention to terminology. The terms modern, modernity and modernisation are used to describe 'the shift from a local market to international capitalism, from production based on self-sufficiency and exchange to a system that responds only to distant consumer markets' (p.7) with the concomitant physical and spatial changes that these imply, although this is not a political economy of colonial space. Wright draws on a range of theoretical and historical literature on imperialism and colonialism as also work on French and English colonial architecture and urbanism; these feed into her account, which is historical rather than theoretical. The book has many seminal themes of which I shall only touch on a few.

Far more than in Britain, French colonies were always seen as social laboratories in which both general rules of social organisation and the difference of cultural particularities were sought. Indeed, the difference between French and British colonial experience, not least with the highly institutionalised colonial urban theory, policy and practice that the French developed in the metropole, is one of the principal lessons of Wright's book. Intense effort is put into creating appropriate regional styles for urban design programmes imposed in the interests of 'cultural identity' and, hopefully, social control. Interest in the colonies by the new generation of social scientists and architect-urbanists was also a response to social decline in France, its leaders worried about social unrest and questions of national identity. In this context, the colonies were seen as places from which the nation could reinvigorate the metropole.

Particularly illuminating are Wright's account of the Ecole Coloniale and her detailed description of Ernest Hebrard's utopian design – in Beaux-Art classicism – for the Centre Mondial in 1913, a 'world capital' linked to all parts of the world for which, however, he could find no takers. Also well treated is the conscious shift in French urban policies in the colonies from those of assimilation (as in Algiers in 1830 or Saigon in 1859 with the physical destruction of the indigenous city), to those of association in the twentieth century, utilising a form of pre-postmodernism, in an attempt to mitigate the negative effects of unsympathetic modernisation. In Morocco, Lyautey perfected the idea of the dual city, preserving tradition for Moroccans and creating modernity for the colonial French (one thinks of today, where multiculturalism is a code word for Others). His efforts to establish in Rabat a Bureau of Antiquities, Fine Arts and Monuments suggest a foretaste of the Aga Khan Program at the Massachusetts Institute of Technology. Though Wright does not persist with the economically oriented narrative hinted at the start, she returns occasionally to this from her largely urban and architectural history, discussing the land issue, for example, and how the space of street systems in Morocco was restructured to provide economic growth and stability for European investors, or the way in which vernacular urban design was linked to the promotion of tourism. Particularly valuable are the more social and political chapters on Indochina and Madagascar, not least because these histories are much less known, Saigon being a classic case of exploitation, and totally oriented to European use. As grand metanarrative was not in fashion in the late 1980s, Wright's carefully documented argument makes a significant contribution to the growing literature in this field.

What conclusions emerge from reading these thought-provoking monographs? First, fewer people in the future will be willing to speak about colonial*ism* in the singular. Second, for the careful reader of the best of these texts, many postmodern insights will seem like *déjà vu*. Indeed, for any serious student of colonialism, the notion of modernity (which still drives many narratives in the Western humanities) is not only increasingly problematic but is certainly open to serious reinterpretation. Third, readers interested in the construction, or alternatively deconstruction of ideas about globalisation and identity might start with a crash course in colonialism. Fourth, most readers of these books will wonder what has happened to the narratives of capitalism, the capitalist world economy, and the role of the colonial and neo-colonial transformation of space within this, not only in relation to the disciplining and formation of the colonial and postcolonial subject but also in regard to the circulation of capital in the environment of colonial and postcolonial countries. Fifth, as the consciousness of the increasingly decentred Western subject flows more widely through the academy, the authors of these books would no doubt write them differently, were they to start anew today. Race, class and gender, though not necessarily in that order, might perhaps feature more in the texts. Sixth, just as the colonies acted as social laboratories in the 1920s, so, in the 1980s, the postcolonies act as academic and writing laboratories, though perhaps with good effect: the historic colonial city (in its various forms) probably prefigures the urban future in both East and West rather better than does the contemporary Western city. Yet the most important unresolved issue of all concerns the question of polysemicity and the meaning of these environments, whether colonial or postcolonial, for their indigenous subjects.

In Paris, staring across the square to the Invalides where Lyautey's elaborate marble tomb rests not far from that of Napoleon, stand two bronze statues of Lyautey and Gallieni, the latter a diminutive figure supported on the heads and shoulders of four female figures symbolising the African and Asian colonies of France. What do the Parisian Algerians, Moroccans, Vietnamese and other postcolonials make of these representations today, if anything?

NOTES

1 From Anthony D. King, 'Writing colonial space: a review article', *Comparative Studies in Society and History*, 37, 3, 1995 © Society for the Comparative Study of Society and History, published by Cambridge University Press and reproduced by permission.

2 Abu-Lughod (1965:429). The obvious question to ask is how far the first half of this observation is still valid.

3 Redfield and Singer (1954:56). For a preliminary historiography on the colonial city, see King (1989).

4 Russell (1860:140).

5 Postimperial is used in a purely technical, rather than political and economic sense to refer to scholars from the one-time metropole. On the inadequacies of postcolonial to represent continuing imperial and neo-colonial realities, see McClintock (1992).

6 Dirks (1992:17).

7 King (1992:342–3).

8 Dossal (1991); AlSayyad (1991); Kosambi (1985, 1990).

9 King (1980, repeated in 1990a).

10 As will be evident below, such essentialist and dualist categories are largely spurious. Nonetheless, we might take note of Ahmad's (1993) strictures about the discourse on 'Third World Literature' in English in the Western academy which totally ignores writing in Indian vernacular languages (Ahmad, 1993).

11 Hamedah (1992).

12 For a useful bibliography, see Williams and Chrisman (1994).

13 For example, Noyes (1992).

14 Gayatri Spivak was a plenary speaker at an international conference, 'Theatres of Decolonisation: Architecture, Agency, Urbanism', in Chandigarh (January, 1995); Edward Said was programmed to be plenary speaker at an international symposium, 'Asian-Pacific Architecture: The East–West Encounter', in Honolulu, at the University of Hawaii (March, 1995), but was unavoidably prevented from attending.

15 Though Edward Said's *Orientalism* (1978) is frequently given as a starting point (see, for example, Parry [1987] and Seed [1991]), that book does not address questions of space and architecture and, as Ahmad points out, is ambivalent in regard to Foucault's work. There is, however, passing reference to these issues in Said's *Culture and Imperialism* (1994: especially, 15, 69, 85, 94, 131, 134, 153, 155, 240, 326).

16 Ahmad (1993).

17 Fanon (1968).

18 See King (1976:22) for early references. Talal Asad (1973) is the standard marker in the development of postcolonial discourse in the social sciences, though as Ranajit Guha points out in his introduction in Bernard Cohn's collection of essays, Cohn was already probing the complexities of the interpenetration of power and knowledge ('the very fabric of colonialism') in his essays of the 1950s and early 1960s (1988:xx). The various writings of Syed Hussein Alatas, Anouar Abdul-Malek, Samir Amin and Susantha Goonatilake would also be relevant here.

19 King (1990b, 1992:346). Philo and Kearns (1993:15) write, 'There is also a sense in which the "colonial city" has now come home … in that the global redistributions of human populations from the nineteenth century onwards have contributed to most urban areas becoming ethnic mosaics, scarred in all too many instances by segregationist and prejudicial attitudes on the part of white "host" groups.' In the United States, because of the problematic meanings (and attitudes) attached to the term colonial, this metaphor has been slow to develop.

20 Williams and Chrisman (1994).

21 Barnes and Duncan (1992); Duncan and Ley (1993).

22 Young (1992); Chakrabarty (1992).

23 This is discussed further in King (1995).

24 Note must also be taken, of course, of the increasing number of south Asian writers (novelists rather than academics), of whom Salman Rushdie is the most prominent, writing about the space of postcolonialism in the British city.

25 Dyos and Wolff (1973).

26 Markus (1993).

27 For an account of the development of similar norms and forms in regard to the development of social welfare and public health in England during the same period, though without the Foucauldian slant, see Lambert (1963).

BIBLIOGRAPHY

Abu-Lughod, J. (1965) 'Tale of two cities: the origins of modern Cairo', *Comparative Studies in Society and History*, 7, 4: 429–57.

Ahmad, A. (1993) *In Theory*, London: Verso.

AlSayyad, N., ed. (1991) *Forms of Dominance: On the Architecture and Urbanism of the Colonial Enterprise*, Aldershot: Avebury.

Asad, T., ed., *Anthropology and the Colonial Encounter*, London: Ithaca Press, 1973.

Barnes, T. and Duncan, J., eds (1992) *Writing Worlds: Discourse, Text and Metaphor in the Representation of Landscape*. London and New York: Routledge.

Bhabha, H. (1983) 'The Other Question: the Stereotype and Colonial Discourse'. *Screen*, 24, 6: 18–36.

Chakrabarty, D. (1992) 'Postcoloniality and the artifice of history: who speaks of "Indian" pasts?' *Representations*, 37: 1–26.

Dirks, N. (1992) 'Introduction', in Nicholas Dirks, ed., *Colonialism and Culture*, Ann Arbor: University of Michigan Press.

Dossal, M. (1991) *Imperial Designs and Indian Realities: The Planning of Bombay City, 1855–75*, Delhi: Oxford University Press.

Duncan, J. and Ley, D., eds (1993) *Place/Culture/Representation*, New York: Routledge.

Dyos, H.J. and Wolff, M., eds (1973) *The Victorian City: Images and Realities*, London: Routledge and Kegan Paul.

Fanon, F. (1968) *The Wretched of the Earth*, New York: Grove reprint. Originally published as *Les Damnes de la Terre*, François Maspero, ed., Paris, 1961.

Guha, R. (1988) 'Introduction', in Bernard S. Cohn, *An Anthropologist Among the Historians and Other Essays*, Delhi and New York: Oxford University Press, pp.vii–xxvi.

Hamadeh, H. (1992) 'Creating the traditional city: a French project', in N. AlSayyad, ed., *Forms of Dominance*, Aldershot: Avebury, pp.241–60.

King, A.D. (1976) *Colonial Urban Development: Culture, Social Power and Environment*, London: Routledge and Kegan Paul.

King, A.D. (1980) 'Colonial cities: global pivots of change', in M.R. Ross and G. Telkamp, eds, *Colonial Cities*, Boston: Martinus Nijhoff, pp.7–32.

King, A.D. (1989) 'Colonialism, urbanism and the capitalist world economy', *International Journal of Urban and Regional Research*, 13,1: 1–18.

King, A.D. (1990a) *Urbanism, Colonialism and the World-Economy: Cultural and Spatial Foundations of the World Urban System*, London and New York: Routledge.

King, A.D. (1990b) 'The new colonialism: global restructuring and the city'. *Intersight*, 1.

King, A.D. (1992) 'Rethinking colonialism: an epilogue', in N. AlSayyad, ed., *Forms of Dominance*, Aldershot: Avebury, pp.339–55.

King, A.D. (1995) 'The times and spaces of modernity or, who needs postmodernism?', in Scott Lash, Mike Featherstone and Roland Robertson, eds, *Global Modernities*, Newbury Park and London: Sage, pp.108–23.

Kosambi, M. (1985) *Bombay in Transition: The Growth and Social Ecology of a Colonial City, 1880–1980*. Stockholm: Alongvist and Wiksell International.

Kosambi, M. (1990) 'The colonial city in its global niche'. *Economic and Political Weekly*, December 22.

Lambert, R. (1963) *Sir John Simon 1816–1904 and English Social Administration*, London: MacGibbon and Kee.

McClintock, A. (1992) 'The angel of progress: pitfalls of the term "postcolonialism"', *Social Text*, Spring, 1–15.

Markus, T.A. (1993) *Buildings and Power: Freedom and Control in the Origin of Modern Building Types*, New York: Routledge.

Noyes, J. (1992) *Colonial Space: Spatiality in the Discourse of German South West Africa 1884–1915*, Philadelphia: Harwood Academic Publishing.

Parry, B. (1987) 'Problems in current theories of colonial discourse', *Oxford Literary Review*, 9, 1–2: 27–58.

Philo, C. and Kearns, G. (1993) 'Culture, history, capital: a critical introduction to the selling of places', in C. Philo and G. Kearns, eds, *Selling Places: The City as Cultural Capital, Past and Present*, Oxford: Pergamon.

Rabinow, P. (1989) *French Modern: Norms and Forms of the Social Environment*, Cambridge, MA: MIT Press.

Redfield, R. and Singer, M. (1954) 'The cultural role of cities'. *Economic Development and Cultural Change*, 3, 53: 73.

Russell, W.H. (1860) *My Diary in the Years 1858–9*, 2 vols, London: Routledge, Warne and Routledge.

Said, E. (1978) *Orientalism*, New York: Pantheon.

Said, E. (1994) *Culture and Imperialism*, London: Vintage.

Seed, P. (1991) 'Colonial and Postcolonial Discourse'. *Latin American Research Review*, 26, 3: 181–200.

Spivak, G.C. (1988) *In Other Worlds*, New York: Routledge.

Spivak, G.C. (1992) *The Postcolonial Critic*. New York: Routledge.

Williams, P. and Chrisman, L., eds, (1994) *Colonial Discourse and Postcolonial Theory: A Reader*, New York: Columbia University Press.

Young, R. (1990) *White Mythologies: Writing History and the West*, New York: Routledge.

Chapter 4: Re-presenting world cities: cultural theory/social practice[1]

INTRODUCTION

If we accept that there is some reality which the term 'world city' represents, I want to look at this principally as a cultural space and see what recent work in social and cultural theory suggests about it.

How can this theory be deployed to say something about the spaces and built environments of the world city? What is the significance of such a world city as a site for the construction of new cultural and political identities or for processes of cultural transformation in general? And what relevance might it have, either for the persistence or modification of existing local, regional or national identities and cultures, or alternatively, for the construction of new transnational ones?

In the context of these questions, therefore, I shall examine a number of issues including the idea of the world or global city as a representation; the context within which this representation has been constructed; and whether the terms 'world city' and 'global city' mean the same or whether each signals a different set of assumptions and presuppositions. Let me begin by clarifying the terms I have introduced.

REPRESENTING THE CITY

In the words of James Donald:

> '(t)he city' does not just refer to a set of buildings in a particular place. To put it polemically, there is no such *thing* as a city. Rather, the city designates the space produced by the interaction of historically and geographically specific institutions, social relations of production and reproduction, practices of government, forms and media of communication, and so forth.

Donald suggests that by calling this diversity 'the city', we ascribe to it a coherence or integrity which it does not have. *The city*, then, is above all a representation. But what sort of representation? By analogy with the now familiar idea that the nation provides us with an 'imagined community', I would argue that the city constitutes an *imagined environment*. It is what is involved in that imagining, 'the discourses, symbols, metaphors and fantasies through which we ascribe meaning to the modern experience of urban living' which, for Donald, is 'as important a topic for the social sciences as the material determinants of the physical environment' (1992:6).

This concern with representation, with what Barnes and Duncan (1992) refer to as the 'discourses, texts and metaphors' through which the city is represented, has cautioned us against the danger of making monolithic claims. It has also, in the process, opened up the opportunity for otherwise marginalised voices, alternate representations, to be heard from below. Equally important, it has redirected our attention from the object of discourse (the city) to the subject constructing it (the author). Ulf Hannerz, one of the more prolific authors on the notion of world or global culture (including world cities) has suggested that there are principally four categories of people who play major parts in the making of contemporary Western world cities: the transnational management class, Third World populations, expressive specialists (or cultural practitioners) and tourists (1993). He also refers to the media who have a special relationship with world cities (1993).

Though I shall make use of Hannerz's categories below, the principal omission from his list is that of the authorial subjects themselves, the academics and scholars who, by exercising their power to name, not only construct the category and the criteria used to define it, but also identify the places to which it refers. That the construction of the category 'world city' is primarily based on an interpretation of some aspects of what are referred to as 'economic data' does not disguise the fact that 'world city' is essentially a *cultural construct*, constituted at a particular time and in particular spaces of the Western academy. We might ask where, by whom and for what purposes is this cultural construct produced.[2] I shall return to this theme below.

We might begin by reflecting on, and distinguishing between, a variety of different concepts: 'the city', 'the world', the 'world class city' (as in 'world class' athlete), 'cities in the world', 'cities of the world', 'world cities' (à la Friedmann) and 'city worlds'. It is the latter, 'city worlds', which scholars actually think about and construct; some of these 'city worlds' are 'world cities'. And just as Gayatri Spivak writes of 'the worlding of the world', we might also speak of the 'cityng of the city'. Indeed, it would not be inappropriate, in the context of our discussion, in terms of what is seen by the West as the resurgence of religious fundamentalism, and the cultural regions in the world where our present set of 'world cities' is *not* located, to include in this list the 'worldly city'; and to ask whether the world's 'world cities' are, in fact, the most worldly of the world's cities (King 1994).

What these reflections show us is that, in addition to working with imagined constructs of 'the city', we are also working with imagined constructs of 'the world'. 'World class city', for example, already assumes a positionality, a standard from which the rest are to be measured, but a standard of what, and according to whom?

The problem with thinking about 'the city' is not only that it is in fact many cities, consisting of many representations, but rather that 'the city' reifies an imagined object, drawing boundaries around it, cutting it off from and excluding those economic, social, cultural, political, religious, administrative relations and flows without which 'the city' would not exist at all. Unlike 'the great Wen', the metaphor with which Dickens characterised London, 'city' makes no reference to the body on which Dickens' excrescence lived. Cities can be distinguished by a large number of criterial attributes (King 1994) only some of which refer to the geographical, economic, political, cultural, climatic or other kinds of contextual space (such as inland, industrial, socialist, Islamic, or winter) which supposedly helps to account for their existence. But cities also exist under scores of quite different metaphors – sin city, city of angels, holy city, and many more. In this context, the number of meanings which 'world city' might have are infinite.

The problem with the 'world' or 'global city' term is that it has been appropriated, perhaps hijacked, to represent and also reify not only just one part of a city's activity (not the only, or even the largest one) but also put at the service of only one particular representation of 'the world' – the world economy. Having myself made use, in a somewhat indiscriminate way, of both world and global city terms and concepts (1990) (which I refer to in more detail below) I am inclined to think, in retrospect, that both are somewhat greedy in what they have appropriated under these labels. As with any over ambitious theory, they occlude as much if not more than they reveal.

An argument can and indeed has been made (Friedmann and Wolff 1982, King 1990, Sassen 1991 and others) that a particular world city has, in relation to a particular economic and administrative sphere, global control capability: but this neither exhausts the function or meaning of the city in relation to the world economy, in relation to 'the world' nor, more importantly and pointedly, the significance or meaning of 'the world' to the city. If it did, God (literally) help us. To begin with, capitalism is essentially a cultural system before it is an economic one. Both the system, or systems (as it exists in many forms) and the subjects which inhabit it, have to be constructed. People are not born to consume.

However, discourse theory, in focusing solely on discursive representations, the way the city is spoken, read or written (Macdonald 1986), takes our analytical attention away from two other representational levels.

As I have suggested earlier, the second is the way the built environment, the physical and spatial form of the city, is itself a representation of economic, social, political and cultural relations and practices, of hierarchies and structures, which not only represent but also inherently constitute these same relations, hierarchies and structures of everyday social life. Here, I refer only to the spatialisation, or materialisation of these social relations, the way they inscribe themselves in the physical world and which have economic, social, physical and behavioural effects.

The third is another symbolic level constituted through visual representation, the semiotic domain where visual signifiers refer to some other signified. This level, as we well know, is a murky area as such visual representations can have infinite meanings, depending on the subjectivity of the viewer. I distinguish between these second and third levels by suggesting that a hospital building, for example, may be understood as a material or spatial representation of social discourses about health (and indeed, is a constituent element of those discourses); a hospital designed in a particular place and at a particular period in time, in Gothic style, say, may be an attempt on the part of its patrons or its architect to fuse the discourses about health with those of religion. Each of these two levels of physical and material representation is a necessary prerequisite for the fourth, the mental constructs which form the discourses (see Donald, above) in which the hospital is subsequently represented (Wolff 1992).

Here, we might draw attention to the immense amount of symbolic capital (Bourdieu 1977) there is invested in the site, history, associations, and cultural meaning of buildings which, as dramatic events in and outside world cities have reminded us, represent and help to constitute, whole regimes of economic, political and cultural power. Within the space of six months, the demolition of the Babri mosque in Ayodhya, the dynamiting of Mumbai's Stock Exchange, the symbolic attack on New York's World Trade Center and the massive explosion by the Hong Kong Bank in the City of London, all undertaken by ideologically, religiously or, in the last case, anti-colonial inspired insurgents, demonstrate the extent to which the world city's 'signature architecture' has upstaged the state's (and the world's) more sober debating chambers as the appropriate site to conduct an alternative international politics. With security controls now blanketing airports, symbolic world city buildings have become (with the conscious, and complicit cooperation of the global media) the obvious site for contesting ideological and cultural regimes, a politics of spectacle beamed into 'the privacy of your own home'.

My third term, culture, is often used in an everyday sense in two senses, as 'way of life' and to refer to the 'expressive arts'. For the purposes of this chapter, I shall refer to an earlier conceptualisation and collapse this distinction between what, in crude terms, we may call older 'anthropological' notions of culture (ways of life, values, beliefs) and 'humanistic ones' (expressive arts, media). By suggesting that culture in its sense of art, literature, film, music, architecture, practices of representation of all kinds, both draws from, and participates in, the construction of culture as a way of life, as a system of values and beliefs which, in turn, continues to affect culture as a creative, representational practice, we can bridge what is often seen as a gap between these different meanings (King 1991:2).

The term 'world city' has been around at least since the later eighteenth century, used by Goethe, apparently, to refer to the cultural eminence of Paris and Rome (Gottman 1989:62). However, given that the language Goethe spoke does not, with the term 'Stadt', distinguish between 'town' and 'city', his reference to 'Weltstadt' may be treated as a neologism necessitated by the German language. In this volume, I am assuming that the meaning attached to it is that given by Friedmann in 1982. I am also assuming that by 'world cities in a world-system' we are also using, at least in a relatively loose sense, Wallerstein's conceptualisation of a 'world-system'. Although both of these concepts have obvious relevance for the understanding of cultural phenomena, this is not an aspect which is particularly well developed in either of them.

'Global', a term used by Sassen, myself and others, is, I believe, used interchangeably with 'world cities', the semantic shift in 1990 probably reflecting the increased frequency of use as well as the growing consciousness of transnational social, cultural, political and religio-ideological movements (from ecological concerns to those of peace), characteristic of the 1980s. Global may, however, also reflect the social theoretical debate on globalisation, by Robertson (1992) and others, gathering pace from the mid 1980s, and premised on totally different (or complementary) bases to the world-system paradigm. The distinction between the two paradigms I would describe principally in terms of the focus of globalisation theory on questions of culture, identity and meaning in representations of 'the world as a single place' compared to the economic and political, neo-Marxist emphasis of the world-system perspective.

GLOBALISATION

Theories of globalisation have been used to refer to a number of processes. McGrew (1992), from which much of the following is drawn, references the writings of Giddens, Harvey, Rosenau, Robertson, Wallerstein and others, citing especially the multiplicity of interconnections that transcend the nation-state (and by implication, the geographically defined societies which make up the inter-state system). Resulting from the development of global networks of communication and knowledge, and systems of global production and exchange, there appears to be a diminishing grip of local circumstances on people's lives: goods, capital, people, knowledge, images, fashions, beliefs, flow across territorial borders and there is said to be, for some at least, a profound reordering of time and space in social life. Globalisation is seen to be the intensification of global connectedness, the constituting of the world as one place. In Giddens' words, it concerns 'the intersection of presence and absence, the interlacing of social events and social relations "at a distance" with local contextualities' (cited in McGrew 1992:67).

In discussions of globalisation, there is considerable slippage between the discourse on 'globe talk' or 'global babble' (Abu-Lughod 1991) and the object/ subject which it is seen to affect – whether nation state, locality or individual subject. Where globalisation in Robertson's (1992:8) terms can mean 'consciousness of the world as a whole' the subject can be collective as well as individual and the ensuing debate about individual, or group cultural or political identity. Yet globalisation in this sense is neither historically nor geographically even: McGrew, for instance, writes specifically of 'Western globalisation'. He sees it as not historically inevitable but occurring to a greater or lesser extent at different times and under different historic conditions. As Frost and Spence ask, 'Are the forces which have created global cities in recent times merely a single phase of development?' (1993:557). Given that deregulation of financial markets can only occur once and, like other decisions, is likely to occur as a response to developments in other financial centres, the answer seems to be 'Yes'. But it is also the case that, with intensive competition between different global cities, the possibilities of deglobalisation have also to be faced.

Globalisation is also seen to have a 'differential reach', with its consequences not uniformly experienced across the globe. Hegemonic states in the inter-state system work to impose a form of world order which attempts to encourage openness, and interdependence, but which also reinforces inequalities of power and wealth both between states and across them.

Initially, popular wisdom saw the outcome of globalisation as a process of cultural homogenisation on a global scale. Later interpretations by McGrew are expressed in terms of five polarised oppositions, and emphasise not only the uneven but also the essentially dialectic nature of the process. The results of globalising influences, whether economic, political or cultural are seen as being inherently contingent on the time, place and circumstances where they apply. McGrew states these oppositions as follows.

1   Universalism vs particularism. As globalisation universalises different spheres of modern social life (the nation state, consumer fashions, etc.), it simultaneously encourages particularisation, by relativising both place and locale, so that the construction of difference and uniqueness results (e.g. in the resurgence of nationalism and the highlighting of ethnic difference).

2   Homogenisation vs differentiation. Just as globalisation produces a certain kind of 'sameness' to surface appearances and social institutions across the globe (city life, technologies, bureaucratisation, etc.) it also results in the rearticulation of the global as a response to local circumstances (people interpret the same thing differently).

3   Integration vs fragmentation. Although globalisation creates new communities which unite people across the national boundaries of the world (international trade unions, multinational companies, etc.) it also fragments and divides within and across traditional nation-state boundaries. Thus labour becomes fragmented along local, sectional, national, ethnic and racial lines.

4   Centralisation vs decentralisation. As globalisation facilitates concentrations of power, information and knowledge (transnational companies etc.), it also provokes local resistances which are also decentralising (new social movements).

5   Juxtaposition vs syncretisation. Globalisation, by compressing time and space, forces the juxtaposition of civilisations, ways of life and social practices. While this leads to the hybridisation of ideas, values, knowledge, institutions, cultural practices (from cuisines to architecture) it also reinforces cultural and social prejudices and boundaries.

Applying McGrew's insights to the understanding of the spatial and environmental dynamics of contemporary world cities is suggestive. Above all, they suggest that whatever is existing in 'the present' is certainly not going to be the end product; space, like the forces which produce it, is constantly in flux. Not least, the powerful forces of globalisation and internationalisation (two quite different processes) on major world cities, also result in the intensification of cultural nationalisms both in and outside those cities. I refer not just to the xenophobic responses of the right but also to the 'reinvention of tradition' and the 'vernacular' by the cultural elites. It is worth quoting Robertson (1992) at this point:

> In a nutshell, globalization involves the universalisation of particularism not just the particularisation of universalism. While the latter process does involve the thematisation of the issue of universal (i.e. global) 'truth', the former involves the global valorization of particular identities.

Robertson sees the contemporary concern with civilisational and societal (as well as ethnic) uniqueness, as exemplified by the increasing emphasis placed on identity, tradition and indigenisation, as being largely premised on globally diffused ideas.

> Identity, tradition, and the demand for indigenization only make sense contextually. Moreover, unique cannot be regarded simply as a thing-in-itself. It largely depends both upon the thematisation and diffusion of 'universal' ideas concerning the appropriateness of being unique *in a context*, which is an empirical matter, and the employment of criteria on the part of scholarly observers, which is an analytical issue.

> (Robertson 1992:130)

Globalisation, seen in this way, does not result in homogeneity but a deepening of particularity. According to this, each world city increasingly becomes the same to the extent that each one becomes increasingly different. The logic of globalisation theory, therefore, is in a sense to deny its own existence. As far as the world city is concerned, it is to recognise that there is indeed a category, but culturally and in many other ways, each one is different.

MIGRATION AND ITS CULTURAL EFFECTS

In the loose kind of 'globe talk' about the multiculturality of cities, attention is often drawn to the mere presence of 'other' nationalities and language groups. That one city has representatives from 102 nations or language groups and another, from 192, is somehow taken as a 'sufficient and necessary' condition of its multiculturality. This question needs addressing both in more detail and with more sophistication.

It might be useful to imagine, from a demographic viewpoint, an idea of what a 'perfect' world city would be, for example, one whose population was composed of a minimum number of representatives (say 1,000) of each nation state, and in proportion to its total population, of each of the almost 200 nations in the world. Irrespective of the artificiality implied by this notion of the 'nationally constructed subject', such an 'international' or 'United Nations' city would in no way get close to the tens of thousands of world ethnic and linguistic groups which made up these nation-states.

The relevance of suggesting this ideal, or perhaps absurd, model, however, is to demonstrate that, from a demographic viewpoint, no so-called world city can, or ever will, in any way approximate to it . In all world cities, there is, with the odd exception, a numerically dominant population from the host society, and in each, the proportion who are 'foreign born' comes from such a diverse range of cultures, religions and ethnicities, and as a result of such historically different circumstances, that the monolithic, even xenophobic category of 'foreign born' can, for all except legal purposes (though this is clearly a highly significant exception) be rejected. From very specific points of view, to assume that 'foreign birth' provides commonality amongst a vast range of peoples, in 20 cities of five continents, is as absurd as suggesting that 'domestic birth' can be used to culturally characterise those born in the host society. Similarly, to suggest that the 15 per cent of the Paris population who are 'foreign born' (sic) and coming primarily from North Africa (Algeria, Morocco, Tunis), Armenia or Mauritius (Ambroise-Rendu 1993); the 29 per cent in New York, over half of whom are from the Caribbean and Central America, with significant proportions from Europe, South America, East Asia and Africa (Bayer and Perlman 1990); and the 18 per cent 'foreign born' in London, from South Asia, Ireland, continental Europe, East, West and South Africa and the Caribbean (King 1990), have somehow more in common than they have in what is different seems to be a somewhat grandiose claim.

Clearly, the historical, cultural and political power (or lack of it) possessed by migrants from different countries, when relocated in the cities of another society, is highly variable. Given that a large proportion are from the Third World, postcolonial societies, their colonial histories, with their linguistic and cultural links (as well as the residual racial stigma attributed by host societies), place different kinds of migrants in very different situations of power and lack of power, irrespective of their relation to the labour market. Their influence on the culture and politics of the dominant society, however, can be considerable. There is no better example than the very considerable influence which postcolonial criticism (e.g. of Edward Said, Homi Bhabha, Dipesh Chakrabarty, Stuart Hall, Gayatri Spivak and many others) has had on the epistemology of the Western academy, at least in the humanities (Spivak 1988; 1991). In terms of cultural politics and critique, quantification is irrelevant.

To speak specifically about space and the built environment. The public display of individual or collective cultural identities through the use of distinctive building types, forms, construction materials, methods, colours and qualities, has, in general, less impact in a city like New York, despite its very many different nationalities and cultures, because the city has only *one* dominant spatial culture: the block by block grid system – a result of the city's historical origins and the devotion of its founders to the commodification of land and the accumulation of capital (Sennet 1991:53). It has also, compared to many cities, a relatively short history. Of course, cultural difference is constituted in different ways in that city and in recent times, the impact of Puerto Rican community activities has modified spatial use (Sciorra 1994).

Yet in particular cities of the Third World, grossly different construction standards, different social, cultural, and construction practices of various regional migrant groups, and immensely different modes of production and standards of living exist side by side, without the 'benefit' of 'planning', in city space. This means that cities like Mumbai, or Delhi, with fewer representatives from other national groups, nevertheless have a much wider variety of historically and culturally constructed physical and spatial environments. The serious issue raised by these comments, of course, is whether we are speaking of cultural diversity or social inequality, a question for New York as well as Mumbai.

Elsewhere I have suggested that frames for understanding social and cultural phenomena in world cities can include the odd idea from the political economic frame of the world system perspective, the culturally oriented frame of globalization, but also the more specifically historical and political frames of postcolonialism (for cities like Singapore, Jakarta, Hong Kong) and postimperialism (for London, Paris or Amsterdam) (King 1993). Extrapolating these frameworks allows us to examine, for example, the very different balances of power between dominant ethnicities, cultures and social groups in, for example, the postcolonial and postimperial city.

These frameworks, however, hardly exhaust the possibilities. For such cities as Jakarta or Colombo, we would need, in addition, to position them in relation to the very specific economic and geopolitical alliances and spaces of recent years.

DISPLACED PLACES

As suggested above, the research of Swedish anthropologist Ulf Hannerz on the 'World System of Culture', has led him to suggest that the transnational nature of contemporary world cities in the West comes especially from four categories of people: the transnational business class, Third World migrant populations, tourists and people he describes as those 'specialising in expressive activities' (1992b).

If we adopt Sharon Zukin's (1991) two spatial categories of 'landscapes of power' and 'the vernacular of the powerless' we can begin to describe the spatial and built environmental representations of these four categories. In this context, the norms and forms of the institutional, spatial and symbolic signs of the international business class (whether transnational headquarters, banks, hotels, offices) conform in most ways to the norms and forms manifest in these same institutions of the hegemonic states in the world order: the USA, Japan, Germany. These are the 'landscapes of power'. More than anything else, these institutions reproduce transnational symbolic forms and styles, in many cases financed by international banks, and often designed by First World international architectural firms (King 1990; Sassen 1991). Here, Lawrence Vale's account of *Architecture, Power and National Identity* (1992) is relevant, concluding as it does that the identities of capitol complexes in postcolonial states were, in effect, those of the architects (often foreign) who had designed them, and political leaders who commissioned them. Equally significant is the top end of international tourism.

Numerically, however, the largest category is that of international migrants, a small proportion of whom are from an international elite, though the largest proportion are the poor and destitute. Here, cultural representation in space takes place in what I shall call the 'double vernacular'. In the first instance, living and working space is appropriated in what was once the working class, vernacular housing of the city, distinguished by its age, location and, in terms of building and architectural form regional identity. Appropriated by incoming migrants, it is transformed into the vernacular of the newcomers, modified by kinship preferences, adapted to meet cultural requirements or to take in tenants and accumulate capital, and modified, by external decoration, to make a statement about symbolic cultural identity. Obsolete neighbourhood buildings, whether warehouses or churches, are transformed into social and cultural spaces, mosques, temples and social clubs. We may refer here, to the spaces of the Portuguese in Toronto, Puerto Ricans in New York or Bangladeshis in East London.

The fourth group Hannerz describes as a small number of people who yet maintain a rather high profile in world cities, people concerned with culture in a narrower sense, specialising in expressive activities – cultural practitioners – international groups of professionals in art, fashion, design, photography, writing, music.

I have already indicated one small but significant category that Hannerz omits here, academics and scholars. Another, however, is that of architectural and urban design practitioners. It is these who, in their design work, provide the surface representations, the final garment cladding the combined interests of the institutional investors, the financial industry, real estate speculators and the elite of the corporate world. These are some of the main brokers in the economy of signs in the world city. Like each of the previous three groups, one of the principal identities of their multiple identity is 'global', providing that we understand here that 'global' is, in fact, a very local and restricted category. The professional values they subscribe to encompass both an 'international' architectural practice determined principally by the values of the market, the contestatory discourse of the postmodern, and increasingly, in Robertson's (1992:130) terms, a particular concern with 'tradition, identity and indigenization'. Their design response depends upon the 'thematisation and diffusion of universal' ideas concerning the appropriateness of being unique *in a context* (ibid.).

Elsewhere, Hannerz has proposed four typical frameworks for examining cultural process in world cities organised as 'a flow of meaningful forms between people: the market, the state, forms of life, and movements'. In the market framework, people relate to each other as buyer and seller, and meaning and meaningful form have been commoditized.

The second framework of cultural process Hannerz sees as the state, not as a bounded physical area but as organisational form. The state engages in managing meaning by fostering the idea that the state is a nation, and constructs people as citizens. Some states more than others promote 'cultural welfare', that is, meanings and meaningful forms are held to certain intellectual and aesthetic standards. Third is the form of life framework where the cultural flow occurs merely between fellow human beings in their mingling with one another, a free and reciprocal flow going on as we observe one another and listen to one another in everyday situations. The fourth framework is that of movements, more intermittently part of the cultural totality than the other three – a major influence in recent decades – women's, environmental, ecological and peace movements (1992).

Hannerz's frameworks provide scope for understanding various processes in the world city: factors affecting the constructions of identity, the opportunities provided by the market and forms of life which take on material representations.

For ethnographer Arjun Appadurai, the central challenge is to study the 'new cosmopolitanisms' of the world city. Here, in addition to the idea of displacement, a central concern is with the idea of deterritorialisation, not only of the transnational corporations and money markets, but of ethnic groups, political forms which operate in ways that transcend specific territorial boundaries and identities (Appadurai 1991:192).

Elsewhere, Appadurai (1990) has offered suggestive concepts for exploring different dimensions of the global cultural flows in major world cities, including the idea of the ethnoscape (the landscape of ethnically differentiated persons who constitute the shifting world); the technoscape (the global configuration of technology); the mediascape (images of the world created by media) and ideoscapes (ideologies of states and counter ideologies of movements).

The process of deterritorialisation is, however, simultaneously one of reterritorialisation. Where Appadurai (1991) suggests that deterritorialisation creates new markets for film companies, impresarios and travel agencies which thrive on the need of the relocated population for contact with its homeland, the reterritorialisation occurs, culturally, in the world city spaces where these processes take place. In many more ways than one, the world city becomes a place where the symbolic economy of new cultural meanings and representations takes place (Zukin 1994). At one level, the juxtaposition of cultures, the contestations, the redefinitions of identity, the cultural politics, the fractured identities, become the very material from which new cultural conflict arises, yet simultaneously, these also provide the new cultural content for the movies, videos, theatre or literature. In the ten years between 1983 and 1993, seven out of ten of the novels winning the London-based publishing industry's Booker Award in the UK were written by immigrant authors. Ethnic restaurants and neighbourhoods are commodified for the overlapping interests of the international business community and tourists. What were once ethnic ghettoes are cleaned up, and put on show – to simulate the colonial experience but without the tropical heat (McAuley 1987).

In this context, the representation itself becomes the reality. After years of circulation, the world city metaphor is used by city governments, financial elites and the cultural industries as a mirror in which to assess their own fortunes, or mobilize their competitive image.

NOTES

1 From Anthony D. King, 'Representing world cities: cultural theory/social practice', in Paul L. Knox and Peter J. Taylor, eds, *World Cities in a World System*, 1995 © Cambridge University Press.
2 Were a bomb to fall on the conference hall in which a large majority of world and global city theorists were assembled, would the 'world city' disappear?

BIBLIOGRAPHY

Abu-Lughod, J. (1991) 'Going beyond global babble', in A.D. King, ed., *Culture Globalization and the World-System*, London: University of Minnesota Press and Macmillan, pp.131–8.

Ambroise-Rendu, M. (1993) 'The migrants who turned Paris into a melting pot', *Guardian Weekly*, 27 June, p.14.

Appadurai, A. (1990) 'Disjuncture and difference in the global cultural economy', *Public Culture*, 2, 2: 1–24.

Appadurai, A. (1991) 'Global ethnoscapes; notes and queries for a transnational anthropology', in R.G. Fox, ed., *Recapturing Anthropology: Working in the Present*, Santa Fe: School of American Research Press, pp.191–210.

Barnes, T. and Duncan, J.S. (1992) *Writing Worlds: Discourse, Text and Metaphor in the Representation of Landscape*, London and New York: Routledge.

Bayer, D. and Perlman, J. (1990) 'Here is New York – 1990'. Paper presented at the Conference on Megacities of the Americas, State University of New York at Albany, 5–6 April.

Bourdieu, P. (1977) *Outline of a Theory of Practice*, trans. Richard Nice, Cambridge: Cambridge University Press.

Donald, J. (1992) 'Metropolis: the city as text', in R. Bocock and K. Thompson, eds, *Social and Cultural Forms of Modernity*, Cambridge: Polity Press in association with the Open University, pp.1–54.

Friedmann, J. and Wolff, G. (1982) 'World city formation: an agenda for research and action', *International Journal of Urban and Regional Research*, 6: 309–44.

Frost, M. and Spence, N. (1993) 'Global city characteristics and Central London's employment', *Urban Studies*, 30, 3: 547–58.

Giddens, A. (1990) *The Consequences of Modernity*, Cambridge: Polity Press.

Gottman, J. (1989) 'What are cities becoming centres of? Sorting out the possibilities', in R.V. Knight and G. Gappert, eds, *Cities in a Global Society*, London, Newbury Park and New Delhi: Sage, pp.58–67.

Harvey, D. (1989) *The Condition of Postmodernity,* Oxford and Cambridge, MA: Blackwell.

Hannerz, U. (1992) *Culture, Cities and the World*, Amsterdam: Centrum voor Grootstedeljk Onderzoek.

Hannerz, U. (1993) 'The cultural role of world cities', in Anthony Cohen and Katsuyoshi Fukui, eds, *The Age of the City*, Edinburgh: Edinburgh University Press.

King, A.D. (1990) *Global Cities: Post-Imperialism and the Internationalization of London*, London and New York: Routledge.

King, A.D., ed. (1991) 'Spaces of culture, spaces of knowledge' in *Culture, Globalization and the World-System: Contemporary Conditions for the Representation of Identity*, Minneapolis and London: University of Minnesota Press and Macmillan.

King, A.D. (1993) 'Identity and difference: the internationalization of capital and the globalization of culture', in P.L. Knox, ed., *The Restless Urban Landscape*, Englewood Cliffs: Prentice Hall.

King, A.D. (1994) 'Terminologies and types: making sense of some types of dwellings and cities', in L. Schneekloth and K. Franck, eds, *Building Type and the Social Ordering of Space*, New York: Van Nostrand Reinhold.

London Planning Advisory Committee (LPAC) (1991) *London: World City Moving into the 21st Century*, London: HMSO.

Macdonald, D. (1986) *Theories of Discourse*, Oxford: Blackwell.

McAuley, I. (1987) *Guide to Ethnic London: A Complete Handbook to the Many Faces of London and Its Ethnic Neighborhoods. Everything from Restaurants and Shops to Historical Walks and Cultural Celebrations*, London: Michael Haag.

McGrew, A. (1992) 'A global society?', in S. Hall, D. Held and T. Macgrew, eds, *Modernity and Its Futures*, Oxford: Polity Press in association with the Open University, pp.61–116.

Robertson, R. (1992) *Globalization: Social Theory and Global Culture*, London, Newbury Park and Delhi: Sage.

Rosenau, J. (1980) *The Study of Global Interdependence*, London: Frances Pinter.

Sassen, S. (1991) *The Global City: New York London Tokyo*, Princeton: Princeton University Press.

Sciorra, J. (1994) 'Metaphors of home: Puerto Rican vernacular architecture in New York City', in A.D. King, ed., *Re-Presenting the City: Ethnicity, Capital and Culture in the 21st Century Metropolis*. London: Macmillan.

Sennet, R. (1991) *The Conscience of the Eye*, New York: W.W. Norton.

Spivak, G.C. (1988) *In Other Worlds*, New York: Routledge.

Spivak, G.C. (1991) *The Post-Colonial Critic*, London and New York: Routledge.

Vale, L.J. (1992) *Architecture, Power and National Identity*, New Haven: Yale University Press.

Wolff, J. (1992) 'The real city, the discursive city, the disappearing city: postmodernism and urban sociology', *Theory and Society*, 21: 553–60.

Zukin, S. (1991) *Landscapes of Power*, Berkeley: University of California Press.

Zukin, S. (1994) 'Space and symbols in an age of decline', in A.D. King, ed., *Re-Presenting the City: Ethnicity, Capital and Culture in the 21st Century Metropolis*, London: Macmillan, pp.43–59.

Chapter 5: Postcolonialism, representation and the city[1]

INTERROGATING THE CITY

Postcolonial criticism may be briefly described as an oppositional form of knowledge that critiques Eurocentric conceptions of the world. More fundamentally, in Mangin's words, 'the term postcolonial refers not to a simple periodisation but rather to a methodological revisionism which enables a wholesale critique of Western structures of knowledge and power, particularly those of the post-Enlightenment period'; it demands 'a rethinking of the very terms by which knowledge has been constructed' (Mangin 1995:2). For Achille Mbembe, postcoloniality is 'the specific identity of a given historical trajectory, that of societies recently emerging from the experiences of colonization' (Mbembe 1992:2). These two definitions neatly embody the idea of the postcolonial as an epoch, as a problematic, and as a form of expression and identity (Simon 1998:230). Yet postcolonial criticism, as a new awareness or consciousness, is not just one thing; it can be distinguished from postcolonial theory as well as colonial discourse analysis, among others (Moore-Gilbert 1997, ch.1). And for obvious reasons of continuing neo-colonialism and imperialism, neither the term (McClintock 1992; Shohat 1992) nor the discourse (Dirlik 1997) go unchallenged. For Hall,

> In the re-staged narrative of the post-colonial, colonisation assumes the place and significance of a major, extended and ruptural world-historical event. By 'colonisation', the 'post-colonial' references something more than direct rule over certain areas of the world by the imperial powers. I think it is signifying the whole process of expansion, exploration, conquest, colonisation and imperial hegemonisation which constituted the 'outer face', the constitutive outside, of European and then Western capitalist modernity after 1492.
>
> (Hall 1996:249)

In the literature I am citing above, postcolonial criticism has principally emerged in anglo-phonic literary studies, and cultural studies more generally, especially from the mid to late 1980s (Moore-Gilbert 1997; Williams and Chrisman 1994). Three questions may be asked. Given the existence of anti-colonial nationalisms at least from the early twentieth century and the formal ending of most modern European colonial regimes in the two decades after 1947, why has a consciousness of colonialism in the making of the modern world and, not least, in the construction of its forms of academic knowledge, only fully surfaced in the Euro-American academy in the late 1980s and 1990s? Why has it emerged most prominently in regard to the humanities and not (or only later) in the social sciences? What is the connection, if any, between these (more recent) forms of postcolonial criticism and earlier studies of colonial space and urbanism?

As suggested elsewhere (King 1997), postcolonial criticism is an outcome of the new conditions of knowledge production that have emerged since the late 1970s and, in particular, in relation to the postcolonial diasporic transmigration of 'Third World' intellectuals. By *trans*migration I refer both to the frequent movement of the transmigrant between being 'abroad' and 'back home', as well as the electronic/telematic connection between both places. It is these which enable postcolonial subjects (as well as others) to translate the social, political and cultural capital gained in one setting into the social, political, cultural (and often economic) capital in another (after Schiller *et al.* 1995). Here, the capital is essentially intellectual as one-time 'Third World' intellectuals have entered the Western (especially Euro-American) academy making, in recent decades, a significant impact on the cultural politics of knowledge creation, questioning traditional canons, and making space for diversity by developing new theoretical paradigms (McDowell 1995). Postcolonial scholars have not only challenged imperialism from the perspective of their previously marginalised positions in the 'Third World' but also, in regard to discriminations of race, class, gender, sexuality and ethnicity, from the position of internally colonised populations within the metropole. The real, as well as cultural, racism of the Western academy, has also provided the context for the development of the discourse.

To summarise, therefore, critical perspectives in the humanities which draw on Foucault's insights into the 'power/knowledge' relationship in the form of postcolonial studies have largely been developed in tandem with diasporic movements of postcolonial scholars to the metropole. In the social sciences, to over-simplify, somewhat comparable, though different critical perspectives on the implications of imperialism in the construction of knowledge emerged, some years earlier, with the movement of scholars in the opposite direction (i.e. from the metropole to the postcolony). These would include (prior to Foucauldian influences), oppositional voices in 'Development Studies' (for an overview, see Slater 1995), critiques in anthropology (Asad 1973; Cohn 1988) and in debates on 'the sociology of development and the underdevelopment of sociology' of Andre Gundar Frank, and others in the late 1960s (see King 1995a). Though as Slater points out, the major weakness in the (mainly) Marxist accounts here was 'the failure to theorize subjectivity and identity' (Slater 1995:71).

Yet the failure of these various critical perspectives to fully interact must be accounted for not by the gaps between countries or languages but those that occur across the campus, *between* disciplines. For example, Moore-Gilbert writes in 1997 that 'colonial discourse analysis now operates across an ever broader range of fields, including the history of law, anthropology, political economy, philosophy, historiography, art history, and psychoanalysis' (1997:9) but makes no reference to studies in geography, planning, urbanism or architecture. In his magisterial study of the impact of imperialism on the formation of knowledge and culture Edward Said does better in that, at least in passing, he refers to the impact of imperialism on metropolitan capitals and to the spatial transformations in colonial cities (Said 1994; see also King 1995a). There are, perhaps, other explanations to be offered.

I have suggested elsewhere one possible reason why a serious postcolonial critique was slow to develop in regard to architecture and urban studies (see Chapter 3). The early exponents of postcolonial criticism focused on a critique of literary and historical writing and, as I have indicated, were located in the humanities of the Western academy. But with some exceptions (Home 1996; King 1976, 1990b), it did not address, in any significant way, the impact of imperialism on the spatial disciplines of architecture, planning and urbanism more generally, either in the colony or, indeed, in the metropole.

The renewed interest in these issues in the American academy in the late 1980s, also drawing to varying degrees on Foucault's 'Power/Knowledge' paradigm (Metcalf 1989; Rabinow 1989), has as much to do with issues of theory in the Western academy (Wright 1991; AlSayyad 1991) as with urban policy and practice in the postcolony. Where the colonial city concept has been mobilised as a metaphor to represent the increasingly ethnically and spatially segregated situation of Western cities (King 1990a; Philo and Kearns 1993[2]), revisionist discourses of 'the global' (King 1990b) as well as poststructuralist approaches (Jacobs 1996) have led to studies on the imperial as well as the (technically) postimperial city (Driver and Gilbert 1998).

The more conscious use of the deconstructive methods of postcolonial criticism to the understanding of colonial architecture, space and urbanism have, with occasional exceptions, principally been the outcome of three conferences organised by a group of architects, academics and critics under the title of 'Other Connections' and, in a deliberate attempt to avoid the influence of 'Western hegemonies', took place in Singapore (1993), Chandigarh (1995) and Melbourne (1997). In a selection of papers from the first two of these, *Postcolonial Space(s)*, the editors suggest that 'Postcolonial space is a space of intervention into those architectural constructions that parade under a universalist guise and either exclude or repress differential spatialities or often disadvantaged ethnicities, communities or peoples.' The essays, 'located at the interstices of a number of disciplines including architecture, literary theory, cultural studies and philosophy' and informed by 'poststructuralist theory, psychoanalytic interpretations and feminist studies' are seen as investigating 'questions of representation and interpretation, issues of difference and identity' (Nalbantoglu and Wong 1997:7).

Earlier studies on colonial urbanism provided a political, social, cultural and behavioural interpretation of the physical and spatial forms of the colonial city, principally from the position of the coloniser, emphasising their social and cultural effects, and in relation to issues of social and cultural identity (King 1976). In challenging universalist approaches, newer studies emphasise questions of representation, difference and identity, including issues of race and gender. What seems to have been lost, however, is an acknowledgement of the real forces of *neo*-colonialism, and with globalisation, the exploitative relations of global capitalism with its gross inequities (see Dirlik 1997).

The major contribution of the more general postcolonial perspectives to the study of the city (and not only the 'postcolonial' city) is in the recognition of the essential reciprocity of colonial processes, in the questioning of simple binary dichotomies (between coloniser/colonised, East/West) and in acknowledging the uniqueness of particular colonial situations. In Said's words, the colonial relationship is best understood in terms of 'Overlapping Territories, Intertwined Histories'; it requires a questioning of those categories 'presuming that the West and its culture are largely independent of other cultures' (Said 1994:134). In specifically urban terms, these perspectives are illustrated in Yeoh's study of the 'contested terrain' of colonial Singapore where 'the spaces of everyday life were developed, sustained, renegotiated, distorted or countered by a Chinese counter-discourse in the everyday resistance of the colonized' (Yeoh 1996; see also Kusno 1998).

DECENTRING AND RE-CENTRING STUDIES OF THE CITY

What are the implications of postcolonial criticism for urban studies more generally? The first would seem to be for a decentring of Eurocentric conceptions of the world, not only in terms of society, space and culture, but equally in terms of temporality and history; to contest the view, in Chakrabarty's terms, that all histories tend to begin and end with Europe (Chakrabarty 1992). In this context, there are numerous reasons to challenge the taken for granted assumption that the 'natural' study of contemporary urbanism should properly begin with the so-called 'industrial capitalist, modernist city' in the West, an assumption probably made by urbanists since Adna Ferrin Weber in 1899. Without reference to the larger, often colonial space economies, markets and systems of urbanisation and culture of which it was a part, there is no 'autonomous' understanding of the 'Euro American' capitalist industrial city. Moreover, though not denying the global importance of the relationship between capitalism and industrial urbanism, there have been other systems of cities in the course of world history (Chase-Dunn 1985), and more than one urban revolution. But such reasoning apart, we can also ask whose city, whose history is being privileged? Whose 'global explanation' is being foisted on the world?

'Modern', 'modernist' and 'modernity' are equally ambiguous, non-transparent terms. The problem with 'modernity' is to assume that it is a historical term, referencing time or history (without reference to space) rather than a cultural one that references a way of life. If modern means 'now', 'of the present', we need to know whose 'now' and whose 'where' is being privileged. As the English word 'modern' has been around since the sixteenth century (King 1995b) it is evident that notions of modernity are ever-changing, inflected by such things as religion, politics, ideology. Different understandings of modernity exist simultaneously in different places, and under very different conditions. Colonial modernity is different from metropolitan modernity; Islamic modernity from Christian or 'secular' modernity; postmodern modernity from premodern modernity. If one of the characteristics of the contemporary 'modern' Western city is its ethnic, racial, and cultural diversity, this was characteristic of late eighteenth-century Batavia (Java) (Taylor 1983) long before it was characteristic of London or Paris.

In McDowell's words, 'Recognizing different ways of knowing does not mean abrogating responsibility for distinguishing between them' (1995:281). We need to recognise where theories come from, the conditions that produce (and also circulate) them, how exclusive as well as inclusive they attempt to be, whose interests are advanced by them, and where. Forms of knowledge reflect the worlds and spaces of the powerful; they also reflect their own times.

Given the hegemony of Western forms of knowledge and the dominance of English-language publishing worldwide, it is not surprising that if we read some of the most widely circulating urban studies in the last two decades, it seems that an apparent unity has descended over many of the world's cities in that they have been largely narrated through one or the other (inter-related) systems of representation. On one hand, the concepts and narratives of a disciplinary urban political economy (e.g. the *International Journal of Urban and Regional Research* in the 1980s) have had the effect of reducing the vast diversity of different topographies, polities, geographies, ethnicities, landscapes, peoples, memories, architectures, cultures, histories, religions, languages, identities and differences of all kinds into a uniform collective whole, to be selectively understood as a series of urban social movements, cases of collective consumption and instances of state intervention. On the other hand, with the invention of concepts of both the world and global city, stemming largely from a dominant American academy based either in Los Angeles or New York (with regional offices elsewhere) new paradigms have been launched, the result of which, in prioritising so-called 'economic criteria', has focused (if not fixed) for a decade the attention of many urban scholars on perhaps 30 or 40 cities, all but three or four of them either in Europe or the United States (Knox and Taylor 1995; Knox 1995). As Duncan points out in relation to Burgess' 'concentric zone' theory of the city in the infamous Chicago School of urban sociology, its effect was to ensure that all cities were made to defer to the form of Chicago (Duncan 1996:259). Similarly, the effect of the 'world' and 'global city' paradigm has been to prompt scholars as well as municipal officials worldwide to ask 'Is this, or is this not a "world city"'? Those that don't make the grade have, to some degree, dropped off the screen. The fixation on a particular socially constructed notion of 'the economy' and 'the accumulation of capital' without reference to the historical, cultural and global conditions in which this has taken place and without reference to what, in other cities worldwide, gives meaning to people's lives leaves many questions unanswered.

I am not, of course, dismissing these two dominant paradigms offhand (not least as I have also been implicated in producing them). It is rather that such theories create particular social and cultural worlds that have meaning to those who use them. To imagine they are universally applicable, however, that they in any way give insight into the many different meanings of particular places, or can, without reference to the particular histories, politics, memories, or subjectivities, capture the highly diverse identities which exist in particular cities is an illusion.

Here, perhaps the most striking absence in cross-cultural urban studies is reference to the institutions, power, and growing influence in many cities worldwide of religious movements, old and new. I refer here not simply to specific cities worldwide where the promotion or defence of particular religious identities have (often, for centuries) been the defining force in the space and politics of the city – Belfast, Jerusalem, Beirut, Tehran, Varanasi, Rome, Istanbul – but also to the fact that, in a universe where worlds are shaped by particular religious *world*views, it might be worth asking why so-called 'world cities' are overwhelmingly only in one of those worlds, conventionally understood as 'Christian', and mostly in Protestant states.

Cities are not only sites of financial and economic activity, but also of symbolic and cultural capital. Particular sacred cities worldwide have, in recent years, become the sites for staging major religio-political struggles. In these, the essential element of the urban, namely, the building as symbolic signifier, as marker of sacred space, has become the pre-eminent site of religious and often violent political struggles – in India, Ayodhya, Amritsar, Mumbai; in the Middle East, Makka, Jerusalem; in Sri Lanka, Kandy; to say nothing of Waco in Texas, Jonesville, or the World Trade Center in New York. In Europe, new identities are inscribed, old ones violated, by the desecration of cemeteries or commemorative monuments. Sacred texts are stuck, like graffiti, onto one-time working class walls. In the 1998 riots in Jakarta, shops of Indonesian ethnic Chinese were destroyed, except for those displaying Islamic signs. That I write here from an agnostic position should not inhibit the recognition that subjects live in worlds (not least urban worlds) that are made and lived in through religious beliefs and worldviews or, alternatively, as secular responses to them. New York's or London's trumpeting of being 'global' (an inflated form of nationalism, or neo-imperialism) is not unconnected to many other cities being simply 'national'. If urban studies are to address issues of ethnicity, religion, nationalism, cultural identity, they need a language, and a set of concepts to do so. The question is not simply who is writing the city, or even where s/he is coming from. It is rather the positionality, and the theoretical language adopted.

NOTES

1   From Anthony D. King, 'Postcolonialism, representation and the city', in Gary Bridge and Sophie Watson, eds, *A Companion to the City*, 2000 © Wiley.
2   Philo and Kearns (1993:15) write 'There is also a sense in which "the colonial city" has now come home … in that the global redistributions of human populations from the nineteenth century onwards have contributed to most urban areas becoming ethnic mosaics, scarred in all too many instances by segregationist and prejudicial attitudes on the part of white "host" groups'.

BIBLIOGRAPHY

AlSayyad, N. (1991) *Forms of Dominance: On the Architecture and Urbanism of the Colonial Enterprise*, Aldershot: Avebury.

Ahmad, Aijaz (1992) *In Theory: Classes, Nations, Literatures*, Delhi: Oxford University Press.

Asad, T. (1973) *Anthropology and the Colonial Encounter*, London: Ithaca Press.

Bhabha, H. (1994) *The Location of Culture*, London and New York: Routledge.

Chakrabarty, D. (1992) 'Postcoloniality and the artifice of history: who speaks for "Indian" pasts?' *Representations* 32 (Winter) 1–27.

Chase-Dunn, C.K. (1985) 'The system of world-cities 800–1975' in Michael Timberlake, ed., *Urbanisation in the World-Economy*, New York: Academic Press.

Cohn, B.S. (1988) *An Anthropologist Among the Historians and Other Essays*, Delhi: Oxford University Press.

Dirlik, A. (1997) *The Postcolonial Aura: Third World Criticism in the Age of Global Capitalism*, Boulder, CO: Westview Press.

Driver, F. and Gilbert, D. (1998) 'Heart of empire? Landscape, space and performance in imperial London', *Environment and Planning D: Society and Space*, 16, 1: 11–28.

Duncan, J.S. (1996) 'Metrop(e)olis or Hayden White among the urbanists', in A.D. King, ed., *Re-Presenting the City: Ethnicity, Capital and Culture in the 21st Century Metropolis*, London and New York: Macmillan and New York University Press, pp.253–68.

Fanon, F. (1968) *The Wretched of the Earth*, New York: Grove Reprint. Originally published as *Les Damnes de la Terre*. Francois Maspero ed., Paris, 1961.

Foucault, M. (1980) *Power/Knowledge*, New York: Pantheon Books.

Guha, R. (1988) 'Introduction', in B.S. Cohn, *An Anthropologist Among the Historians and Other Essays*, Delhi: Oxford University Press.

Hall, S. (1996) 'When was the "post-colonial"? Thinking at the limit', in Iain Chambers and Lidia Curti, eds, *The Post-Colonial Question: Common Skies, Divided Horizons*, London and New York: Routledge, 242–60.

Home, R. (1997) *Of Planting and Planning: The Making of British Colonial Cities*, London: Spon.

Johnston, R.J., Taylor, P.J. and Watts, M.J., eds (1995) *Geographies of Global Change*, Oxford: Blackwell.

King, A.D. (1976) *Colonial Urban Development: Culture, Social Power and Environment*, London and Boston: Routledge and Kegan Paul.

King, A.D. (1990a) 'The new colonialism: global restructuring and the city', *Intersight* 1.

King, A.D. (1990b) *Global Cities: Post-imperialism and the Internationalisation of London*, London and New York: Routledge.

King, A.D. (1995a) 'Writing colonial space: a review essay', *Comparative Studies in Society and History*, 37, 3: 541–54.

King, A.D. (1995b) 'The times and spaces of modernity (or who needs postmodernism?)', in Scott Lash, Mike Featherstone and Roland Robertson, eds, *Global Modernities*, Newbury Park and London: Sage, 108–23.

King, A.D. (1997) 'Locution and location: positioning the postcolonial' in Vikram Prakash, ed., *Theatres of Decolonisation: Architecture/Agency/Urbanism*, Seattle, WA: College of Architecture and Urban Planning, University of Washington, Vol 2. 295–310.

Knox, Paul (1995) 'World cities and the organisation of global space', in R.J. Johnston, Peter J. Taylor and Michael J. Watts, eds, *Geographies of Global Change*, Oxford: Blackwell, 232–47.

Knox, P. and Taylor, P.J., eds (1995) *World Cities in a World-System*, Cambridge: Cambridge University Press.

Kusno, A. (1998) 'Beyond the postcolonial: architecture, urban space and political cultures in Indonesia'. PhD dissertation, State University of New York at Binghamton.

Mangin, P., ed. (1995) 'Introduction', in *Contemporary Postcolonial Theory: A Reader*, London: Arnold.

Mbembe, A. (1992) 'The banality of power and the aesthetics of vulgarity in the postcolony', trans. J. Roitman, *Public Culture*, 4, 2.

McClintock, A. (1992) 'The angel of progress: pitfalls of the term "post-colonialism"', *Social Text*, 31/32: 1–15.

McDowell, L. (1995) 'Understanding diversity: the problem of/for theory', in R.J. Johnston, P.J. Taylor and M.J. Watts, eds, *Geographies of Global Change*, Oxford: Blackwell, 280–94.

Metcalf, T.R. (1989) *An Imperial Vision: Indian Architecture and Britain's Raj*, Berkeley: University of California Press.

Moore-Gilbert, B. (1997) *Postcolonial Theory: Contexts, Practices, Politics*, London: Verso.

Nalbantoglu, G.B. and Wong, C.T., eds (1997) *Postcolonial Space(s)*, Princeton: Princeton University Press.

Noyes, J. (1992) *Colonial Space: Spatiality in the Discourse of German Southwest Africa*, Philadelphia: Harwood Academic Publishing.

Philo, C. and Kearns, G. (1993) 'Culture, history, capital: a critical introduction to the selling of places', in C. Philo and G. Kearns, eds, *Selling Places: The City as Cultural Capital, Past and Present*, Oxford: Pergamon.

Prakash, V., ed. (1997) *Theatres of Decolonisation: Architecture/Agency/Urbanism*, Seattle, WA: College of Architecture and Urban Planning, University of Washington, 2 vols.

Rabinow, P. (1989) *French Modern: Norms and Forms of the Social Environment*, Cambridge: MIT Press.

Said, E. (1978) *Orientalism*, New York: Pantheon.

Said, E. (1994) *Culture and Imperialism*, London: Vintage.

Schiller, N., Basch, L. and Blanc-Szanton, C. (1995) 'From immigrant to transmigrant: theorising transnational migration', *Anthropological Quarterly*, 68, 1: 48–63.

Shohat, E. (1992) 'Notes on the postcolonial', *Social Text*, 31/32: 91–113.

Simon, D. (1998) 'Rethinking (post)modernism, postcolonialism, and posttraditionalism: South–North perspectives', *Environment and Planning D: Society and Space*, 16, 2: 219–45.

Slater, D. (1995) 'Trajectories of development theory: capitalism, socialism and beyond', in R.J. Johnston, P.J. Taylor and M.J. Watts, eds, *Geographies of Global Change*, Oxford: Blackwell, 63–76.

Taylor, J.G. (1983) *The Social World of Batavia*, Madison: University of Wisconsin Press.

Williams, P. and Chrisman, L., eds (1994) *Colonial Discourse and Postcolonial Theory: A Reader*, New York: Columbia University Press.

Wright, G. (1991) *The Politics of Design in French Colonial Urbanism*, Chicago: Chicago University Press.

Yeoh, B.S.A. (1996) *Contesting Space: Power Relations and the Urban Built Environment in Colonial Singapore*, Oxford: Oxford University Press.

Chapter 6: Cities: contradictory utopias[1]

INTRODUCTION

Having worked for many years in sociology and urban studies (including the field of 'development'), I moved some time ago into the realms of art history and cultural theory. A disciplinary change in mid life is hardly as revolutionary as a change of sex but it does open new perspectives. If words such as 'development' or 'globalisation' didn't figure 20 years ago in most art historians' vocabularies, art history does, nonetheless, have a number of key conceptual concerns, two of which I shall first briefly explore: positionality and representation. I shall then – prompted by this collection's theme of 'Global Futures' – address the editor's invitation to write 'a critical Utopia for the world's cities'.

POSITIONALITY

The problem of position, the space from which we speak, political, ideological, dominant or subaltern – is not unknown to scholars in the field of development studies. At least some of the apparent insights of postcolonial criticism, audible from the mid to late 1980s, have a certain similarity with debates between a Third World intelligentsia and development scholars in the 1960s. Questioning the assumption that history begins and ends with Europe, reiterated by Chakrabarty (1992), Prakash (1990) or even Said (1978, 1993), in a postcolonialist discourse in the humanities, had its precursors among historians and social scientists of India (Romila Thapur), Egypt (Anouar Abdel Malik) or Sri Lanka (Susantha Goonitilake) in the 1960s , to cite only a few. The perspective of 'the Other', seen not just from a (subaltern) below, but from a Eurocentric 'centre', was viewed as the margins. It was most clearly exposed in the contested inter-cultural encounters of development studies and also the social sciences, 20 or 30 years before it emerged again in the 1990s, in the postcolonial humanities textbooks of the metropole (Ashcroft *et al.* 1995; Williams and Chrisman 1994; see also Dirlik 1996; King 1997).

What difference have the realities, as well as discourses, of globalisation made to issues of positionality? The question is not simply whether the subaltern can speak (Spivak 1988) but whether she (or he) can set the agenda. If so, where, and how, is it set and what is to be discussed, not least in regard to 'global futures'? Have 30 years of an apparent 'time-space compression' (Harvey 1989) made the question of position redundant? It is because of these political and epistemological concerns, that I start with some of the initial assumptions.

GLOBAL FUTURES

Having in the last 15 years made considerable use of the terms global or globalisation, I am concerned, especially, about their viability in particular contexts (King 1997a, 1997b).

Global can be used in at least two senses; metaphorically, referring to the total whole or, more literally, as referring to, or encompassing, the entire terrestrial globe. In certain cases, global/globalisation seem entirely appropriate – aspects of economic globalisation in the 1980s (24-hour trading in financial services, worldwide property marketing, satellite broadcasting, global production and marketing, global warming). I am less convinced with its application in the realm of the human, social and cultural. As a term used to further a particular economic and ideological agenda, it is at once both too broad and too narrow. Because all 'global' discourses 'stress the importance of transnational forces, the practices of coding and decoding everyday practices that disrupt, disturb, and even deny the identity of the global are not revealed' (Kusno, in King 1997a). Above all, the discourse on the global is positioned, understandably enough, not only in the place from which it comes but from where it can be fuelled, disseminated and consumed. And because of the absence of other discourses, from where it can expand.

In brief, the very concepts of the global and globalisation have depended on the *material* conditions that have produced and given access to them – satellites, telematics, electronic communication, air travel, the distribution of globally marketed commodities, etc. It is hardly necessary to state that relatively few have access to these resources. Globalisation, wherever it touches down, is a highly partial, very uneven process (McGrew 1992; Scott 1997). Talking about the global is a highly privileged discourse for some, and for others, is totally irrelevant (O'Byrne 1997). As a metaphor, the term global – with its connotations of the singular, unitary, total – is, in many ways, the most ineffective metaphor to identify what we're looking for, namely, the desires, wishes and aspirations for the future of individuals and groups in a myriad different sites all over the world. We might think whether those of us who flew to this conference are those who construct the discourse of the global; those whom we flew over, probably do not.

REPRESENTING THE CITY

In the context of these issues, therefore, writing a 'critical utopia for the world's cities' assumes we have adequate theoretical tools to do so. What can we say of those that already exist?

By far the most dominant paradigm in urban studies for over two decades has been that of urban political economy though with some moves into the postmodern (Harvey 1989; Watson and Gibson 1995). While the predominantly economic discourse of world and global cities initiated from the early 1980s (Knox and Taylor 1995), and the collapse of Eastern European regimes, both offered new analytical spaces, this largely structuralist theoretical paradigm has not been able to handle new concerns with identity, representation and cultural difference that have arisen in relation to the city. Nor has that particular discourse been very adept in addressing questions of urban and architectural symbolism central to these concerns.

On the other hand, much of the theoretical literature in cultural studies dealing with representation as 'the production of meaning through language, discourse and image ... of how visual images, language and discourse work as systems of representation' (Hall 1997) has not had as its object of study the built and symbolic spaces of the city.

The obvious exception to this is the burgeoning field of postcolonial theory and criticism which, having been largely concerned with literary studies for a decade (Moore-Gilbert 1997) has, as discussed in the previous chapter, been linked more closely to urban and architectural studies. While the essays in *Postcolonial Space(s)* (Nalbantoglu and Wong 1997) were offered as 'a reminder of the colonial past and a salutary gesture towards the future', the Marxism which sustained the urban political economy paradigm for 20 years seems – in this work – to have been relegated to obscurity. Capitalism is so taken for granted as to be absent from the debate. Of more interest in this context is the work of Yeoh (1996) which addresses the agency of indigenous peoples in the cultural translation process that gave meaning to colonial space.

UTOPIAS

It might be useful here to begin by reminding ourselves of the basic features of 'Utopia' of Sir Thomas More (1477–1536), as well as the conditions prevailing on his book's first publication in 1516.

More's imaginary society was founded on the basis of a belief, or ideology – a passionate religious belief for which its originator was ultimately to pay with his life; a society where people practised a form of Christian communism, participating with complete equality in all activities relating to housing, clothing, food, education, government, war and religion. What was common for full citizenship for all Utopians was a belief in a good and just God who ruled the world. Such an over-riding commitment to a religious faith has characterised many, if not most utopian experiments, from that of the Pilgrim Fathers to the followers of Joseph Smith and the Latter Day Saints.

In the second place, Utopia was envisioned as a 'society' and not a city. In early sixteenth-century England a city was a much more distinctive, and different, part of the society than in our own day (in the West, at least), when life outside the city is not too different from life within it.

Third, the actual territory of Utopia was represented by More as an *island* located at the limits of what, in 1516, was still a world without boundaries, though close enough to a 'New World' which suggested everything the imagination made possible. Since then, by and large, the history of utopian settlements has been one of *fleeing* from the social and political disasters created by humankind and attempting to establish *new* societies and settlements in some near-to-pristine environment. We need hardly remind ourselves that the conditions of More's time no longer prevail; the collective abandonment of social, political or environmental chaos is neither a socially responsible option, nor even – except at an individual level – a practical possibility.

Indeed, of the contradictory meanings implicit in the contemporary use of the term 'utopian', 'a place or state of ideal (social and political) perfection', as against 'an impractical scheme for social and political improvement' (Penguin 1982) neither really addresses the conditions and material results of five centuries of capitalism, imperialism, colonialism, environmental degradation, namely, not how to abandon existing settlements and establish new ones but how to improve the ones we actually have.

In this context, we need to have a much better historical understanding of the historically contingent concepts with which we try to understand and, above all, order and decide our worlds. In thinking of utopias we need knowledge as much as imagination. Much more needs to be known of the history of so-called 'Third World' and colonial cities. As I've suggested elsewhere,

> the culture, society and space of early twentieth century Calcutta (now Kolkata) or Singapore pre-figured the future in a much more accurate way than did that of London or New York. 'Modernity' was not born in Paris but rather in Rio.
>
> (King 1991:8)

If after the collapse of the great social experiments of the twentieth century, we are now witnessing a 're-feudalisation' of society in Europe and America, with an increasing retreat into suburban fortresses (Ellin 1997), we could benefit by knowing more of feudalism.

A CRITICAL UTOPIA FOR THE WORLD'S CITIES?

It was conventional wisdom that, over the last four decades of the twentieth century, 'First' and 'Third World' cities had, in certain specific ways, and to varying degrees, become increasingly similar. The ever-widening gap between the rich and poor, the potential of some to earn astronomically high salaries (or in other legal and illegal ways, to accumulate vast wealth) and others to become permanent members of an unemployed, impoverished underclass; the simultaneous production of luxurious high-rise apartments and office towers and low-rise, street-level poverty and homelessness; the spread of fortress-like enclaves of residential privilege alongside the increase in street crime and social marginalisation; socially, the existence of ethnic, racial and cultural diversity and spatially, ethnic, racial and cultural segregation; the heights and depths of conspicuous consumption as well as the heights and depths of crime, disease and drugs. In terms of social, racial and spatial segregation, cities in the 'First World' as well as the 'Third', increasingly took on the characteristics of historic colonial cities (King 1976).

The 'logic of the market', left unchecked, simultaneously exacerbated but also reduced the scale of economic and social divisions between different spatial categories in the following ways. Extrapolating what had occurred in the last 30 years of the twentieth century, in what at the time were the 'Third World' countries in Asia, differences were reduced between cities and the countryside, as had happened historically in the West – yet simultaneously exacerbating such differences in Asian 'Third World' cities. Differences between the rich and poor in both other 'Third World' as well as 'First (and previously 'Second') World' cities also became more extreme. Finally, through the same logic of the market and the processes of global capitalism, as economic, social and spatial differences in all cities increased, the differences between the various cities themselves, worldwide, in fact became reduced. Put another way, the economic, technological, and social profile of cities worldwide became increasingly similar though cultural differences remained.

Spatially – by which I refer to their architecture, urban design and physical and spatial form – cities also, in some ways, became increasingly alike (at least in the gaze of the globalised population who moved between them), the result of the international transfers of construction materials, consumer products, architectural and planning ideologies, 'starchitects' and transportation technology. In other ways, however, partly because it was in the interests of capital – which 'lives and works through difference' (Hall 1991) – to make them different, partly because of the tendency of globalisation to 'exacerbate the concern with identity' (Robertson 1992), and partly due to the inherent lasting effects of cultural difference (Nederveen Pietersee 1996), they also stayed, or even became, increasingly different.

These tendencies had become more evident in the last decades of the twentieth century – but they were also much older than that. For what had long been globalised (yet Western-centred) professions of city planning, architecture and urban design, now invariably seeking to retain, or give their particular city a distinctive visual and spatial image, the extent to which they could make each of them different was a measure of the degree to which all of them became the same – though again, only in the gaze of the 'external' observer. In the gaze of the international traveller, 'real' difference was evident only in cities where there was no local consciousness of their *global* existence.

THE RISE OF URBAN GOVERNMENT

Given the degrees of difference between cities, and the imperative (see above) that each society or community had as much control as possible over their own agendas and desires, in and for the future, powers of government and control previously developed and implemented at world, state, or regional level were gradually, yet massively, shifted to the level of each individual city.

By the middle of the twenty-first century, cities, as the principal loci of population worldwide, and the centres (especially) of intellectual labour, cultural production, information processing, politics, communication and consumption, were in a far better position to take over many functions, and also services, previously provided and delivered at the level of the nation state. Even in the 1980s, certain cities were already conducting their own foreign policies, particularly as far as these concerned their economic well-being (Kirby and Marston 1995). Despite the near universal access to electronic communication that was to develop by the mid twenty-first century, cities, as social units, and their governments, were still to be far more spatially accessible to their citizens than nation-states and their governments had been to their subjects. As much smaller social units of population, cities provided much greater possibilities for different political and constitutional choice: where the majority took the form of city republics, a number of others (especially in what was previously the USA) chose to be monarchies; others (especially in what was once the Soviet Union, and in other one-time colonial states) preferred to be bureaucracies; still others, theocracies or enlightened dictatorships.

This shift to the city as the organising space of social and political life can best be understood as part of a larger historical trajectory. In ancient times, the social, political and spatial organisation of people had been in empires, a system that had been revived in more recent memory. The dismantling of over-large geopolitical units of authority had begun in the mid twentieth century with the collapse and subsequent disintegration of the major European empires. The outcome of this disintegration, the tripling of the number of nation-states (from 67 to 186 between 1945 and 1990) had been a major phase in the nation-forming period of humankind. Prior to the French Revolution there had been some 20 of what we would now recognise as nation-states. Between the Congress of Vienna (1815) and the formation of the United Nations (1945), the number had tripled, from 23 to 67 (Birch 1989).

This organisation of people along 'national' territorial lines had largely, though not entirely, been governed by geographical factors – peoples, widely distributed across territories, were divided by oceans, rivers, mountains, deserts. The nationality principle was based on 'where you lived was who you are', logical enough when virtually all the world's peoples were dispersed through rural areas. As recently as 1800, for example, less than 3 per cent of the world's population was urban (Clark 1998) so that organising scattered populations administratively into territorially based nation-states in the nineteenth and twentieth centuries had made sense.

Yet the expansion of nation-states in the twentieth century was, in the early decades of the new millennium, to be recognised as only a temporary solution to the problems of identity, territory and government. It had been an expected and 'natural' outcome, the result of decades (sometimes centuries) of colonial rule that had given postcolonial peoples little option but to follow the example of their imperial European rulers – irrespective of the illogical ethnic or territorial base on which such nation-states were built. Half a century of so-called independence from the 1950s, the increasing consciousness of their still postcolonial status at the millennium, made such states increasingly open to new forms of political, economic and territorial organisation.

The shift to forms of city states and city identities had resulted from five major developments, evident at the close of the twentieth century, and that were to continue into the twenty-first. The first was a further destabilising of the notion of fixed national identities resulting from the collapse of the Soviet empire in 1989 and the subsequent turmoil associated with the remaking of national identities in an increasingly globalised world. This collapse was only a sequel to the equally ambiguous identity situation which had been created in many postcolonial states, 30 years earlier – a situation, for example, where people could move through three or four national identities in a lifetime (e.g. British Indian, Pakistani, Bangladeshi).

The second development was the massive increase in mobility and migration which had grown in the twentieth and twenty-first centuries – some permanent, some temporary, some long term, some short, though in total resulting in a massive diaspora of different peoples worldwide, with personal and kinship connections, property, business and personal interests diffused across different states. The identity effects of such transmigrations (Glick Schiller *et al.* 1995) were never singular. People increasingly came to have multiple identities, deploying them to their advantage wherever they happened to be.

The third development came from the influence of the electronic media. Here, despite the fact that electronic communications – television, cell phones, Internet, the Web – theoretically enabled people to make completely free decisions as to where they lived, because of the constant introduction of new, 'improved' products and the need to constantly update software and other equipment, the demographic effects of these constantly changing new technologies was to keep people close to sources of supply, in or near the cities.

The effect of these developments was to loosen, or 'soften up', the attachment of people to singular national identities, to singular places of origin, not necessarily to erase or dismiss them but rather, to make people available for something else in addition.

The fourth development was demographic. Few world leaders (or indeed, the population at large) had noticed that 1996 had been the year in which 50 per cent of the world's population had become urban. 'Despite its symbolic significance, this historical event went largely unrecognized and unnoticed' (Clark 1998:85); this, despite the fact that reports in 1988 had already suggested that a figure of 60 per cent would be reached by 2025 (United Nations 1988) and that cities of one million inhabitants, just over 100 in 1960, would be nearing 700 in 2025, a figure that was roughly similar to that for cities of half a million inhabitants. By 2015, many large cities (almost 30 by 2015), with over ten million inhabitants, were already much larger than many small states (Oxford University Press 1996). In this situation, it was hardly surprising that many visionaries had already seen the nation state as an increasingly obsolescent form of social, spatial and political organisation.

The fifth development was to take place in east and southeast Asia, which had rapidly overcome the temporary economic crisis of the 1990s. In some postcolonial states (South Korea, Hong Kong, Taiwan, Malaysia, Indonesia, Singapore) the high rates of economic development and growth had, by the early twenty-first century, pushed what was often a rural population into cities, cities themselves built to the very highest standards, 'modernised', offering an opportunity to be not simply like others in the Western world but, in fact, to be much better off in every way. In this context, Shanghai had long since overtaken Manhattan as the paradigmatic example of a certain version of 1930s 'modernity' and was to occupy this somewhat obsolescent role for many decades.

The real model of global living came to be Hong Kong. The citizens of this city, by far the wealthiest in the world by the year 2020, had, through an act of unprecedented collective self-reflexivity not unconnected to the interaction between capitalist and socialist values, come to realise two foundational truths. The first was a realisation of the essentially mimetic nature of its first strivings for modernity which, in following the (Western) example of New York, had resulted in an imitative version of Manhattan. However, now (2020) that Manhattan was itself largely a heap of ruins following the gradual decline, and then collapse of its financial trading function (taken over by Kuala Lumpur and Hong Kong), the people of Hong Kong came to realise the false values on which their first 'global city' had been built – a total commitment to profit-hungry capitalism and a way of manifesting this, in the skyscraper skyline, that was totally dependent on Western, especially American, forms of design.

By 2020 such values had gone through a 180 degree turn. While still the richest city in the world, the citizens of Hong Kong had become committed to the ideas of an ecologically sound environment. The skyscrapers had been demolished, making way for low-rise, energy-efficient offices and 'green' apartment complexes. Parks, greenswards and commons were interspersed throughout the city where citizens could be seen daily practising the old discipline of Tai-chi, exercising minds and bodies. No longer confined to the cramped and obsolete colonial space of 'Victoria Island' and the so-called 'New Territories', the city with its 15 million inhabitants was evenly spread out over the mainland, communications provided by a highly efficient rapid transit system. In being thus encouraged to return to their cultural roots, the Chinese population (as well as the large proportion of cosmopolitan inhabitants) attained a new harmony of living, something previously dreamt of, but never attained, by earlier utopian city planners. In terms of livability indices – clean air, freedom from crime, longevity, social and spiritual happiness, it had the highest ranking in the world.

As the economic and political significance of the nation-state shrank as a result of economic globalisation (already predicted in the 1980s and 1990s), and as the worldwide system of cities came into its own, major alliances were formed, not only between cities in geopolitical blocs such as the European Community, NAFTA, SEATO, and others, but also between groups of cities specialising in the production of particular services and products, and between those with similar ideological and political outlooks. No longer competing for the favour of investments from multinational companies, individual cities as well as city alliances regulated the opportunities which multinational companies required in order to operate (not least as they also needed to compete with the highly efficient city corporations, each of which had largely specialised in terms of function, commodity production or the like). Multinational corporations, no longer footloose, yet with no other opportunities to exist, readily agreed to be taxed in order to pay for infrastructure. Alliances between workers in cities worldwide no longer made it possible to threaten them with undisclosed plans to shift production to other sites.

In order to bring the system of city governments about, urban political infrastructure was strengthened and national levels scaled down. The culturally diverse populations which both colonialism and global capitalism had located in cities both encouraged diversity and difference in cities and also provided popular support to sustain it. Because of this diversity, large parts of the (especially rural) world previously excluded from the world economy (ineffectively operated and administered through the competing and contradictory apparatus of private capital and the nation-state) were brought into the world economy, by a much larger, proactive policy run by the alliance of cities. What were, at the end of the twentieth century, single-issue parties – greens, ecologists, feminists, animal rights and peace activists – began in the new millennium to target and win over particular cities. Subsequently, through these smaller social units than the state, they were able to diffuse their influence through city alliances.

National governments, while still continuing to exist, had their influence (as well as their costs) substantially reduced. Their task, however, was still considerable as they were responsible for those parts of the nation-states which did not come under the jurisdiction of cities, not least the vast areas of agricultural land and the production of food that goes with this. Quite early on they surrendered their responsibility to RRGs (Rural Regional Governments) who held equal status and power to governments of the city. Jurisdiction of the seas, as well as concerns about fishing, marine recreation and the like were the responsibility of coastal cities.

By the fourth decade of the twenty-first century, only 20 per cent or less of the populations of what, in the 1990s, were nation-states, lived in non-urban areas, governed by RRGs. In their international capacity, national governments were also needed to oversee specific environmental, transportation and other matters. Security and defence, however, were transferred to alliances of city governments, logically enough, as here were the main centres of population.

The major shift in responsibility was at the supranational level where, from the late nineteenth to the end of the twentieth century, a myriad of organisations had arisen to oversee, develop, and provide economic and political relations and exchange between different *nation-states* at the level of the *international*. With the demise of the nation-state, and the replacement of the concept of national identity with city identity, a system of *intercity* relations was put into place. The world became an immense beehive of citizens, each one committed, on one hand, as a Parisian, San Franciscan, Tokyan, Muscovite, Lahori, Delhiwallah, not only to her or his own city but to the idea of city government itself. The very innumerability of major cities in the world (well over 3,000), making it impossible for any one person (or government) to remember them all, was also a factor in the disappearance of the idea of nationality.

The United Nations, which had emerged in the middle of the twentieth century as the epitome of the era of the nation-state (even though there had been fewer than twenty-five of such units of social organisation at the beginning of the previous century), though still continuing – at a level very much reduced in scale and cost – to deal with the semi-redundant apparatus of the nation-state, was eventually replaced by a new body, the United Cities Organisation (UCO). As City Representatives were in constant electronic communication, there was much less need for a more permanent institution or building (the abandonment of which was to greatly reduce the influence of both the United States, as well as New York, in world affairs). Instead, the UCO met in one of the world's largest cities every two years, moving round from one to the other. Building on the administrative and logistic structures developed during the era of nation-states, such as the Olympic Games and the World Cup, the UCO was therefore able, over the brief space of a century, to totally transform what, in the 1990s, had been the most over-crowded, dilapidated, polluted, unendowed, badly constructed and congested 50 cities in the world. Carefully pooling and deploying resources gathered on a global scale, combining these with taxes levied on multinational corporations and cooperating with the governments of individual cities, the UCO was able not only to eliminate global poverty but also gradually evened out the distribution of excesses and wants among the cities of the world. In addition, because of its relation to the grass roots of all urban problems and their solutions, the UCO was also able to eliminate the major environmental problems that had been of such concern in the previous century.

Having access to the bulk of the resources formally belonging to the United Nations, the UCO, in close touch with its individual members, was able to address, in a much more realistic and rational way, the principal social problems which had occurred in the world in the second half of the twentieth century, especially after the threat of the Cold War had disappeared in 1989. It had suddenly dawned on the Secretary-General of that august body (the UN) – at the stroke of midnight as the second millennium turned into the third – that by far the largest proportion of the world's problems were of an urban nature, and if not inherently 'urban', nonetheless erupting in cities – crime, drugs, pollution, poverty, ignorance, terrorism, disease, riots, racism, sexism, global warming, famine, traffic congestion, political corruption, social, racial and sexual oppression, and many more. With the active support of sympathisers worldwide, the creation of the UCO had taken only 20 years. By 2020, as all one-time 'national' as well as 'international' politicians were elected by their urban constituencies, lived in their cities, and so were immediately accessible to the inhabitants, urban conditions rapidly improved. Particular administrative, technical, or social ideas to improve the quality of urban life, found to be effective in one or more particular cities, were quickly disseminated round the world (Perlman 1995).

With populations largely located in well-planned, yet also architecturally and spatially immensely varied cities, systems of public transport were much improved and developed. By this time, the vast majority of the population lived in a form of accommodation and settlement that had slowly evolved through the nineteenth and twentieth centuries. Just as the interaction of social, architectural and spatial developments had given rise to the neologism 'suburbia' in 1895 (Oxford English Dictionary 1989), and the multiethnic transmigration of populations had, a century later, spawned 'ethnoburb' (Li 1998) so, by the 2040s, the total multicultural diversity of massive major cities worldwide, created by total global mobility, had given rise to the metropolitan 'globurb'.

As the problems of poverty and starvation had, by this time, been largely resolved, leading politicians recognised that the main life-threatening disease was overeating and obesity, brought about by a combination of the consumption of industrialised food, marketed by multinational corporations, and irrational forms of individualised, city-polluting transport. By 2030, so committed were people to eradicating obesity worldwide, which was creating immense strain on hospital facilities and health-maintenance organisations, that in addition to laying down intricate webs of cycle routes in all the world's cities, most people walked between their various destinations. The 415 million automobiles worldwide that had fouled the air of cities in the declining decades of the twentieth century, the oil and gas fuelling of which had not only endangered the future of the planet but led to the loss of millions of lives in futile wars (fought around the oil-producing states of the Middle East), were now recycled and put to better use. The millions of people previously employed in their production – especially in the cities of Japan, the United States, Britain and Germany – were in this way released to be engaged in more satisfying, and socially useful work.

Early on the morning of 6 July 2036, in the crystal clear air of east London's Tower Hill, the silence broken only by the cry of seagulls above and the lapping of the waves against the shore of the River Thames below, 200 tourists from every corner of the world, waiting to visit the Tower of London, were suddenly startled, and then amazed to see a clear, bright, technicolor likeness of a figure they quickly recognised as Sir Thomas More – head intact, and with what appeared to be a smile of satisfaction. Five hundred years after his execution, his image rose over their heads, moved slowly into the sky and floated off towards the celestial city....

NOTE

1   From Anthony D. King, 'Cities: contradictory utopias', in Jan Nederveen Pieterse, ed., *Global Futures: Shaping Globalisation*, 2000 © Anthony D. King.

BIBLIOGRAPHY

Ashcroft, B., Griffiths, G. and Tiffin, H., eds (1995) *The Post-Colonial Studies Reader*, London and New York: Routledge.

Benjamin, W. (1995) 'Paris: capital of the nineteenth century', in W. Benjamin, *Reflections, Essays, Aphorisms, Autobiographical Writings*, New York: Schoken.

Birch, A. (1989) *Nationalism and National Integration*, London and Boston: Unwin Hyman.

Chakrabarty, D. (1992) 'Postcoloniality and the artifice of history: who speaks of Indian pasts?', *Representations*, 37: 1–27.

Clark, D. (1998) 'Interdependent urbanization in an urban world: an historical overview', *The Geographical Journal*, 164, 1: 85–95.

de Certeau, M. (1988) *The Practice of Everyday Life*, Berkeley: University of California Press.

Dirlik, A. (1994) 'The postcolonial aura: Third World criticism in the age of global capitalism', *Critical Inquiry*, 20, 2: 328–56.

Durrschmidt, R. (1997) 'The delinking of locale and milieu: on the situatedness of extended milieux in a global environment', in J. Eade, ed., *Living the Global City*, London and New York: Routledge, pp.56–72.

Eade, J., ed. (1997) *Living the Global City*, London and New York: Routledge.

Ellin, N., ed. (1997) *Architecture of Fear*, New York: Princeton Architectural Press.

Fisher, J., ed. (1995) *Global Visions: Towards a New Internationalism in the Visual Arts*, London: Kala Press.

Friedmann, J. (1995) 'Where we stand: a decade of world city research', in P. Knox and P.J. Taylor, eds, *World Cities in a World-System*, Cambridge: Cambridge University Press, pp.21–47.

Glick Schiller, N., Basch, L. and Blanc-Szanton, C. (1995) 'From immigrant to transmigrant: theorizing transnational migration', *Anthropological Quarterly*, 68, 1: 48–63.

Hall, S. (1991) 'The local and the global: globalization and ethnicity', in A.D. King, *Culture, Globalization and the World-System: Contemporary Conditions for the Representation of Identity*, London: Macmillan, pp.19–40.

Hall, S., ed. (1997) *Representation: Cultural Representation and Signifying Practices*, London: Sage.

Harvey, D. (1973) *Social Justice and the City*, London: Arnold.

Harvey, D. (1989) *The Conditions of Postmodernity*, Cambridge: Blackwell.

Kapur, G. (1995) 'A critique of "internationalism"', in J. Fisher, ed., *Global Visions: Towards a New Internationalism in the Visual Arts*, London: Kala Press.

King, A.D. (1976) *Colonial Urban Development*, London and Boston: Routledge and Kegan Paul.

King, A.D. (1990) *Global Cities: Postimperialism and the Internationalization of London*, London and New York: Routledge.

King, A.D. (1991) 'Introduction: spaces of culture, spaces of knowledge', in A.D. King, ed., *Culture, Globalisation and the World-System: Contemporary Conditions for the Representation of Identity*, Binghamton: Department of Art and Art History, State University of New York at Binghamton, pp.1–18.

King, A.D. (1994) 'Terminologies and types: making sense of some types of buildings and cities', in Karen Franck and Lynda Schneekloth, eds, *Ordering Space: Types in Architecture and Design*, New York: Van Nostrand Reinhold, pp.127–44.

King, A.D., ed. (1996) *Re-Presenting the City: Ethnicity, Capital and Culture in the 21st Century Metropolis*, London: Macmillan and New York University Press.

King, A.D., ed. (1997a) *Culture, Globalization and the World-System: Contemporary Conditions for the Representation of Identity*, London: Macmillan, 1991; second North American edition, with new preface, University of Minnesota Press.

King, A.D. (1997b) 'Locution and location: positioning the postcolonial', in Vikram Prakash, ed., *Theatres of Decolonization: Architecture/Agency/Urbanism II*, Seattle: College of Architecture and Urban Planning, University of Washington, pp.295–310.

Kirby, A. and Marston, S. (1995) 'World cities and global communities: the municipal foreign policy movement and new roles for cities', in P.L. Knox and P.J. Taylor, eds, *World Cities in a World-System*, Cambridge: Cambridge University Press, pp.267–79.

Li, W. (1998) 'Anatomy of a new ethnic settlement: the Chinese *ethnoburb* in Los Angeles', *Urban Studies*, 35, 3: 479–501.

McGrew, A. (1992) 'A global society?', in Robert Bocock and Kenneth Thompson, eds, *Social and Cultural Forms of Modernity*, Oxford: Polity, for the Open University.

Moore-Gilbert, B. (1997) *Postcolonial Theory*, London: Verso.

Nalbantoglu, G.B. and Wong Chai, T., eds (1997) *Postcolonial Space(s)*, Princeton: Princeton University Press.

Nederveen Pieterse, J. (1996) 'Globalization and culture: three paradigms', *Economic and Political Weekly*, 8 June: 1389–93.

O'Byrne, D. (1997) 'Working class culture: local community and global conditions', in J. Eade, ed., *Living the Global City*, London and New York: Routledge, pp.73–89.

Oxford University Press (1996) *Atlas of the World*, Oxford: Oxford University Press.

Penguin (1982) *Dictionary*, Harmondsworth: Penguin.

Perlman, J. (1995) 'The megacities project'. Paper presented at a conference on World Cities in a World System, Washington, April.

Prakash, G. (1990) 'Writing post-Orientalist histories of the Third World: perspectives from Indian historiography', *Comparative Studies in Society and History*, 32, 2: 383–408.

Robertson, R. (1992) *Globalization: Social Theory and Global Culture*, London, Thousand Oaks and New Delhi: Sage.

Said, E. (1978) *Orientalism*, New York: Pantheon.

Said, E. (1993) *Culture and Imperialism*, London: Chatto and Windus.

Sassen, S. (1991) *The Global City: London, New York, Tokyo*, Princeton: Princeton University Press.

Scott, A., ed. (1997) *The Limits to Globalization*, London and New York: Routledge.

Smith, N. (1984) *Uneven Development: Nature, Capitalism and the Production of Space*, Oxford: Blackwell.

Spivak, G.C. (1988) 'Can the subaltern speak?' in Larry Grossberg, Cary Nelson, Paula Treicher, eds, *Cultural Studies*, London and New York: Routledge.

Spivak, G.C. (1997) 'City, country, agency', in Vikram Prakash, ed., *Theatres of Decolonization: Architecture/Agency/Urbanism*, Seattle, WA: College of Architecture and Urban Planning, University of Washington, Seattle, pp.1–22.

United Nations Center for Human Settlements (Habitat) (1988) *Global Report on Human Settlements*, Oxford: Oxford University Press.

United Nations Center for Human Settlements (Habitat) (1996) *An Urbanising World: Global Report on Human Settlements*, Oxford: Oxford University Press.

Watson, S. and Gibson, K. (1995) *Postmodern Cities and Spaces*, Oxford: Blackwell.

Williams, P. and Chrisman, L., eds (1994) *Colonial Discourse and Postcolonial Theory: A Reader*, Brighton: Harvester.

Yeoh, B. (1996) *Contesting Space: Power Relations and the Urban Built Environment in Colonial Singapore*, Oxford: Oxford University Press.

Methodologies

Case studies in globalisation and imperialism

Chapter 7: Actually existing postcolonialisms: colonial urbanism and architecture after the postcolonial turn[1]

The internal mental structures of colonial power outlive their epoch. Habits of thought, from the most inconsequential practices of everyday life through to the most highly formalized systems of philosophical abstraction, still reproduce inherited and often unseen colonial mentalities.

(Bill Schwartz 'Actually existing postcolonialism' 2000:16)

INTRODUCTION

In this chapter I focus quite narrowly on what is represented as 'actually existing' postcolonial urbanism and architecture as well as 'actually existing' postcolonial writing on this topic. In both cases, of course, these are textual representations – but as representations don't exist independently of the material realities they attempt to represent, I will not labour this point here.

At what was possibly the first conference or workshop to be held on 'Colonial Cities' over 30 years ago my paper concluded with the following statement: 'What my unilateral view' (on the colonial city) 'has underplayed is the contribution of the indigenous society and culture. The next book on 'colonial' or 'ex-colonial' cities might come from representatives of those cities themselves' (King, 1985:27).[2] I did not imply at that time, nor do I here, that 'location' should be treated as an 'essence' which, irrespective of other factors, would give the indigenous inhabitants of the one-time colonial city a privileged insight. As Young writes in his book, *Postcolonialism* (2001),

> Nowadays, no one really knows where an author 'is' when they read a book, apart from guarded information about institutional affiliation on the dust jacket, and nor should it matter. The difference is less a matter of geography than where individuals locate themselves as speaking from, epistemologically, politically, culturally and politically, who they are speaking to and how they define their own enunciative space

(Young 2001:62)

While I would, in principle, agree with this, it is also the case that, generally speaking, it is statistically more likely that members of the one-time colonised society (rather than that of the coloniser) are not only fluent in the colonial as well as the national language, but possibly also in local and regional languages of the one-time colonised state. They may also have better knowledge of (if not always access to) local sources. Exactly *where* scholars do their research, where they write it up, and the intellectual, social, political, cultural and other environments which influence their subjective identities may have more or less importance. Hence, while accepting Young's statement, I have in the following account nevertheless aimed to identify interpretations which are not only recent but also produced primarily by indigenous scholars from the one-time colonised society.

The works I address here fall into one or both of two categories. First, postcolonial studies of contemporary or near contemporary developments in postcolonial cities which have a particular focus on urban space and form, socio-spatial structure and aspects of architectural design. The second category, what I shall call 'postcolonial writings', are accounts by scholars who, in giving agency and voice to the (historically) once-colonised, are both contesting and re-writing the history, geography and architecture of the one-time colonial city or 'colonial urbanism' broadly conceived. In either case, scholars might be located, permanently or temporarily, in the post colony, post metropolis, any other part of the anglophonic postcolonial empire (e.g. USA, Australia, Canada, Singapore or elsewhere). Though the majority of the accounts refer to South and Southeast Asia, this chapter by no means attempts to be comprehensive. Its purpose is rather to foreground some questions raised in the accounts and ask about conditions that gave raise to their production.

POSTCOLONIAL URBANISM: KOLKATA, DELHI, MUMBAI

If one of the most pressing analytical questions is to see 'what the colonial and the postcolonial have done to each other' (Kusno 2000), the next is to ask what the global is doing to the postcolonial, and vice versa. This is addressed by Sanjoy Chakravorty in 'From colonial city to globalizing city? The far-from-complete spatial transformation of Kolkata' (Chakravorty 2000).

As with other studies, urban geographer Chakravorty nests his analysis of the spatial structure of Calcutta in a three-phase frame of political economic development: colonial economy during the first global period; postcolonial (or command) economy during a nationalist period; and reform economy during the second global period (ibid.:57). He makes a number of assertions. That while the colonial city was 'deeply divided' between colonisers and natives it 'would be wrong to assume that this spatial division was strictly enforced' (p.65). Nonetheless, the thrust of his argument is to show that 'this basic structure, created in the eighteenth century, still dominates the spatial pattern of work and home in the city' (p.66). With independence in 1947, 'the spatial divisions of the colonial city (demarcated by class and race barriers) were largely retained, with the native upper class (capital and land owners, political leaders and top government officials) now occupying the privileged space once occupied by the colonizers' (p.67). The new (postcolonial) space retained much of this inheritance with the race divisions being replaced by class divisions with some residential segregation by occupation, religion, caste and ethnicity continued into the postcolonial period.

With the coming of the 'new' economy and the 'post-reform city', a more significant change has taken place in Indian society, where there is increasing (and more acceptable) social, cultural, and technological polarization (p.70) with new town projects, and an expanded international airport, though with these new towns, 'colonies' named after specific corporations (e.g. AVB colony, MAMC colony), apparently following well-worn (colonial) Public Works Department practices.

Concluding that Kolkata's spatial structure 'cannot be separated from its political economic history' (p.72) Chakravorty states that it is quite different from its more colonial counterparts, 'the more segregated, hierarchical, monolingual Chennai (Madras) or the dynamic, polyglot, recently chauvinistic Mumbai'. Unlike Mumbai and Delhi, Kolkata has not been plagued by communal riots and 'the bourgeois planning apparatus has worked and continues for the benefit of the upper classes' (p.74).

Chakravorty's analysis might be fairly characterised as a straightforward political economic narrative. Another recent paper on a similar topic, though in this case referring to Delhi, demonstrates that postcolonial analysis can be more political. Cultural geographers Chatterjee and Kenny (1999) argue that, despite five decades of independence, attempts to bridge the vast spatial, social, economic and infrastructural inequities, as well as religious, cultural and lifestyle differences, between old and new Delhi, the legacy of hegemonic colonial planning, and create a single capital symbolising the unity and identity of the nation, have yet to be resolved. In offering reasons for this, the authors point to the essential ambiguities of the postcolonial: the fact that 'the replacement of previous hierarchies of space, power and knowledge has not been complete'; 'Muslim, Hindu and western socio-cultural norms co-exist, albeit uneasily, in Delhi's built environment' (p.96). Multiple identities produce a multiplicity of spatialities.

While the book *Bombay: The Cities Within* (1995), by architect Rahul Mehrotra and journalist Sharada Dwivedi, is clearly about colonial and postcolonial Bombay (since 1996, officially known, in a consciously postcolonial gesture, by its precolonial name of Mumbai), the narrative does *not* take a politically conscious postcolonial position, as implied in Sidaway's second interpretation of that term. The treatment of the historical evolution of the built environment of Mumbai is treated even-handedly, without any particular reference to the power hegemonies, and even apolitically. The book 'looks at the city with a sense of nostalgia while also with the intention of portraying aspects of the past that have continued relevance in terms of … approaches to the physical forms that result from these….' The book treats urban form as 'the text of the city' (p.6). As the Introduction begins by stating that 'Bombay was not an indigenous city but was built by the

British expressly for maintaining trade links with India' (p.9) the colonial presence is taken for granted, a *fait accompli*, not worth contesting. Whether writing of the many ancient as well as more recent Hindu shrines, sacred tanks, Buddhist temples, Muslim mosques, Moghul palaces or British colonial administrative, commercial or government buildings, all are treated as resources or heritage and not as material objects on which to exercise a cultural or socio-political critique. There is no large ideological divide or difference read into the activities and policies of city planners before or after 1947. As the authors have a deep commitment to urban design and conservation, every building, every space, is regarded as a neutral, unpoliticised historical and aesthetic resource. 'Today', they write, 'the city's image comprises of strange yet familiar juxtapositions – a roadside Hindu shrine abuts St Thomas's Cathedral, chimney stacks are dwarfed by skyscrapers, fishing villages and slums nestle at the foot of luxury apartments, and bazaars occupy the Victorian arcades' (p.309) . In 'One space, Two Worlds', the social (and also urban design) critique is reserved for the major force which is seen to have impacted and dominated the city in the last four decades, 'distress migration'. Only at this point is there a passing reference to the potential of colonial power:

> Undoubtedly, the urban poor as well as rural migrants have always formed an identifiable element among urban developments in Mumbai. However, formerly under colonial rule their direct contact with, and influence on the city was very limited, both worlds lived in different spaces. Today, the city is clearly comprised of different worlds … but (they) are also united by their sheer physical presence in the city. But in the proposals by city authorities, there's 'a sense of induced dualism' which relegates the homeless poor to the periphery.

POSTCOLONIAL SUBURBS: THE METAMORPHOSIS OF THE BUNGALOW

Where the previous articles address the spatial and social forms of the city, the following three speak, at least initially, to the architectural and social form of the building, not least the distinctively colonial product, the bungalow–compound complex (King 1976; 1984), and also to the suburban spatial forms its parameters help to construct. In more than five decades following Independence, how do Indian (and other) scholars see what has happened to both the idea, and reality, of the sprawling colonial bungalow, its expansive, space-consuming suburban setting, its role as a symbol of status, and, not least, its significance as a subject of scholarly investigation? The answer depends, to different degrees, on where the postcolonial bungalows are, to whom they belong (public or private) and who are occupying them.

Anita Sinha's essays on 'The Bungalows of Lucknow' (1999) traces 'continuities and changes in the Lucknow cantonment from the colonial to the postcolonial era'. She concludes that 'the landscape retains its colonial image in large part because it is governed by the zoning regulations and bylaws of a century ago'. Despite alterations to the bungalows to meet the needs of the extended

Indian families who live in some of them, she suggests that 'the continuity of colonial imagery in the post-colonial era implies the internalization of colonial values by planners and residents of the cantonment' (p.57).

Like other cantonments in India, that at Lucknow was a major constituent part of the 'colonial landscape of power' – physically manifest in its spatial separation from the indigenous city and segregation according to racial group and military rank. However, because the cantonment depended heavily on Indian manpower (for servants) and financial resources, 'the separation was never complete'. The continuity of colonial values is largely attributed to the fact that today Lucknow cantonment forms the headquarters of the Central Command of the Indian army with almost one-third of its population consisting of army personnel. Though the names of Indian politicians and army generals name the streets and a dozen Hindu temples (also a gurdwara and mosque) have been constructed, Lucknow cantonment 'has not seen any drastic changes in the half century since independence' (p.57). Despite the persistence of the typical colonial social maldistribution of space, with 90 per cent of the cantonment population living on 7 per cent of the land, the two bodies responsible for the cantonment manage it according to the (colonial) Cantonment Act of 1924, their 'conceptual framework … shaped by colonial ideas' (p.58). Sinha quotes a senior military official: 'bungalow area is seen as sacrosanct … land cannot be carved out of it to accommodate the civilian population of the bazaars' (p.58). Sinha's interviews with residents of 15 bungalows, undertaken in the 1990s, reveal interesting differences between civilian owners and army officers. While the Cantonment Board forbids modifications exceeding 10 per cent of the structure, civilian owners had adapted the bungalow's internal space to accommodate extended family needs (in one case, rooms being divided up among seven siblings). Owing to the ever-increasing costs of servants (between 10 and 20 of whom maintained the extensive spaces of the bungalow in colonial times), maintaining the bungalows and compounds (from one to five acres in area) was a major problem. On the other hand, senior army officers and wealthy civilians kept their bungalows in good colonial style: lawns to the front, orchards at the rear, occasionally a bar for evening parties at the back, the occasional badminton court. On average, according to Sinha, each compound had 30–40 mature trees.

Sinha maintains that the colonial bungalow 'has had a profound impact on Indian residential architecture'. It was adopted by the Indian elite in the last century and the new housing in the post-Independence era shows its influence … (even though) 'the adoption of its form has never been total' (p.61). She cites a study of a new residential enclave in south Delhi inhabited by retired officers of the ICS and the military as 'a representation of colonialism in a decolonized space'. The 'colony' is governed by by-laws that do not permit parking and vending on its tree-lined streets. Similar middle class and upper-income developments have occurred in other Indian cities (p.62).

Interestingly, Sinha states that, in Lucknow, half a century after Independence, 'there are no signs of a post-colonial sensibility with regard to planning the physical environment' (p.62). Though no longer 'overtly a symbol of the Other or representative of its cultural hegemony, the cantonment's image 'speaks of the past'. It 'sustains colonial traditions of social inequalities' previously between Europeans and Indians, now between the 'wealthy and lower income Indians'. The future of the cantonment and its bungalows, Sinha concludes, is 'dependent on the military's ability to support its resource-intensive infrastructure' (p.62).

If Sinha (as an architectural and landscape historian) highlights the larger structural, institutional, and also locational factors which keep (even modified) colonial environments in place and the structural economic, social and spatial inequities which go with them, American social anthropologist Thomas Rosin provides both a methodologically different study and one with an unexpected outcome. Rosin charts the social biography of the transformation of a single bungalow where he stayed, at various intervals over two decades, in one of the new colonies of garden suburbs built in Jaipur in the 1950s. These new colonies, 'modeled on the civil lines and cantonments that once housed the British colonial elite' after Independence 'embodied Nehru's vision for a modern India', one where 'the educated middle class would lead the nation in uniting science and technology into the very construction of their daily lives'. The idea of the garden suburbs of bungalows was to replace the fortress-like courtyard houses (*havelis*) that existed in the old walled cities (such as Jaipur).

The original two-storey bungalow, its design much influenced by colonial PWD concepts and 1940s modernistic codes of design, was located in one of these many new colonies, built around administrative cities, and favoured by middle class professions, government servants and entrepreneurs. Drawing on his continuing research over 30 years, Rosin shows how the individual bungalows, originally on their own plots, have, through incremental building, outwards and upwards, been totally transformed over a space of three or four decades. In order to accommodate additional family members, provide facilities for servants and renters, create space for working at home, secure the owner's livelihood and provide for the inheritance of offspring, the enlarged and extended bungalows have produced a space 'similar to an old city ward with towering courtyard houses abutting the property lines' (169). This, of course, has been achieved only with many violations to the building code, including linking up walls to the houses next door, removing trees and shrubs, and excluding access to sunlight.

Rosin positions his study in the context of a number of statements by Indian and other commentators from the 1970s to the 1990s which have predicted that 'the older *havelis* are no longer being built', having ceded their place in the culture to suburban house-types derived from the villa – i.e. a house 'whose external space is outside its walls'. This view, that the suburban villa or bungalow would replace the courtyard house, a view which 'echoes throughout the literature on vernacular architecture in India' (including Sinha's above), according to Rosin, is based on a very short-term, insufficiently observed long-term perspective.

Rosin's anthropological interpretation suggests that the values of public interest and community-wide planning which underpinned the original concept of the garden village have been subordinated to the 'primacy of the family and its sovereignty in relationship to its neighbors' remains'. The transformation of the bungalow suggests that questions of lifestyle, class identity and taste that prompted middle class emulation of the bungalow lifestyle 50 or more years ago have, in practice, proven less important than deep-seated dispositions about the family, descendants and the transmission of heritage.

I move now from accounts of actually existing postcolonial spatial conditions in the late 1990s to actually existing postcolonial scholarship and writing, research, that is, which brings back into the 'sometimes unilateral' accounts of colonial urbanism and architecture the voice of the one-time colonised, the agency of the indigenous, both in contesting and resisting the one-time colonial voice.

POSTCOLONIAL WRITING

Exemplary of these approaches is the opening paragraph from Siddhartha Raychaudhuri's essay:

> Processes of transformation in cities in the non-western world during the colonial period have often been described as one-way processes through which European colonial regimes restructured the physical and social environments of the cities and established their dominance there … (and) the ordinary residents of the city had hardly any voice in those developments.

(Raychaudhuri 2001:677)

Seeking to remedy this view, Raychaudhuri's study of the 'non-western' city of Ahmedabad in the first half of the twentieth century was a process where a section of the Indian elite contested the restructuring being attempted by the government in order to effect their own reorganisation of the city centre, in the process, helping the elite themselves to establish their hegemony in the city. In focusing especially on the spatial organisation of the city, the article suggests that the Ahmedabad experience could also have implications for the transformation of other cities in the 'non-western world' under colonialism. Summarising her findings, the author suggests that, by the 1940s, the Indian business elites had been the major players in structuring the city. And its town planning arrangements were carried out according to their own agenda. The changes that had resulted also reflected and facilitated the rise of new social and important political classes who, with control over municipal bodies, exercised both coercive power and moral hegemony among large sections of the city's population, particularly the emergent working class and the increasingly self-conscious Muslim population. In this way, they constructed their own forms of modernity, with neighbourhoods organised according to different caste, religious and regional identities, brought together forming new working class loyalties and new forms of identity. What distinguished this urban, spatial and social transformation in Ahmedabad, according to Raychaudhuri, and made it different from other Indian cities, such as Mumbai and Kolkata, was precisely that the indigenous elites had played the significant role in bringing about the changes, whereas in the other cities it had been the colonial government, giving it a 'distinctive character'.

Drawing on other existing literature, the author maintains that in other colonial cities such as Cairo, Rabat, Kuala Lumpur and Jakarta, the late nineteenth- and twentieth-century changes were marked by attempts (on the part of the government) 'to foster colonial difference'. This had not been effected in Ahmedabad, where the Indian elites had ensured that the organisation and use of space in the city had been mediated by concern for local traditions and practices. The new social and cultural order, while promoting new national ideas, linguistic and literary forms, new forms of history and domesticity, while all essentially 'modern', were also not 'western'.

Arguing that similar developments might have taken place elsewhere, the author argues for more research on the role of indigenous elites in indigenous cities (rather than colonial port towns where colonial military, economic and political power was strong). Here, in more inland and intermediate centres, she suggests, is where local elites resisted colonial rule. It is also in these locations that the elites used the 'massive infrastructure of the ever-growing postcolonial state' to promote the development of Indian capitalism. Extending her findings across a larger area, Raychaudhuri hypothesises that the 'substantial number of elites who assumed power in post-colonial states hailed from urban areas', their power gained, at the national level, through first getting established in the inland and intermediate cities.

There are parallels here, though at a local rather than national scale, in Jyoti Hosagrahar's innovative study of what she calls 'indigenous modernities'. Based on the assumption that the many studies on imperial Delhi have uncritically adopted a set of binary classifications where colonial/indigenous, European/native, old/new are unquestionably taken to represent 'modernity' and 'tradition', and where the scholarly lens has focused disproportionately on 'imperial' New Delhi, Hosagrahar instead shines her investigative light on the 'old' city. Here, both the social and spatial forms of the merchants' space of the old city of Shahjehanabad, never historically static, never unchanging, continued to be transformed throughout the building program, but more by the ongoing social, economic and cultural agendas of the merchant occupiers. Hosagrahar's sophisticated architectural history, based on interviews with long-term, oral histories, Urdu novels, and analysis of existing structures, de-emphasises the divide between the *haveli* and the bungalow landscape of early colonial settlement. 'Beneath the apparent opposition', she writes, 'was a charged interconnection between the two spaces. The new residents of Delhi responded to the new model of urban life in a variety of ways by disdaining and rejecting, mocking and mimicking, participating and conniving and learning and accepting (Hosagrahar 2001:36). From the sources she cites, the new 'colonial' environment offered opportunities for some Indian residents to construct new identities, a way of identifying with the new by rejecting the old or, when occasion demanded, of moving between the two. The *havelis*, 'not a timeless or changeless house form, gradually became home to a new petite bourgeoisie'.

The inherently *dynamic* nature of social (and spatial) analysis is also central to Rosin's study referred to above. This brings an implicit message of caution for any attempts to construct 'snapshot' categories of social and spatial analysis, frozen in one point of time. This is also a theme which runs through Meera Kosambi's (1990:2775–81) perceptive reading and critique of my *Urbanism, Colonialism and the World-Economy* (1990a). Any attempt to create a constructed type not only conceals changes over time but also space. This not only applies to notions about the 'colonial city' but the vaguer concept of 'colonial urbanism' which, dependent on its global location, might extend between 50 and 300 or 400 years. Moreover, by primarily focusing on the colonial, Kosambi (echoing Raychaudhuri, and Hosagrahar above) suggests that transformations in the indigenous settlement get ignored.

Moving from South to South East Asia, I have left Brenda Yeoh's *Contesting Space: Power Relations and the Urban Built Environment in Colonial Singapore* (1996) to the end of this section even though it was published some years before the other works discussed. Yeoh's thorough and detailed study showing how the built environment of colonial Singapore was shaped 'by conflict and negotiation between colonial institutions of control … and Asian communities who lived and worked in the city' is probably one of the first, and most carefully documented accounts which challenged the notion of the colonial city as being simply a product of 'dominant forces' without attending to the 'underside … the conflict and collision, negotiation and dialogue' with the colonised population. Looking especially at the everyday life in the city, and the 'contested space' of modifications to streets, public areas and housing, struggles over the installation of utilities or the naming of spaces, Yeoh sees the colonial urban landscape as 'a terrain of discipline and resistance' where the colonised 'must be seen as knowledgable and skilled agents with some awareness of the struggle for control, not just passive recipients of colonial rule' (p.14).

CONCLUSION

Reading these books and essays it is difficult not to arrive at two or three conclusions. First, that while all of the essays above address what I have called 'actually existing postcolonialism', or postcolonial issues, and are, ipso facto, written with a postcolonial consciousness, none of them actually cite, or make use of any of the theoretical literature normally associated with 'postcolonial theory and criticism'. Does this deserve a comment? The exception, not mentioned so far, is the edited collection *Postcolonial Space(s)* (1997). In the words of the editors, 'Postcolonial space is a space of intervention into those architectural constructions that parade under a universalist guise and either exclude or repress different spatialities of often disadvantaged ethnicities, communities or peoples' (Nalbantoglu and Wong 1997:7). While the chapters successfully contest the boundaries of what 'architecture' is usually taken to be, the commitment of contributors to exploring innovative poststructuralist, psychoanalytic, feminist, and other approaches, characteristic of postcolonial theory in literature, need also to be read alongside older accounts that acknowledge the persistent and material factors of uneven development worldwide (Smith 1984) and the corporate *knowledge* influence of global capitalism.

The second conclusion turns me back to the quotation from Young (2001) cited at the start, and the note I appended to this, about the respective insights in issues of colonialism and postcolonialism offered by scholars from the once-colonised and once colonising societies. One is tempted to suggest that it is the 'grand theories' and metanarratives that have come (and still continue to come) from the one-time metropolitan location. Most recently, these include the 'modelling' of Southeast Asian cities within larger trajectories of urban development where postcolonial cities are projected to develop into one or the other of 'four unique forms of postcolonial [urban] space' (Yeoh 1996:462). Alternatively, other once-metropolitan scholars argue that postcolonial cities will converge with metropolitan urban forms 'as a result of the inexorable logic of globalization'; 'the postcolonial city as a distinct type is an "unusual and transitory experience" eventually to be eclipsed by the globalizing city' (Yeoh 1996:462).

For Kusno (2000), the problem of postcolonial studies has been a tendency to undertake a critique of colonial discourse around a broad, often undifferentiated critique of 'the West', without acknowledging that colonialisms come in many forms. Recognising historical differences between various colonial states he argues that, until the demise of Suharto's 'New Order' regime in 1998, Indonesia in fact continued as a colonial regime in all but name. Contesting a key theme in much postcolonial criticism, he argues that colonialism in Indonesia did not bring about a displacement of indigenous culture; as Indonesians were encouraged by Dutch orientalist discourse to remain 'Indonesian', they never thought of themselves as part of a colonial legacy.

A more fundamental point is raised by Kosambi: 'the search for the intellectual antecedents of the current debate about the "colonial city"', she writes, 'becomes an interesting exercise in the sociology of knowledge, spanning the social science literature of the last four decades. Among the shifting perspectives and underneath ideological camouflages, the concept has remained, for a long time, both elusive and chameleonic' (1990:2777). As for Yeoh, she asks as to what extent can 'postcolonial' endure as a meaningful category (of urban analysis)? 'How essential is the influence of empire for understanding the contemporary city'? (2001:463). A better understanding and assessment of postcolonial impacts can only come about through a wider range of works on urban space which 'give greater credence to diverse voices, different mediums of representation and therefore different perspectives on the city' – including a whole variety of different analytical frames.

NOTES

1 Anthony D. King, 'Actually existing postcolonialisms: colonial urbanism and architecture after the postcolonial turn', in Ryan Bishop, John Phillips and Wei Wei Yeo, eds, *Postcolonial Urbanism: Southeast Asian Cities and Global Processes*, 2003 Taylor and Francis Group LLC.
2 The workshop, held at the Centre for Studies of European Expansion, University of Leiden in May 1980, was attended by various European scholars who had previously published on the topic of colonial cities. Virtually none of the participants were indigenous subjects of the one-time colonial cities and in the extensive bibliography assembled by the workshop organisers, few titles were identified as coming from indigenous scholars.

BIBLIOGRAPHY

Alsayyad, N. (2001) *Hybrid Urbanism: On the Identity Discourse and the Built Environment*, Westport: Praegar.

Chakravorty, S. (2000) 'From colonial city to globalizing city? The far from complete spatial transformation of Calcutta', in Peter Marcuse and Ronald van Kempen, eds, *Globalizing Cities: A New Spatial Order*, Oxford and Malden: Blackwell, pp.56–77.

Chatterjee, S. and Kenny, J. (1999) 'Creating a new capital: colonial discourse and the decolonisation of Delhi', *Historical Geography*, 27: 73–98.

Cohen, P. (2000) 'From the other side of the tracks: dual cities, third spaces, and the urban uncanny in contemporary discourses of "race" and "class"', in G. Bridge and S. Watson, eds, *Companion to the City*, Oxford: Blackwell, 324–5.

Dick, H.W. and Rimmer, P. (1998) 'Beyond the Third World city: the new urban geography of Southeast Asia', *Urban Studies*, 35: 100–9.

Hosagrahar, J. (2001) 'Mansions to margins: modernity and the domestic landscape of historic Delhi, 1847–1910', *Journal of the Society of Architectural Historians* 60: 24–45.

King, A.D. (1976) *Colonial Urban Development: Culture, Social Power and Environment*, London and Boston: Routledge.

King, A.D. (1984) *The Bungalow: The Production of a Global Culture*, 2nd ed., Oxford: Oxford University Press.

King, A.D. (1985) 'Colonial cities: global pivots of change', in R. Ross and G. Telkamp, eds, *Colonial Cities: Essays on Urbanism in a Colonial Context*, The Hague: Leiden University Press, pp.7–32.

King, A.D. (1990a) *Urbanism, Colonialism and the World-Economy*, London and New York: Routledge.

King, A.D. (1990b) *Global Cities: Postimperialism and the Internationalisation of London*, London and New York: Routledge.

King, A.D. (2002) 'Cultures and spaces of postcolonial knowledges', in K. Anderson, M. Domosh, S. Pile, and N. Thrift, eds, *Handbook of Cultural Geography*, London: Sage, 81–98.

Kosambi, M. (1990) 'The colonial city in its global reach', *Economic and Political Weekly*, 22 December, 2775–881.

Kusno, A. (2000) *Beyond the Postcolonial: Architecture, Urban Space and Political Cultures in Indonesia*, London and New York: Routledge.

Loomba, A. (1998) *Colonialism/Postcolonialism*, London and New York: Routledge.

Mehrotra, R. and Diwedi, S. (1995) *Bombay: The City Within*, Bombay: Indian Bookhouse.

Nalbantoglu, G. and Wong, W.B.T. (1997) *Postcolonial Spaces*, Princeton: Princeton University Press.

Perera, N. (1998) *Decolonising Ceylon: Colonialism, Nationalism, and the Politics of Space in Sri Lanka*, New Delhi: Oxford University Press.

Raychaudhuri, S. (2001) 'Colonialism, indigenous elites, and the transformation of cities in the non-western world: Ahmedabad (Western India) 1890–1947', *Modern Asian Studies* 35, 3: 677–726.

Rosin, T. (2001) 'From garden suburb to old city ward: a longitudinal study of social process and incremental architecture in Jaipur, India', *Journal of Material Culture*, 6, 2: 165–92.

Schwartz, B. (2000) 'Actually-existing postcolonialism', *Radical Philosophy Review*, 104: 16–24.

Sidaway, J. (2000) 'Postcolonial geographies: an exploratory essay', *Progress in Geography*, 24, 4: 591–612.

Sinha, A. (1999) 'The bungalows of Lucknow', *Open House International*, 24, 2: 56–63.

Smith, N. (1984) *Uneven Development: Nature, Capital and the Production of Space*, Oxford: Blackwell.

Wolfe, P. (1997) 'History and imperialism; a century of theory, from Marx to postcolonialism', *American Historical Review*, 102, 388–420.

Yeoh, B.S.A. (1996) *Contesting Space: Power Relations and the Urban Built Environment in Colonial Singapore*, Kuala Lumpur: Oxford University Press.

Yeoh, B.S.A. (2001) 'Postcolonial cities', *Progress in Human Geography*, 25, 3: 456–68.

Young, R. (2001) *Postcolonialism: An Introduction*, London: Blackwell.

Chapter 8: Internationalism, imperialism, postcolonialism, globalisation: framing vernacular architecture[1]

INTERNATIONALISM

In November 2004 as I was packing my books to ship to England, discarding scores accumulated both before and during my 17 years in the USA and reflecting on which ones I might need for this talk, I picked up a book I'd had for years but never seriously studied. Published in London by the prestigious Architectural Press in 1939, it was called *Weekend Houses, Cottages and Bungalows* (ed. Alan Hastings). It had an introduction by Hugh Casson, to become one of the most prominent architects in post-war Britain.

I'm not one of those historians who gets involved with 'High Architecture' but I couldn't help notice, among the 50-odd architects whose work it illustrated, the names and designs of some whom, over 70 years later, architectural historians have subsequently canonised as pioneers of the so-called 'Modern Movement' in Britain: i.e. Lubetkin and Tecton, Wells Coates, Erno Goldfinger, F.R.S. Yorke, Clive Entwistle with Le Corbusier, among others. But the biggest surprise was to suddenly find a name which instantly transported me, in time and space, from upstate New York to an obscure place in Lancashire, England, near where I grew up – which is, I guess, what many of us would take as the paradigmatic 'local'.

I very much doubt if the name of architect Frank Waddington has ever appeared in anyone's PhD – even in a footnote – let alone in any publication on architectural modernism. Yet his name is permanently engraved on my memory. Two of his paintings adorned our home when I was small and today, his brilliant 1932 caricature of my father (who knew him as a friend and business associate) hangs in my study (Figure 8.1). The location of the house which, partly because of its general 'anonymity' and present day taken-for-granted-ness, I'm going to call an example of Vernacular Modernism (Figure 8.2), is at Hoghton, near Preston, a village about half an hour's bike ride from my childhood home.

What we know as 'Modernism' was supposedly the first 'international style' of architecture. The name was first promoted by two prominent Americans, architectural historian Henry-Russell Hitchcock and architect Philip Johnson, in their

Figure 8.1
Frank Waddington's
caricature portrait of the
author's father, 1932
(author's collection).

FRANK WADDINGTON, F.R.I.B.A.

PRESTON, LANCS

THE PLAN shape was governed by
the shallow depth of site. The living-
room had to face the front, which has
an unobstructed view.

CONSTRUCTION. Walls: 11 in. cav-
ity brickwork; Ravenhead rustic fac-
ings finished with off-white distemper.
Parapet walls finished with 2 in. thick
black faience coping. Roofs: timber
joists covered with 1 in. T. & G. boards,
and three layers of compressed bitu-
men felt and compound, finished with
pebble. Sun balcony finished with
½ in. fine Bitu-macadam.

FINISHES. Plaster walls, with wash-
able distemper finish. Floors: oak
boards in living-room and hall; deal
boards to first floor; red "Gran-
wood" blocks to kitchen and larders.
Doors: mostly "Venesta" flush panel.

SERVICES. Electric fires. Cooking
by gas, and gas water heater.

COST. Approximately 1s. per ft. cu.

Figure 8.2
Vernacular Modernism
in a house designed by
Frank Waddington,
Hoghton, near Preston,
Lancashire, England,
1939 (source: Alan
Hastings, ed., *Weekend
Houses, Cottages, and
Bungalows*, 1939).

book, *The International Style: Architecture since 1922,* written to accompany an exhibition with the same name at New York's Museum of Modern Art in 1932. The notion of the 'international', (in 1780, a new word according to the *Oxford English Dictionary*), of course, presupposes that of the 'national'. What is being assumed here, therefore, is that 'architecture' – by which I mean buildings designed by designated architects – is best categorised, or understood, according to the national territories from where it originates, or where it exists. *Inter*national, therefore, must imply something that is present in and/or appropriate to all nations, irrespective of culture, level of economic development or geographical location. Yet in the Hitchcock and Johnson book, illustrating the work of some 40 architects – most prominently Corbusier, Oud, Gropius and Mies van der Rohe – a mere 15 countries were represented. Except for Japan, all were in the West, and apart from a few names in the United States, Europe, especially Germany, dominated.

Now to suggest that this was an 'International Style' when less than a quarter of the 60-odd nation states in existence at that time had any sign of it, strikes me as something of an exaggeration. And in any case, how adequate is the idea of the nation (i.e. people) or nation-state (political entity) for categorising, or interpreting either 'high' or 'vernacular architecture'?

Quite apart from their geographically limited notion of the international highlighted here, we could also ask whether the architectural style described as international was one produced by the collective agency of nations as such, or of individual subjects within nation states; or better, between individual subjects who were members of a particular (architectural) profession that existed in any numbers only in the richer, economically developed regions of Europe and America, some of which were imperial powers? (Eighty years later, there is still only about one architect for every 42,000 people in India compared to one for every 2,000 in the United States or the United Kingdom, and many fewer in sub-Saharan African countries.) And did the connection (the 'inter') take place between nations, or supranationally? Or even globally (irrespective of any intervention by, or reference to any nation as such)? Or was it simply an outcome of some architects pursuing a particular ideology in the context of high-tech, high-energy materials, and capital-intensive building and design practices located in the urban areas of advanced industrial capitalism?

If, like Hitchcock and Johnson in 1932, we treat 'modernism' simply as a 'style' and without asking whether there were more important historical conditions explaining its origin, maybe we can say that it began in Germany and moved to the US. But did it? According to Reyner Banham's excellent study of American industrial building and European modern architecture (Banham 1986), the inspirational sources for Walter Gropius and others in the 'Modern Movement' in Europe were the multi-storeyed daylight factories and massive concrete elevators being built by American engineers at the end of the nineteenth century. For the commercialised grain-producing areas of capitalist North America, these were at once the containers as well as the symbol of the national economic surplus.

So, if both the construction materials and architectural forms of the 'Modern Movement' have their origins in this particular system of economic and social organisation (or mode of production), I'm inclined to say that the house is a product not just of an 'International Style' but rather the *architectural* style of 'International Capitalism', as it had developed in Euro-America. In this case, therefore, we're looking at buildings – whether 'High Architecture', or indeed any vernacular building or landscape – as *primarily* the products of a particular political, economic, social and also cultural system. This is what architectural historian Dell Upton referred to in his 2004 VAF lecture, as the 'dominant socio-cultural interpretation' (Upton 2004).

(In passing, can we, today, refer to a vernacular of international capitalism, with particular building forms and spaces found in every country in the world? Highways, gas stations, airports, suburban shopping malls, theme parks, luxury hotels, franchised fast food outlets, gated communities and the rest, and site and services shacks in the poorest cities? How does this compare with one or the other of the one-time socialist regimes in eastern Europe with collectivist housing and socialised welfare?)

However, in 1932, more than 80 per cent of the world consisted of colonies, protectorates, dominions or commonwealths held mainly by the major European (and also American and Asian) imperial powers, especially in Africa, Asia, the Middle East and Australasia (and also, for most of their history, in South America). These were places not mentioned by Hitchcock and Johnson. In this context, therefore, we're not speaking about a world of nations, or nation-states, but a world of empires and colonies, not an 'international' but an 'intercolonial' or 'interimperial world', even though it was also a world of myriad different cultures, most of which, incidentally, had not gone through the experience of industrialisation and urbanisation which, in Central and Western Europe, had provided the conditions for the invention of the so-called modern movement. A world which, though consisting of technically 'independent' states for the last 50 or more years, the West has (largely) referred to as the 'Third World' (or more recently, the Global South).

IMPERIALISM

In the last few years we have learnt a great deal about how so-called 'Modern Movement' forms of architecture and urban design were transplanted to various parts of this world as part and parcel of imperial, colonial, and postcolonial regimes, and overwhelmingly deployed, under unequal relations of power, as part of an ideology of domination, exploitation and 'modernisation'. As there isn't space to discuss this in any detail, let me mention some key studies. As Mark Crinson has written, 'Imperialism figures hazily, if at all, in most surveys of modern architecture' and rarely, I would add, in studies of vernacular architecture. In *Modern Architecture and the End of Empire* (2003), Crinson has charted British imperial developments in Iraq and Persia in the 1940s, Ghana in the 1950s, Malaya in the 1960s and Hong Kong in the 1980s. Zeynep Celik (1997) and others have shown how French control over Algeria permitted Le Corbusier to carry out his experiments there. In India, as Norma Evenson (1989), Jon Lang and the Desais (1998), and Peter Scriver and Vikram Prakash (2007) have shown, Modernist design was part of the colonial capitalist construction of its major, as well as minor, cities. Gwen Wright (1991) and Paul Rabinow (1989) have provided us with fascinating studies of colonial developments in South East Asia and Morocco.

Mia Fuller (2006) has opened up the hitherto unknown story of Italy's attempt to bring 'social modernity' to their east and north African settler colonies, and James Holston, in his excellent study of *The Modernist City* (1989), has charted its socially and spatially transformative impact on Brazil. In almost all of these cases, the introduction of 'Modernist' design has depended not only on the unequal relations of colonialism but also on an architectural self-colonisation by the locals. The impact of 'Modernism' – especially in terms of materials, technology, the influence of imagery – on 'ordinary buildings and landscapes' can only be described as colossal. But perhaps the two biggest effects of the 'Modernist' penetration of architecture has been, first, to equate a certain genre of buildings with what is seen as a socially progressive style of life: being 'modern' implied, for the bourgeoisie, a 'Modernist' environment. The second, and equally profound outcome, has been to create something called 'traditional' building or, alternatively, the 'vernacular'.

Yet as James Holston points out, it is not possible to generalise about what the social, political or cultural meaning attached to Modernist design actually is. For Sukarno, the architect-president of newly independent Indonesia, it was to be a sign of both modernity and nationalism (Kusno, 2000). The same can be said for Nehru's postcolonial sponsorship of Corbusier's designs for Chandigarh (Prakash, 2002). These, however, are some of the issues which can be addressed under the general rubric of the *postcolonial*, discussed below. At this point, I wish to return to Binghamton and my preliminary thoughts about what I have called 'vernacular modernism'.

VERNACULAR MODERNISM

Binghamton is a small rust-belt city in up-state New York. Ten minutes' walk from what was once my timber-framed Colonial Revival home (Figure 8.3), and sticking out like a sore thumb between the 'anonymous' ranch houses and split-levels of the 1950s and 1960s (Figure 8.4), is what a local historian has described as the 'first example of International Style architecture' in the city (Figure 8.5) (Spanfelner, 2002). The house was built in 1934, for Dr Willy Schmidt, a German chemist and physicist, sent by Agfa corporation to set up the first organic photo-chemical research lab in the plant Agfa had recently taken over from the photographic corporation Ansco. Schmidt, with two doctorates and wide-ranging interests in art and music, brought to the innocent natives of Binghamton the architecturally invasive ideas of the Bauhaus which, between its opening in 1919 and its closure

Figure 8.3
Lincoln Avenue,
Binghamton, New York
(2004 photograph,
author).

Figure 8.4
Leroy Street,
Binghamton, New York
(2004 photograph,
author).

Figure 8.5
Anonymous Modernism,
Leroy Street,
Binghamton, New York
(2004 photograph,
author).

by the Nazis in 1933, had shifted its location from Weimar to Dessau (the home of Agfa) in 1927.

The Bauhaus had acquired an architecture department only in 1927. In that year they appointed a professor, Hannes Meyer, a Marxist intellectual interested in land reform, cooperative movements and a fervent belief that it was 'the architect's job to improve society by designing functional buildings that would improve the lot of the common man' (Whitford 1988:180). As he wrote in 1928,

> Building is not an aesthetic process … architecture which produces effects introduced by the artist has no right to exist. Architecture which 'continues a tradition' is historicist … the new house is … a product of industry and as such is the work of specialists: economists, statisticians, hygienists, climatologists, experts in … norms, heating techniques.

As for the architect, 'He was an artist and is becoming a specialist in organization … building is only organization: social, technical, economic, mental organization'.

Meyer's most important commission in Dessau was to construct an experimental housing-project where an entire planned estate was built for a large number of workers with standardised components, produced on site, that drastically reduced transport costs (Whitford 1988). However, while Dr Schmidt had brought the style and design from Germany he left Meyer's radical political and social agenda behind. Instead of building collective housing for Agfa's workers, he adapted his Bauhaus vision to the individualised market-oriented plots of Binghamton. Here, as in myriad similar cases elsewhere, whenever ideas and designs are transplanted, they inevitably get translated. And where Schmidt commissioned the design from Europe, the local builder branched out on his own. Abandoning the timber-built, balloon framed houses of the local vernacular (Figure 8.6) he built three or four modest prefabricated concrete houses in 'the manner of the Bauhaus' in a cheaper part of town (Figure 8.7). Like Waddington's house in Lancashire, these were to become part of what I've called 'vernacular modernism'.

Today, there's no trace of Agfa Films in Binghamton. The company's plant, bought and sold a dozen times since Dr Schmidt came to town, was taken over and demolished by Eastman Kodak in 1998. In fact, there's hardly a trace of industry in Binghamton which, in the 17 years I spent there, has gone where labour is cheaper, the Deep South or booming China. Yet the particular social hierarchy and division of labour represented by Dr Schmidt's Bauhaus house, and Agfa films, with its links to Germany and the Dessau Bauhaus, like earlier abandoned economies, has left strata-like deposits on the local landscape.

Yet this was not the first time that foreign elements had penetrated the colonial urban landscape of up-state New York (King 2004:ch.11). As I continued my fieldwork, backing up the road to capture, in my viewfinder, a broader, more architecturally inclusive view of where this instance of local vernacular modernism had taken place, I found my four-sided image blocked on one side by a characteristic 1940s American bungalow, which almost obscured the object of my attention (Figure 8.8).

Figure 8.6
Beethoven Street,
Binghamton, New York
(2004 photograph,
author).

Figure 8.7
Modernist Vernacular,
West Side, Binghamton,
New York (2004
photograph, author).

Figure 8.8
West Side, Binghamton,
New York (2004
photograph, author).

POSTCOLONIALISM

As most of us know, the idea and name of the bungalow (first identified in 1659 in what is now Bangladesh) was introduced into the West (in Britain) at the end of the 1860s and, probably from England, into the United States, in the early 1880s (King 1984) (Figure 8.9). As a type it grew to maturity in California and then, for all kinds of reasons, came to be the first vernacular house type to be found throughout suburban America.

If we're trying to explain the bungalow's presence in all these different places we'd need to look at a historically, politically and, especially, geographically much broader conceptual framework, an imperial or colonial space economy and mode of production with its origins in South Asia, its generative core in Europe and with its presence scattered in many different parts of the world. And were I writing this book again today I'd make far more use of postcolonial theory and criticism, an approach which demands, according to one commentator, 'a rethinking of the very terms by which knowledge has been constructed' (Mongia 1996:2).

There have been many definitions of 'postcolonialism' but I shall cite that of geographer Derek Gregory, who describes it as

> a critical politico-intellectual formation that is centrally concerned with the impact of colonialism and its contestation on the cultures of both colonizing and colonized peoples in the past, and the reproduction and transformation of colonial relations, representations and practices in the present.

As 'there have been many colonialisms' the 'post' especially brings into consciousness those of the sixteenth to the twentieth centuries 'in such a way that our understanding of the present is transformed' (Gregory 2000).

There are two features about postcolonial theory and perspective that I want to emphasise here. First, unlike 'internationalism', which represents the world as consisting of different nations, or nation-states, postcolonial perspectives are more interested in representing the world (or parts of it) as a system of one-time colonies under the regime of one-time empires.

Second, one, if not the most significant objectives of postcolonial criticism, to use Chakrabarty's phrase, is to 'provincialise Europe', to counter Eurocentric representations of the world and write postcolonial histories of their own society from a 'native' point of view. In Chakrabarty's much-cited phrase, 'Third World historians feel a need to refer to works in European history; historians of Europe do not feel any need to reciprocate' (1992:2). Relatively few scholars in the US have, as far as I know, looked at American architectural historiography from this particular postcolonial position. The American situation, as we know, is complex. The origins of the United States are simultaneously those of a colonialist society (in relation to its native people) and also a postcolonial society (in relation to the metropolitan power). Yet structurally, what the United States shares with all other postcolonial regimes, in South and Southeast Asia, Africa, the Middle East, which mainly achieved their independence after 1945 is that, almost 200 years earlier,

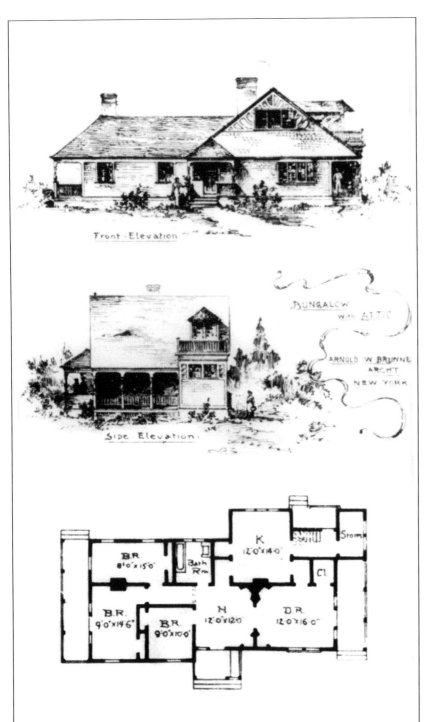

Figure 8.9
A.W. Brunner, *Cottages, or Hints on Economic Building*, 1884.

and as a postcolonial society 'avant-le-lettre', the US has not only 'provincialised Europe' (and increasingly, the rest of the world) in writing its own national (and specifically nationalistic) cultural and architectural histories but has done so by writing them primarily in relation to itself. This is where Dell Upton's comment about vernacular architecture's 'thinly disguised nationalistic, even patriotic agenda' (Upton 2004) strikes me as very valid.

In brief, if we are interested in 'using global theory to help look at vernacular architecture and landscapes' (the remit for this lecture) we must first and foremost be concerned about positionality, about taking a position. Why should we actually *want* to do this? The answer is obviously one of cultural politics. A glance at architectural history book titles in any library will confirm that, for most countries in the world, by far the most common classificatory category or framework is that of the nation state, whether this refers to questions of building type, social process, style or any other theme. The significance of the bungalow, for me, was in the opportunity it provided to open up doors to the particular political, cultural and global historical conditions which produced it, doors which open into the variously theorised fields of imperialism, colonialism, postcolonialism, postimperialism, globalisation, among others.

GLOBALISATION

Over the last few decades an increasing number of scholars have realised that the nation state is an inappropriate unit in which to understand changes taking place in the contemporary world. Students of the city, for example, have shifted their focus from studying the city *qua* city, either in relation to itself or to others like it, to studying the city in relation to the society where it exists, and from the 1990s, on studying the city in relation to the world, or usually, the world economy (King 2004; 2007). How can we understand this transnational space in a way that makes sense for interpreting the social meaning of vernacular buildings?

I have proposed elsewhere that we might take an eclectic approach. I understand globalisation here in terms of Robertson's pithy definition as 'a process by which the world becomes a single place' (1992). Notions of the modern world system which emphasise the geographical expansion of the capitalist world economy, from the sixteenth century, are, to a limited extent, useful, not least because the perspective is historical and also recognises the hegemony of particular states at different times in the 'world system' (the Netherlands in the seventeenth century, Britain in the nineteenth, the United States in the twentieth). Yet as postcolonial scholars have suggested, world-system theorists have paid insufficient attention to the material culture consequence of colonialism and give inadequate attention to the individual in a mechanistic representation of humankind. Powerful civilisations like India and China figure too little in this Western-centric representation. Nonetheless, insights from all theories can spin off other ideas. Broader frameworks can be seen in *The Global Cities Reader* (2006) where the editors bring together 50 readings by scholars who, from the late 1970s have aimed to examine cities through a global lens. Though the dominant frame for the earliest essays tends to be that of world-systems, emphasising economy rather than culture, a number of contributors address how processes of globalisation have impacted architecture and the built environment, raising provocative questions for students of vernacular architecture.

Globalisation can be understood as a speeding up in the degree of global interconnectedness. In his edited book, *Globalization in World History*, Anthony Hopkins (2002) not only puts forward the idea of different phases of globalisation in world history, the archaic (prior to 1600), proto (from the eighteenth century), modern (from the nineteenth century, and including the imperial phase), and postcolonial phases (after 1950), but also how it might be understood in the world outside the West – in Eurasia, Africa, China, including Islamic phases of the process, as well as in Europe and the Americas. Similarly, Jan Nederveen Pieterse treats globalisation as a 'long term historical process involving ancient population movements, long distance cross-cultural trade, the spread of world religions and the diffusion and development of technologies due to inter-cultural contact' (2004:24– 5). This latter emphasis on the roles of migration, trade, religion, and communications technology is invaluable for a globally oriented study of vernacular landscapes.

The problem with the metaphor (and the term) of 'globalisation' is that 'the globe' connotes a singular entity and hence, globalisation as a singular process, which it is certainly not. The interconnectivity is best represented by a language not only of flows and spaces, but also of very particular networks, threads and agencies.

CONCLUSION

What I have tried to suggest in these comments are some possible ways in which we can follow these threads, through larger theoretical frames. Some of these ideas, like that of a social and spatial division of labour, a space economy, a mode or form of production, might be helpful in explaining the actual existence of vernacular buildings and landscapes. Why they are where they are, when they are, how they're used, how they disappear, what they leave behind. Other ideas, about cultures existing far from their place of origin, about cultural traces in language, might help to tell us what buildings and landscapes look like, and why, how they might change their uses. We should be concerned not only with the wide-ranging spatial and social contexts in which buildings and landscapes are produced, but the equally wide ranging spaces in which they're consumed. Nothing is so practical as a good theory. But grand theoretical and historical ideas must also be informed, as well as transformed, by empirical investigation and fieldwork.

NOTE

1   From Anthony D. King, 'Internationalism, Imperialism, Postcolonialism, Globalisation', *Perspectives in Vernacular Architecture*, 13, 2, 2006/2007 © Vernacular Architecture Forum.

BIBLIOGRAPHY

Banham, Reyner (1986) *A Concrete Atlantis: US Industrial Building and European Modern Architecture 1900–1925*, Cambridge, MA and London: MIT Press.

Bozdogan, S. (2001) *Modernism and Nation Building: Turkish Architectural Culture in the Early Republic*, Seattle: University of Washington Press.

Celik, Zeynep (1997) *Urban Forms and Colonial Confrontations: Algeria Under French Rule*, Berkeley, CA: University of California Press.

Chakrabarty, Dipesh (1992) 'Provincialising Europe: postcoloniality and the critique of history', *Cultural Studies*, 16, 1: 337–57.

Chattopadhyay, S. (2004) *Representing Calcutta: Modernity, Nationalism and the Colonial Uncanny*, London and New York: Routledge.

Crinson, Mark (2003) *Modern Architecture and the End of Empire*, London: Ashgate.

Evenson, N. (1989) *The Indian Metropolis: A View Towards the West*, New Haven: Yale University Press.

Fuller, M. (2006) *Moderns Abroad: Architecture, Cities and Italian Imperialism*, London and New York: Routledge.

Gregory, D. (2000) 'Postcolonialism', in R. Johnson, D. Gregory, D. Smith, eds, *The Dictionary of Human Geography*, Oxford: Blackwell.

Hastings, A. (1939) *Week-end Houses, Cottages and Bungalows*, Westminster: The Architectural Press, 7–18.

Hitchcock, H.R. and P. Johnson (1966) *The International Style: Architecture Since 1922*, New York: W.W.Norton.

Holston, J. (1989) *The Modernist City: An Anthropological Critique of Brazil*, Chicago: University of Chicago Press.

Hopkins, A.G., ed. (2002) *Globalization in World History*, London: Pimlico.

Hosagrahar, J. (2005) *Indigenous Modernities: Negotiating Architecture and Urbanism*, London and New York: Routledge.

King, A.D. (1984) *The Bungalow: The Production of a Global Culture*, London and New York: Routledge and Kegan Paul.

King, A.D. (2004) *Spaces of Global Cultures: Architecture, Urbanism, Identity*. London and New York: Routledge.

King, A.D. (2007) 'Boundaries, networks and cities', in A. Cinar and T. Bender, eds, *Locating the City: Urban Imaginaries and the Practices of Modernity*, Minneapolis: University of Minnesota Press.

Kusno, A. (2000) *Behind the Postcolonial: Urban Space and Political Cultures in Indonesia*, London and New York: Routledge.

Lancaster, C. (1983) *The American Bungalow*, New York: Abbeville Press.

Lang, J., Desai, M. and Desai, M. (1998) *Architecture and Independence: The Search for Identity in British India and Ceylon*, Delhi: Oxford University Press.

Mongia, P. (1996) *Contemporary Postcolonial Theory: A Reader*, London: Arnold.

Oxford University Press (1989) *Oxford English Dictionary*, Oxford: Oxford University Press.

Pieterse, J.N. (2004) *Globalisation and Culture*, Lanham, MD: Rowman and Littlefield.

Prakash, V. (2002) *Chandigarh's Le Corbusier*, Seattle, WA: University of Washington Press.

Rabinow, P. (1989) *French Modern: Norms and Forms of the Social Environment*, Cambridge, MA: MIT Press.

Robertson, R. (1992) *Globalization: Social Theory and Global Culture*, London: Sage.

Scriver, P. and Prasad, V., eds (2007) *Colonial Modernities: Building, Dwelling and Architecture in British India and Ceylon*, London and New York: Routledge.

Spanfelner, K. (2002) 'Bauhaus in Broome: The International Style in the Southern Tier', in Ronald Chipper, ed., *Ansco: Cameras, Construction and Community*, Binghamton: Roberson Museum and PAST, pp.10–28.

Upton, D. (2004) 'What now?' Keynote Address. Annual Conference of the Vernacular Architecture Forum (online).

Whitford, F. (1988) *The Bauhaus,* London: Thames and Hudson.

Wright, G. (1991) *The Politics of Design in French Colonial Urbanism*, Chicago: University of Chicago Press.

Chapter 9: Postcolonial cities, postcolonial critiques[1]

INTRODUCTION

The editors of the collection in which this chapter was originally published acknowledge two basic postcolonial premises. They refer to 'the powerful geographies of colonization' linking the development of urban centres in the West with the genesis of colonial space, and they connect this to 'the palpable presence of people from other cultures and continents in our midst'. This, 'for centuries, has been the normal case in the world that is *not* Europe'. Revising this paper six months after the conference, following terrorist bombings in London, the earthquake in South Asia and its aftermath, riots in French cities, and the continuing war in Iraq, it is apparent that the 'postcolonial presence' assumes daily a new significance, the subtext of this chapter.

In accepting these two premises, however, my aim in this chapter is to discuss recent postcolonial writing on cities both outside and inside Europe. I first briefly address recent writing on the topic of colonial cities by postcolonial authors indigenous to those cities. I then address recent scholarship on the postcolonial city, understood as it is, in different ways, and the cross-over between notions of the post-imperial, postcolonial and global city. While all these categories are inter-related, the obvious distinction between them is the political and historical framework within which each is conceived and represented. The central issue concerns the question of representation, especially the power of representation to affect both the understanding of the city as well as policies adopted towards it.

Most urbanists would probably agree that the most influential representation of the city in recent years has been that of the 'world' or 'global city'. Yet while the criteria for identifying 'world cities' are clearly stated (Beaverstock *et al.* 2000; Keil and Brenner 2006), they are not particularly useful for addressing issues of global or local security posed by religious or other ideologically driven groups, or policies of education or language conceived in relation to specific cultural histories and contemporary political identities. While acknowledging that 'world city' populations are racially and ethnically diverse and frequently characterised by social and spatial polarisation, the 'world city' model ignores the religio-cultural origins of the city's populations and the geopolitico-historical conditions explaining their presence. While the concept of 'postcolonial' would, in many cases, be analytically more useful, this is not its most important use. However, it does serve to illustrate that any city's 'reality' is inseparable from its representation.

Until the early 1980s, 'postcolonial' simply meant 'after the colonial' and referred to peoples, states and societies who had experienced a formal decolonisation process. Subsequently, 'postcolonial' has come to mean 'an attitude of critical engagement with colonialism's after effects and its constructions of knowledge' (Radcliffe 1997:1331).

> Postcolonialism is a critical politico-intellectual formation ... centrally concerned
> with the impact of colonialism and its contestation on the cultures of both
> colonizing and colonized peoples in the past, and the reproduction and
> transformation of colonial relations, representations and practices in the present.
>
> (Gregory 2000:612)

Postcolonial criticism also assumes a knowledge of colonial histories in the contemporary world, not only of major European imperial powers but also of the USA, Russia and Japan. By the early twentieth century, Europe held a grand total of 85 per cent of the earth as colonies, protectorates, dependencies, dominions and commonwealths (Said 1993:14). At the heart of much postcolonial critique is an assumption succinctly expressed in the title of Chakrabarty's book, *Provincializing Europe* (2000). In addressing the topic of postcolonial cities, therefore, both usages – a period following colonisation and a critical conceptual position – need deploying.

CITIES: COLONIAL AND POSTCOLONIAL

Not only are the 'colonial city' and the 'imperial city' umbilically connected in terms of economic linkages as well as cultural hybridisation, but their 'post-equivalents' cannot be disentangled one from the other and need to be analysed within a single 'postcolonial' framework of intertwining histories and relations (Yeoh 2001:457).

As Yeoh suggests, to write about the postcolonial city presupposes some minimum knowledge of its predecessor, the colonial city, including its historiography.[2] Though embracing, for geographers, 'a variety of urban types and forms' it may nonetheless be generalised as 'a distinct settlement form resulting from the domination of an indigenous civilization by colonial settlers' (Pacione 2001:450–1), the focus here being on the colonial city established by Europeans mainly in the nineteenth and early twentieth centuries in Asia and Africa.

Important here, and bringing the second meaning of 'postcolonial' into play, we need to recognise that both the concept of, and most of the literature on the colonial city comes from Euro-American scholars (principally English and American, some French and Spanish), and is written in these languages. Not only is the colonial city apparently a colonial product, so also is its representation.

Ethnic origin, geographical location or political position alone should not, of course, be treated as an essentialism giving indigenous inhabitants of the one-time colonial city a privileged insight into its characteristics.[3] It is rather that these mainly 'non-indigenous' studies – which might be described as the first critical 'postcolonial' accounts of colonial cities, produced in the three or four decades following independence – locate the topic, understandably perhaps, within a European or Euro-American frame. As Indonesian scholar Abidin Kusno has written about these various studies of colonial urbanism (e.g. King 1976; Rabinow 1989; Metcalf 1989; Wright 1991), 'to what extent have studies centered on European imperialism themselves "colonized" ways of thinking about colonial and postcolonial space?' (Kusno 2000:6).

Similar views can be found in *Urbanism: Imported or Exported: Native Aspirations and Foreign Plans* (2003), where the editors refer to 'a sense of unease' among young researchers regarding the 'content, methods and tone' of much recent literature on the formation of modern cities, particularly in 'developing countries': a feeling that

> it often did not adequately convey the complexity of power relations and flows....
> In particular, the local elements are under-represented ... and where they are
> present they are often dealt with as recipients of actions rather than as actors ... a
> significant part of the literature on colonial urbanism has been written based on
> strictly metropolitan sources, rather than ... local archival material.
>
> (Nasr and Volait 2003:vii–xx)

In what follows, therefore, I refer to recent revisionist writing on the colonial city as exemplary of what might be called an indigenous 'critical postcolonial' perspective. Themes include the agency of the indigenous population in producing the colonial city, the indigenous appropriation of the city and the larger narrative within which the city is framed.

WHEN WAS THE COLONIAL CITY?

The stereotypical representation of the colonial city is best expressed by Frantz Fanon:

> The colonial world is a world divided into compartments. It is probably
> unnecessary to recall the existence of native quarters and European quarters, of
> schools for natives and schools for Europeans; in the same way we need not
> recall apartheid in South Africa. Yet if we examine closely this system of
> compartments, we will at least be able to reveal the lines of force it implies. This
> approach to the colonial world, its order and its geographical layout will allow us
> to mark out the lines on which a decolonized society will be organized.
>
> (Fanon 1968:37–38)

Fanon's words were written over 45 years ago (1961). Whether in relation to the original, supposedly 'decolonised' postcolonial city, or alternatively, in the supposedly post-imperial city, are they still applicable? We don't know because, in one sense, the goal posts have been moved.

Irrespective of changing conditions, at what point in historical time, does the 'colonial city' morph into a different category? Is its subsequent identity (and representation) destined to be either 'postcolonial' or to be transformed (if so, by whom?) into a 'world' or 'global city', as suggested, for example, in regard to one-time colonial cities in Asia by Dick and Rimmer (1998) or Skeldon (1997)? As Cooper and Stoler point out, peoples' histories are made up 'of more than the fact that they were colonized' (1997:18). For Goh (2005), Singapore remains a paradigmatic example of a city that occupies both identities and exploits them to advantage. What is not considered here, however, 50 years after independence, are the persistent social and spatial maldistributions of resources (schools, jobs, transport, income) among the population in some postcolonial cities (King 2004). But are such inequities 'postcolonial' through neglect, are they the result of oppressive, neocolonial regimes following independence, or has the nature and conditions of the debate changed, as in postcolonial, postapartheid South Africa? (Murray and Shepherd 2006).

THE COLONIAL CITY REVISITED: 'INDIGENOUS' POSTCOLONIAL CRITIQUES

Different perspectives, interpretations and representations of the colonial city result from the use of different sources, frameworks and methods. Yeoh's study, *Contesting Space: Power Relations and the Urban Built Environment in Colonial Singapore*, is based on a detailed study of local archives. It is perhaps the first account challenging the notion of the colonial city as being simply a product of 'dominant' (Western) 'forces' and representing the city as the product of indigenous agency (1996:9–14). Two other examples are worth citing because they address what is perhaps the most central feature said to characterise the colonial city, namely the racial, social, and spatial divide between the indigenous city and European colonial settlement.

Hosagrahar's study of 'old Delhi' between the 1850s and 1950s, examines transformations in the indigenous city during a century of colonial presence, this latter first represented by a 'typical' colonial urban settlement of 'civil station' and military cantonment and, from 1911, the new colonial capital of New Delhi. Eschewing binary classifications between colonial/indigenous, new/old, European/native, 'modern'/'traditional', she investigates the spatial development of Delhi over a century using an array of different source materials, including contemporary interviews. 'Beneath the apparent opposition' she writes, 'was a charged interconnection between the two spaces'. The residents of Delhi responded to the new model of urban life by 'disdaining and rejecting, mocking and mimicking, participating and conniving, and learning and accepting' from the colonial Western lifestyle. The new colonial settlement offered opportunities for some Indian residents to construct new identities, a way of identifying with the new by rejecting the old and, on occasion, moving between the two spaces (Hosagrahar 2005).

Chattopadhyay's *Representing Calcutta: Modernity, Nationalism and the Colonial Uncanny* (2005) brings yet another perspective to the 'colonial city' and its supposedly defining attributes. She reads the city primarily as the cradle of Bengal nationalism, subverting its colonial representation as a space marked simplistically by the Manichaean division between the 'European city' and the 'black town'. While such labels certainly exist in European maps and the Anglophone colonial literature, in Bengali accounts of the city she examines, Chattopadhyay finds no evidence of these or comparable terms.

What these studies show is the contested and ambiguous space of 'the colonial city' represented in these recent accounts, postcolonial in both senses of the term. It was, and is, a space too complex and unpredictable for easy classification. While these latest studies might be based on previously unexamined indigenous language sources or the interrogation of official colonial accounts, they also frame the 'colonial city' within a different narrative. Most commonly it is the discursive space of 'modernity', or the role of the city's inhabitants in the emergence of a collective (and resistant) national, regional or perhaps gendered identity. In Kusno's study of Jakarta, he states '(m)odern architecture and urbanism in the colonial and postcolonial world have generally been understood in relation to European domination'. Instead he 'explores the theme from another perspective: as a colonial gift inherited by the postcolonial (society and) state' (Kusno 2000:cover). He takes the Western obsession with (over-simplified) 'east–west' antagonisms and redirects his focus on political relations within the region. Regarding Indonesia, he foregrounds the persistence of colonial oppression in the supposedly 'postcolonial' regimes themselves.

POSTCOLONIAL CITIES/POSTCOLONIAL CRITICISM

Compared to colonial cities, postcolonial cities have received far less academic attention.[4] There are some obvious explanations.

As stated, postcolonialism is concerned with colonialism's after effects, including its constructions of knowledge. Dependent on different authors, its politico-intellectual formation can be informed by poststructuralist, feminist, psychoanalytic and other perspectives. It is also an intellectual position that has been criticised from different viewpoints. The most trenchant criticism suggests that it 're-orient(s) the globe once more around a single, binary opposition: colonial/postcolonial … (such that) Colonialism returns at the moment of its disappearance' (McClintock 1992; King 2004).

Resistance to representing 'fully independent' states and cities as largely uninfluenced by the colonial past is one explanation why 'postcolonial' does not figure as an analytical category. For other (and not just 'Western') urbanists, the 'world space' in which they operate, prior to the imagined 'global' of the late 1980s, is the (obsolescent?) one of the 'three worlds' conceived in 1953 (Wolff-Phillips 1987). Though the 'Third World city' concept was probably in circulation before Tinker's *Race and the Third World City* (1971), representation of many postcolonial cities has been subsumed within this ideological framework. Here, postcolonial cities are viewed through the lens of 'Third World problems': air pollution, megacity size, traffic management, 'slums' and water scarcity. Questions about religious or cultural identity and subject formation do not figure here. What Venn (2006) refers to as 'the neglected interface between urban studies and development studies' (see also Robinson 2005), means that cities in different continents are not only represented through different theoretical and methodological frameworks but their inter-connections are ignored. While a postcolonial perspective does make this connection, it is clear that 'world', 'global', 'colonial/postcolonial', 'First/Third World' cities are all labels invented in the West.

POSTCOLONIAL CITIES

How is the postcolonial city recognised? This depends on how the term is understood. Cities are not necessarily postcolonial in the same way.

Yeoh suggests that 'for some, postcolonialism is something fairly tangible' (2001:456). In one interpretation of this 'tangibility' Bishop et al., referring to Singapore, argue, 'post (after) doesn't necessarily indicate either that the colonizers have gone away ... or that the conditions of postcolonialism have necessarily changed much from those of colonialism, despite appearances' (2003:14). Here, postcolonialism is seen as the failure of decolonisation.

Elsewhere, I have referred to 'actually existing postcolonialism' (King 2003), particularly as manifested in the spatial environments of one-time colonial urban landscapes used to help institutionalise (and also symbolise) social relations of exclusion, segregation and privilege based on race, class and power and which, 50 years after independence, continue to do so, albeit in modified form.

Yeoh (2001) provides an extensive review of literature on the geography of postcolonial cities, focusing on themes of identity, heritage, encounters. Dependent on our viewpoint, these may (or may not) be seen as belonging to a more positive interpretation of 'postcolonialism', one adopting a non-Western 'occidentalist' perspective, and viewing the one-time colonial city as 'a gift' (Kusno 2000).

The postcolonial city is 'an important site where claims of identity different from the colonial past are expressed and indexed, and, in some cases, keenly contested' (Yeoh 2001:458). This is seen especially in regard to matters of space, architecture and urban design, the public signs of often fiercely contested political and social positions. Many studies detail the various ways in which postcolonial states and cities have both engaged with and simultaneously distanced themselves from their colonial past, aiming to construct new citizen identities with a consciousness of national culture. States have built new capitals or capitol complexes (Perera 1998; Vale 1992); toponymic reinscription aims to reclaim the cultural space of city streets (King 1976; 2004; Yeoh 1996); modernist design attempts to create new images for the nation (Kusno 2000). Constructing 'the world's tallest building' has become an essentially competitive strategy for postcolonial nations to make claims on others' definitions of modernity, or establish them as 'global players' (King 2004). A recent contender, a 710-metre skyscraper planned for Noida, near Delhi, according to the architect, aims 'to show the world what India can do' (*Guardian* 29 March 2005). Such projects are thought to provide a nation's leaders and perhaps, its people, with a new, more positive identity.

An increasing number of authorities have argued for the preservation of the architecture, urban design and planning of one-time colonial cities, including UNESCO's International Committee on Monuments and Sites (ICOMOS). Unprecedented rural migration and what are seen as over-dependence on state-led development projects imposing Western urban models are behind attempts to prevent 'the disappearance of the Asian city', including its colonial history (Logan, 2002; Lari and Lari, 2001). In this perspective, 50 years after independence, the symbolic significance of colonial buildings has lost its old political meaning. New generations see colonial urban design as generating tourist revenue rather than prompting memories of colonial oppression.

Yet few such reports represent buildings and spaces not just as aesthetic but also cultural, social and political phenomena. The elite Dutch colonial suburb of Menteng, outside Jakarta, with its Art Deco houses and spacious tree-lined boulevards, continues, as in colonial days, to house the rich and powerful elite (including ex-President Suharto). In South Korea's capital, Seoul, the neo-baroque Japanese Government-General headquarters building, constructed in 1926 from the designs of a German architect, and after 1945 used as the City Hall and subsequently the National Museum of Contemporary Art, was in 1995 unceremoniously demolished – significantly, on the 50th anniversary of Korea's liberation from Japan. It restored the appearance of South Korea's Gyeongbok Palace, 'the most important symbol of (our) national history' and the seat of the 500-year-old Korean Choseun Dynasty (Kal 2003).

CITIES: POSTCOLONIAL OR POSTIMPERIAL?

So far I have assumed that 'postcolonial' refers only to those cities in formerly colonised societies and 'postimperial' to those one-time imperial capitals such as Paris, Lisbon or London. However, the distinction between postcolonial and post-imperial can be ambivalent. Labelling London as (technically) post-imperial foregrounds its earlier imperial role. Yet for postcolonial migrants from South Asia London may also (like them) be postcolonial. And as the one-time metropole has been powerfully influenced by postcolonial forces, 'postcolonial' is now used to describe it, particularly in regard to its ethnic and racial composition. Whether we live in a postcolonial world or, more accurately, in *The Colonial Present* (Gregory 2003), colonial and postcolonial histories of migration and memory not only distinguish the population, politics and public culture of one postcolonial city from another, but also from other 'world' or 'global cities' such as Frankfurt or Zurich.[5]

For example, over half of the almost 30 per cent foreign-born population of New York are from the Caribbean and Central Americas, with significant proportions from Europe, South America and South and Southeast Asia (Salvo and Lord, 1997). Any explanation for the presence of, for example, English-speaking migrants from the Caribbean, or South and Southeast Asia,[6] must recognise colonial and postcolonial histories. This is equally so with the Spanish-speaking migrants from the Caribbean and Central and South America. In London, of the roughly 25 per cent of 'foreign-born' population, the large majority are principally from postcolonial countries, particularly South/Southeast Asia, Ireland, East, West and South Africa, the Caribbean, North America and Australia, as well as from continental Europe (Merriman, 1993; Benedictus, 2005). In Paris, the more than 15 per cent of foreign-born are primarily from postcolonial North Africa (Algeria, Morocco, Tunisia), Armenia, or Mauritius (Ambroise-Rendu, 1993).

These distinctively postcolonial migrations clearly have major influences on the economy, society, culture, politics, spatial environments and, in cases, security, of the city. They bring to the so-called 'global city' a variety of vibrant but also very specific postcolonial cosmopolitanisms. Powerful postcolonial minorities bring their influence to bear on government policies, both domestic (immigration, employment, educational or welfare) or foreign (international disputes, disaster relief and the conduct of war).[7] Multiple temporalities co-exist in urban space as also do multiple spatialities, extending the real and the virtual space of the city and its inhabitants to other urban and rural locations round the world (Venn 2006).

The growing outsourcing of employment from North America and the UK to the large Anglophone labour market in Indian cities (especially, call centres), generating employment and a boom in office building, cannot be understood without a postcolonial frame (King 2004). In Paris, as the riots of November 2005 have exposed, most postcolonial minorities are in the *banlieues* which, already 'in the 1990s, have become a byword for socially disadvantaged peripheral areas of French cities' (Hargreaves and McKinney 1997:12). Structurally equivalent to British and American inner-city areas, and seen as ghettoes, the *banlieues* provide a space to develop 'a separatist cultural agenda marked by graffiti, music, dancing and dress codes' with which the *banlieusards* (suburb-dwellers) reterritorialise the 'anonymous housing projects' (ibid.). In Britain, the inner suburban landscapes of postcolonial London are regenerated and transformed by South Asians, who, 'though united by belief, are nonetheless divided along national, ethnic and sectarian lines' (Nasser 2003:9). In Britain's 'second city' of Birmingham, the largest group of 80,000 South Asian Muslims are from Pakistan, comprising 7 per cent of the city's population (ibid.:9). Leicester, with 28 per cent of its 280,000 population from South Asia, is said to be 'the largest Indian city in Europe'. Though Vietnamese scholar P. Norindr writes 'policies of colonial urbanism help to explain race and class divisions in Western metrocentres of today' (1997:114), we need to recognise that individual urban authorities have their own distinctive policies regarding housing, planning and education. In multicultural societies, members of particular communities (like the British overseas) frequently stay together, with their own shops, social centres and places of worship.

Long after the formal end of empire, postcolonial memories continue to affect the use of space. Jacobs (1996) shows how the continuity of discourses over historic sites in the City of London, remembered as 'the economic centre of the Empire', have influenced decisions about urban design. Yet consciousness of the postcolonial multicultural is also powerfully celebratory. It signifies a changing, vibrant future, a new kind of intellectual milieu created by unique ethnicities, hybridities, and diasporas. New and distinctive cultures develop in geographically and culturally specific 'postcolonial cities'. Whether in the one-time metropole or the one-time colony, postcolonialism creates conditions for both the split, as well as the suture, between 'traditional' and 'modern' identities.

Attributes that distinguish postcolonial populations – a language common with the host society, a shared, if contested, history, some familiarity with the culture, norms and social practices of the metropolitan society, the presence of long-established communities, are features among others which distinguish postcolonial communities and migrants from those of non-postcolonial origin. In this way, 'multicultural' Berlin differs from multicultural London or Vancouver.

I have not addressed here the more metaphorical uses of the terms, yet clearly colonial/postcolonial are also relevant in describing the processes of urbanism in contemporary Europe. Today, newly colonised populations in cities – migrant labour, legal as well as illegal, arrives from all over the world, including Eastern Europe, filling the lowest paid slots in an ever increasingly globalised economy. Labour is colonised by capital.

Sidaway (2000) and Domosh (2004) show how the postcolonial paradigm has now expanded to cover many historical and geographical instances. Though not sufficient in themselves, postcolonial histories, sociologies and geographies are nonetheless key to understanding a plethora of issues, and not only in the multicultural, postcolonial/post-imperial global cities of Melbourne, or Toronto. 'Postcolonial vision' results from postcolonial migration and globalisation (Hopkins 2002). It is a comparative, cross-cultural, and cross-temporal perspective. Despite its ambiguity, the paradigm provides one among many ways of reading the contemporary city.

NOTES

1   From Anthony D. King, 'Postcolonial cities, postcolonial critiques', in Helmut Berking, Sybille Frank, Lars Frers, Martina Löw, Lars Meier, Silke Steets, Sergej Stoetzer, eds, *Negotiating Urban Conflicts: Interaction, Space and Control*, 2003 © Helmut Berking and Martina Löw.

2   See King (1985) and (1989).

3   While the location of an author is less important than the position from which she or he speaks – epistemologically, politically, culturally – it is statistically more likely that authors from (or with connections to) the one-time colonised society are not only fluent in the colonial as well as the national language, but possibly also in local and regional languages of the once colonised state. They may also have better knowledge of local sources. Given the contemporary movement of scholars between locations worldwide,

where they work or write up their research is of less importance. Valid contributions can be made by anyone (see King 2003:170).

4   Googling 'postcolonial city/cities, postkoloniale stadt/staedte, ville/villes postcoloniale', brings up numerous references, mostly book titles. Themes addressed include representation in the arts, sites of tension and citizenship, their role in 'Westernisation' and in flows of capital, migration, terrorism, their shaping by imperial legacies and tradition, questions of subjectivity, multiculturalism, hybridity, nationalism, modernity, globalisation, etc. Specifically mentioned cities include Bombay/Mumbai, Cairo, Calcutta/ Kolkata, Chandigarh, Dakar, Delhi, Jaipur, Jakarta, Lagos, London, Melbourne, Rabat, San Francisco, Sao Paulo, Tunis. Apart from one article on Bombay/Mumbai, I found no reference to religion.

5   How postcolonialism impacts these and other European cities is still to be explored.

6   South Asia (India, Pakistan, Bangladesh) accounts for some 50 per cent of cab-drivers in New York City, and (Anglophone) Indians are prominently represented in the information technology and medical professions in the USA.

7   Media coverage of the four 7 July suicide bombers in London focused almost exclusively on their British citizenship and 'Islamist fundamentalist' identity. Yet the specific motivation of the bombings, widely believed by a majority of the public (though not Prime Minister Tony Blair) to be Blair's complicity in the US-led attack on Iraq, was also seen as a response to the decades-long history of British and US colonial oppression in the Middle East, including Britain's colonial role in early twentieth century Iraq (see Gregory 2003).

The shift in media sentiment towards Pakistani born residents in the UK, in the three months between the July bombings and early October when Pakistan and Indian Kashmir was struck by the most disastrous earthquake in its history, with tens of thousands of victims, was palpable. With over 700,000 residents of Pakistani birth/descent in Britain, mostly from the Kashmir region, and many British nationals, the mood of the tabloid media shifted from suspended suspicion to one of sympathy and shared loss, followed by a major fund-raising campaign for survivors.

BIBLIOGRAPHY

Ambroise-Rendu, M. (1993) 'The migrants who turned Paris into a melting pot', *Guardian Weekly*, 27 June: 14.

Beaverstock, J.V., Smith, R.V. and Taylor, P.J. (1999) 'A roster of world cities', *Cities*, 16, 6: 445–58.

Benedictus, L. (2005) 'The world in one city', *Guardian*, 21 January.

Bishop, R., Phillips, J. and Yeo, W.W., eds. (2003) *Postcolonial Urbanism: Southeast Asian Cities and Global Processes*, New York and London: Routledge.

Chakrabarty, D. (2000) *Provincializing Europe: Postcolonial Thought and Historical Difference*, Princeton: Princeton University Press.

Chattopadhyay, S. (2005) *Representing Calcutta: Modernity, Nationalism and the Colonial Uncanny.* London and New York: Routledge.

Cooper, F. and Stoler, L. (1997) *Tensions of Empire: Colonial Cultures in a Bourgeois World*, Berkeley: University of California Press.

Dick, H.W. and Rimmer, P.J. (1998) 'Beyond the Third World city: the new geography of Southeast Asia', *Urban Studies*, 35, 12: 303–21.

Domosh, M. (2004) 'Postcolonialism and the American city', *Urban Geography*, 25, 8: 742–54.

Fanon, F. (1968) *The Wretched of the Earth*. New York: Grove.

Goh, R.B.H. (2005) *Contours of Culture: Space and Social Difference in Singapore*, Hong Kong: Hong Kong University Press.

Gregory, D. (2000) 'Postcolonialism', in R. Johnson, D. Gregory and D.M. Smith, eds, *The Dictionary of Human Geography*, Oxford: Blackwell.

Gregory, D. (2003) *The Colonial Present*. Oxford: Blackwell.

Hargreaves, A.G. and McKinney, M. (1997) *Postcolonial Cultures in France*, London and New York: Routledge.

Hopkins, A.G., ed. (2002) *Globalization in World History*, London: Pimlico.

Hosagrahar, J. (2005) *Indigenous Modernities: Negotiating Urban Form*, London and New York: Routledge.

Jacobs, J. (1996) *Edge of Empire: Postcolonialism and the City*, London and New York: Routledge.

Kal, H. (2003) 'The presence of the past: exhibitions, memories and national identities in colonial and postcolonial Korea'. PhD Dissertation, Binghamton University.

Keil, R. and Brenner, N. (2006) *The Global Cities Reader*, London and New York: Routledge.

King, A.D. (1976) *Colonial Urban Development: Culture, Social Power and Environment*, London and Boston: Routledge and Kegan Paul.

King, A.D. (1985) 'Colonial cities: global pivots of change', in R. Ross and G. Telkamp, eds, *Colonial Cities: Essays on Urbanism in a Colonial Context*, Dordrecht: Martinius Niehoff.

King, A.D. (1989) 'Colonialism, urbanism, and the capitalist world economy: an introduction', *International Journal of Urban and Regional Research*, 13, 1: 1–18.

King, A.D. (1990) *Global Cities: Postimperialism and the Internationalization of London*, London and New York: Routledge.

King, A.D. (2003) 'Actually existing postcolonialism: colonial architecture and urbanism after the postcolonial turn', in R. Bishop *et al.*, eds, *Postcolonial Urbanism: Southeast Asian Cities and Global Processes*, New York and London: Routledge, pp.167–86.

King, A.D. (2004) *Spaces of Global Cultures: Architecture, Urbanism, Identity*, London and New York: Routledge.

Kusno, A. (2000) *Behind the Postcolonial: Architecture, Urban Space and Political Cultures in Indonesia*, London and New York: Routledge.

Lari, Y. and Lari, M.S. (2001) *The Dual City: Karachi During the Raj*, Karachi: Oxford University Press and Heritage Foundation Karachi.

Logan, W.S. (2002) *The Disappearing 'Asian' City: Protecting Asia's Urban Heritage in a Globalizing World*, New York: Oxford University Press.

McClintock, A. (1992) 'Angel of progress: pitfalls of the term "postcolonialism"', *Social Text* 31/32: 84–98.

Merriman, N. ed. (1993) *The Peopling of London: Fifteen Thousand Years of Settlement from Overseas*, London: Museum of London.

Metcalf, T.R. (1989) *An Imperial Vision: Indian Architecture and Britain's Raj*. Berkeley: University of California Press.

Murray, N. and Shepherd, N. (2006) *Desire Lines: Space, Memory and Identity in Postapartheid South Africa*, London and New York: Routledge.

Nasr, J. and Volait, M., eds (2003) *Urbanism: Exported or Imported? Native Aspirations and Foreign Plans*, London: Wiley.

Nasser, N. (2003) 'The space of displacement: making Muslim South Asian place in British neighborhoods', *Traditional Dwellings and Settlements Review*, 15, 1: 7–21.

Norindr, P. (1997) *Phantasmic Indochina: French Colonial Ideology in Architecture, Film and Literature*, Durham, NC and London: Duke University Press.

Pacione, M. (2001) *Urban Geography: A Global Perspective*, New York and London: Routledge.

Perera, N. (1998) *Decolonizing Ceylon: Colonialism, Nationalism, and the Politics of Space in Sri Lanka*. New Delhi: Oxford University Press.

Rabinow, P. (1989) *French Modern: Norms and Forms of the Social Environment*, Cambridge, MA: MIT Press.

Radcliffe, S.A. (1997) 'Different heroes: genealogies of postcolonial geographies', *Environment and Planning D: Society and Space*, 15: 1331–33.

Robinson, J. (2005) *Ordinary Cities: Between Modernity and Development*, London and New York: Routledge.

Said, E. (1993) *Culture and Imperialism*, London: Vintage.

Sidaway, J. (2000) 'Postcolonial geographies: an exploratory essay', *Progress in Human Geography*, 24, 4: 591–612.

Skeldon, R. (1997) 'Hong Kong: colonial city to global city to provincial city?' *Cities*, 14: 265–71.

Tinker, H. (1971) *Race and the Third World City*, Oxford: Oxford University Press.

Vale, L. (1992) *Architecture, Power and National Identity*, Princeton: Yale University Press.

Venn, C. (2006) 'The city as assemblage', in H. Berking, S. Frank, L. Frers, M. Löw, L. Meier, S. Steets, S. Stoetzer, eds, *Negotiating Urban Conflicts: Interaction, Space and Control*, Darmstadt: Helmut Berking and Martina Löw, pp.53–66.

Wolf-Phillips, L. (1987) 'Why "Third World"? Origins, definitions, and usage', *Third World Quarterly*, 9, 4: 1311–27.

Wright, G. (1991) *The Politics of Design in French Colonial Urbanism*, Chicago: Chicago University Press.

Yeoh, B.S.A. (1996) *Contesting Space: Power Relations and the Urban Built Environment in Colonial Singapore*, Kuala Lumpur: Oxford University Press.

Yeoh, B.S.A. (2001) 'Postcolonial cities', *Progress in Human Geography*, 25, 3: 456–68.

Chapter 10: Notes towards a global historical sociology of building types[1]

WORDS AND BUILDINGS

While the name of a building may tell us its function (bank, museum, police station), it does not necessarily tell us about its form nor its spatial structure. On the other hand, lexical terms that describe a building's form (skyscraper, terrace, tower) do not tell us about its function.

We also know that, in a semiotic sense, the relationship between any particular term, as a signifier, and the object signified is – as Saussure argued – entirely arbitrary. The fact that a term (e.g. stadium, hospital), when spoken about between two members of a given speech community, summons up in the imagination of each a similar image and meaning is not due to any essential meaning in the term as such, but rather to the shared linguistic and cultural experience between both parties. For example, we can say that, in Britain, a generally accepted shared meaning has developed over time regarding commonly experienced types of dwelling such as a detached or semi-detached house. Similar forms in the USA would be known as a single family home and a duplex.

We might therefore argue that the steady globalisation of English, both as a first and second language, together with the ever-increasing access to and circulation of visual media (television, film, photography, newsprint, internet) worldwide in the past half-century, has, with the increased urbanisation of the world's population, reduced, for many of them, the gap in meaning between word and image for many phenomena in the contemporary world. Quite apart from the neo-liberal political agendas in many different polities, these are some of the conditions enabling the terms, concepts and realities of various urban building types, from skyscraper to supermarket, gated community to theme park, to become familiarised and travel worldwide.

I have suggested that, for our purposes, building types might be identified in two principal ways, by names signifying their form and by their use. (For different purposes, they can also be classified according to an infinite number of other criteria – size, construction materials, location, spatial structure, age, architectural style, etc.). We also know that the meaning of terms is not stable. Within any particular speech community, meanings can change over time. The only thing that kiosks – an anglicised Turkish term found in many countries round the world (and first documented in English in 1866) – have in common is often just their name and function. Their form – from a one-person telephone or internet kiosk to an entire floor of a multi-storey building – is quite arbitrary.

Looking lexically at names tells us how particular terms for building types are socially 'loaded'. To speak of convents is to reference gender, religion, and nuns. To speak of churches is, depending on the geocultural frame in which they are mentioned, to reference Christians (for others, it might be Catholics, or Lutherans). To speak of synagogues, is to reference Jews, and mosques, to reference Muslims. In any one speech community, the social meaning of a particular term (as with all terms) depends on context and possibly (like 'estate' in Britain) on the social class status of the speaker. Naming here is being considered in a rather literal and etic (i.e. outsider's) rather than emic (insider's) fashion. The question of what a building is *called*, how it is imagined, and how invested with a unique, culture-specific meaning and spoken of in the local setting, belongs to the realm of ethnosemantics.

In the media, buildings and building types are perennial subjects of synecdoche. We refer to 'the White House', 'the Kremlin', 'Buckingham Palace', 'the Elysée'. Buildings stand for people. 'Branding' is a different practice. 'Branding' buildings helps sell the corporate or state interests of those that own or use them. Particular building types, like Bilbao's Museum, Sydney's Opera House, Frankfurt's 'financial centre' skyscrapers, invested with significant architectural and cultural capital, are used – in *autobahn* signs – to brand the city itself (Figure 10.1).

Figure 10.1
A sign of Frankfurt.

In examining the circulation around the world of concepts of and terms for describing building types, at least three assumptions might be considered. First, whenever the concept travels it never remains the same. It is invariably adapted, re-modelled, placed in a different context. Moreover, even if arriving in apparently similar forms, and given a similar name, the building-as-concept is invested with different social, cultural or ideological meanings. Finally, the varied and different meanings which building types and forms acquire also depend on the varied local environments – whether historical, natural, social, political or spatial – in which they are introduced and embedded.

How do the two nouns 'building' and 'architecture' differ from each other? At the simplest level, where architecture is making buildings with the help of architects and the ideology of architecture, buildings are concrete materialities which have some social function. With European imperialism as the handmaid of global capitalism, the ideological construct of architecture-as-art ('big sculpture'), and technology used to serve this goal, has spread from the West, especially from the eighteenth century, around most of the world. With the development of architecture as a 'profession' distinct from other professions (such as civil engineering) and also from 'vernacular building', a discourse became possible that did not exist before, one that has initiated a long and complex history between the two. In this context, the ways in which 'building' and 'architecture' have become globally transportable are fundamentally different and any history or analysis of the process would require two different methodologies, a task beyond the scope of this chapter.[2]

INDIGENOUS AND NON-INDIGENOUS TERMS

That terms as well as concepts for building types travel between different places and speech communities can be illustrated by reference to the existence, in many languages, of exogenous terms for building types. Mostly, these are likely to result from conditions of propinquity, brought about by travel, trade and tourism. In Britain, for example, abattoir (1900), bistro (1980s), café (1880s), casino (1848), chalet (1883), garage (1902), hotel (1817), maisonette (1970s), pavilion (1766) and restaurant (1861) have been imported at varying times from neighbouring France. Other terms and types defy the rule of propinquity and result from Britain's imperial past, such as bazaar (1826) and bungalow (1869), from colonial India. Like bungalow, villa (1748), from Italy, arrived under the particular economic and social conditions I address in the next section.[3] The entry of the terms and material presence of mosques, Hindu temples and Sikh gurdwaras I discuss below. Of course, other, much older terms which might naively be regarded as 'native' or 'indigenous' to Britain such as castle, cottage or factory, depend on earlier instances of linguistic mobility, whether of Latin and the Roman colonisation of Britain, or Anglo-Saxon, with the invasion of their successors.

BUILT FORMS AND SOCIAL FORMS

Why particular terms, the building types they describe and the social practices they embody are introduced in particular societies at particular times and under particular social conditions is central to my argument. For example, Archer has made interesting and suggestive comments about the term and notion of the villa which entered the English language from Italy in the seventeenth century and the urban and architectural vocabulary during the early years of the industrial revolution and expansion of the bourgeois classes in the early eighteenth century. The villa, in various local transformations, later appeared in other countries in Europe, the United States and, through colonialism, in India, China, Latin America and elsewhere (Archer 1997, 2005; King 2004).

According to Archer (1997:41; 2005), the appearance of the villa marked a critical change in English modes of consciousness, 'a consciousness that began to identify primarily in the autonomous *self* rather than in a social hierarchy or collective'. The villa was instrumental in 'spatially differentiating private from public, by establishing the suburban plot as a site for cultivation of the self (e.g. through leisure pursuits) instead of commerce and politics'. Its broader significance was the contribution it made to the creation of bourgeois consciousness (ibid.; also King 2004:ch.7).

As socially classifying devices, providing us with insights into how social formations are organised, both spatially and temporally, and with reference to institutions and social relationships, such as kinship, nation, ethnicity or religion, and transformative flows between them, we can look at building types from a variety of different perspectives. At the level of the nation-state we can distinguish, for example, between public and private sector provision in housing, education or health care; in the public sphere, between different state-related activities of governance and social control in civil society as represented by the presence of courts, prisons and governance buildings.

Building types are used as symbols of modernity. In the late nineteenth century, the Ottoman Empire introduced into some of the leading cities of its Arab provinces 'buildings that represented a modern way of life' and that offered 'a new urban lifestyle': hotels, casinos, theatres, banks, cafés, municipal offices, public gardens, a government palace, and especially, the urban square, 'a metaphor for modern order', frequently with its clock tower, secularising the time and 'dissociating it from the religious realm, … the call to prayer' (Çelik 2008:129–31, 150). In the twentieth century, new nations adopted from older ones the notion of the capitol building, along with schools, museums and exhibitionary complexes, to project a modern, unified national identity (Vale 2008). Today, Olympic stadiums, with spectacular pyrotechnic and terpsichoric displays, perform a similar function. For centuries, cities have competed with each other to build the tallest cathedral or the most capacious mosque. In today's rampant competition between global cities for capital investment and high- and low-cost labour, constructing the 'world's tallest building' has, for some, become the most spectacular symbol of modernity (King 2004; Black 2008).

Specific building types give places their own distinctive identity. Ever since their introduction, skyscrapers have meant New York, Chicago and America. The Taj Mahal means India. However, some culturally representative types, like the boulevard café in Paris, or the British pub, require significant social, cultural and environmental support. They adapt uncomfortably to their surroundings when transferred elsewhere.

BUILDINGS AND RELIGION

In writing about *Globalisation and Culture* (2004) Pieterse has implicitly criticised the often ahistorical representations of globalisation, defining it as 'a long term historical process involving ancient population movements, long distance cross-cultural trade, the spread of world religions and the diffusion and development of technologies due to inter-cultural contacts' (Pieterse 2004:24–5). Included among these technologies are some of the oldest building types which have accompanied the spread of world religions, for long a major force in accounting for the mobility of urban and building forms across continents.

In and on the edges of Europe, the Roman Empire first established temples to Mithras, Zeus, Jupiter and other Roman gods. After CE 313, when Christianity became the empire's official religion, churches were founded at existing Roman centres including, in Britain, at Colchester, possibly the oldest church in England (CE 320) and probably converted from a Roman temple. Following the fifth-century collapse of the Roman empire in Britain, later Christian revivals were to result in some 500 parish churches built under Anglo-Saxon patronage (Crawford 1990:117). In 2007, there were some 47,000 Christian churches of different denominations (Gledhill 2007).

Examining the relation of buildings to religion (or belief systems in general) serves to demonstrate how different social functions and the building types they generate move over time not only across geographical space (as suggested above) but also between different social institutions, whether church, state, kin group, or other social entity. From the eleventh to the sixteenth century, monasteries established in Britain and Ireland moved to the European continent just as other monastic orders arrived in Britain from there. Monasteries provided a space for contemplation but also became central to the medieval economy. Monks ran farms, provided accommodation for travellers, tended the sick, set up schools and created the earliest libraries. When manufacturing was still a domestic activity, monasteries also established some of the earliest factories (Crawford 1990:54). Similarly, in the Spanish conquest of Central and South America, Church institutions and buildings fulfilled a multitude of social, economic and political functions. Elsewhere, mosques built for collective prayer also include *madrasas* for education and courts from which to exercise Islamic law. Models for these buildings move between continents.

Religious buildings act as markers of population movements, cross-cultural trade and social transformation. The oldest British synagogue opened in the City of

London in 1701, almost five decades after the re-establishment of the Jewish community under Cromwell (1656, and following their earlier expulsion in 1290). Britain's first mosque was founded in Cardiff by Yemini Muslim seamen in 1860 and, like others at Liverpool (1887), and London (1924), were based in port cities.[4] The more recent spectacular growth of mosques, Hindu mandirs (temples) and Sikh gurdwaras in Britain (many converted from redundant churches and workplaces) is an outcome of postcolonial South Asian migration from the 1960s, especially for Muslims from Pakistan and Kashmir (Nasser 2006). Registered mosques in Britain have grown from seven in 1961, 400 in 1990 to almost 1,700 in 2007 (Crawford 1990; Gledhill 2007). The earliest Hindu *mandirs* are believed to have opened in Liverpool and Newcastle in 1958; in 2008, some 150 were registered in Britain. Possibly the earliest gurdwara was opened in Putney, London in 1911 (www.bhatra.co.uk), though others appeared in Liverpool and Newcastle in 1958 (Nasser 2006:378). As Nasser writes, 'The mélange of BrAsian communities in Britain, of diverse ethnic, national and religious origins, creates a complex geography of identities which are activated within particular conditions and circumstances and for particular purposes' (ibid.:375). In this case, the 'large-scale conversion of space for religious and cultural use' has depended on the settlement of women and children and the sudden increase in size of congregations' (ibid.:379).

While we can accept that the built environment represents a particular social order, it is in fact *more* than a mere *representation* of it. Rather than merely reflecting that order, physical and spatial urban form (including specific building types) help to constitute much of social and cultural existence. Much of modern social life would be impossible without the existence of specialised, purpose-built buildings, whether power stations, operating theatres, scientific laboratories or schools. The highly evolved levels of the built environments of contemporary civilisation have become essential for human and social reproduction. Social formations at whatever scale, including the global, are to a large extent constituted through the buildings and spaces that they create. And to state the obvious, in a world of grossly uneven development, disparities between rich and poor are both represented and constituted in the physical and spatial built environments of the richer nations and the poorer, as also between richer and poorer classes within them.

THEORISING THE SPACE OF THE GLOBE

A basic problem in attempting to investigate how ideas about building types, generated in particular societies, subsequently circulate around the world is that, for many years, the notion of 'society' was equated with that of the nation-state and this provided the social and territorial boundaries within which most research and scholarship was undertaken. In their 2007 textbook, *Global Sociology*, Cohen and Kennedy list 22 'Global Thinkers' who have taken a more global view of society. However, they do not distinguish between those who address the 'global' as an economic, geopolitical and social framework, such as Wallerstein or Marx, and others, like Foucault or Weber, whom they cite as 'world class' sociologists in terms of intellectual stature. Common to all is their rejection of the nation-state as an adequate unit of analysis for theorising the contemporary global condition. Yet what they also have in common – with two exceptions – is a lack of reference to the agency and meaning of the spatial and built environment in the construction and maintenance of social life.[5]

Ways of thinking about globalisation historically have been suggested by sociologist Roland Robertson (1992), its principal theorist, and historian Anthony Hopkins (2002). Where Hopkins emphasises the non-Western dimensions of globalisation and explores its historical forms and sequences, Robertson concentrates more on the intellectual development of institutions, concepts and ideas. Like Hopkins, he traces the historical path of globalisation through various phases, which he describes in somewhat telegraphic fashion,[6] i.e. the *Germinal Phase*. In Europe from the early fifteenth to the mid-eighteenth century. The incipient growth of national communities. The accentuation of concepts of the individual and ideas about humanity. The heliocentric theory of the world, beginning of modern geography. Spread of the Gregorian calendar. The second, *Incipient Phase*. In Europe, from the mid-eighteenth century to the 1870s. Sharp shift towards the idea of the homogeneous, unitary state; crystallisation of conceptions of formalised international relations. Increases in legal conventions and agencies concerned with international regulation/communication. The third, *Take-Off Phase*, 1870s to mid-1920s. Global conceptions as to the correct idea of 'national society'; thematisation of national and personal identities; inclusion of some non-European societies in 'international society'; sharp increase in number and speed of global forms of communication; development of global competitions – Olympics, Nobel prizes, implementation of World Time and near global adoption of Gregorian calendar. The fourth, *Struggle for Hegemony Phase*. Mid-1920s to 1960s. Establishment of League of Nations, then United Nations. Principle of national independence established. Prospects for humanity sharply focused by the Holocaust and atomic bomb. Crystallisation of (notion of) Third World. The fifth, *Uncertainty Phase*: 1960s to 1990s. Inclusion of Third World and heightening of global consciousness. Moon landing. Number of global institutions increases. End of Cold War. Societies face problems of multiculturality/polyethnicity. Conceptions of individuals made more complex by gender, ethnic and racial considerations. World civil society, citizenship (Robertson 1992:58–9).

As representations of global history differ according to their geocultural origins, Chinese, African or Indian social theorists would doubtless offer different interpretations of such a schema. Nonetheless, we can see how these ideas could be drawn on to construct a more spatially global, urban/built environment history: the development of the national state with its apparatus of physical boundaries, administrative and government buildings, regional and national services materialised in accommodation for the police, postal services; global time institutionalised by railways, airline time-tables; massive stadia engendered by the

Olympic Games; and, today, neo-liberal consumerism met by giant shopping malls, leisure resorts, theme parks, gated enclaves. Notions of multiculturality and polyethnicity materialised in the west by Chinatowns, Londonistans, mosques and *mandirs*. Or Robertson's 'world as a single place', represented not only by inter-linked systems of real and virtual cities, sharing a vast quantum of urban knowledge and also specific *single* institutional buildings (United Nations in New York), or, as a global system of capitalism, the World Bank in Washington.

Yet among these 'global thinkers' insufficient attention is given to the historical structures of imperialism and colonialism (which I discuss elsewhere) and the role played by these two inter-related global forces in establishing the basic physical/spatial infrastructures of present-day globalisation.

NOTES

1   From Anthony D. King, 'Notes towards a global historical sociology of building types', from Michael Guggenheim and Ola Söderström, eds, *Reshaping Cities: How Global Mobility Transforms Architecture and Urban Form*, 2010 © Anthony D. King.
2   My thanks to Tom Markus for his insights here.
3   Dates in brackets are for earliest documented use in the UK from the *Oxford English Dictionary* (1980).
4   Yemeni Muslim sailors working on steamships came from British-colonised Aden in the nineteenth century and settled in various British ports (see Islam and Britain before the twentieth century. www.paklinks.com/gs.religion-scripture/189302-first mosque-built-uk).
5   The primary exceptions are Michel Foucault and David Harvey.
6   I have greatly abbreviated the original list of features in the following phases.

BIBLIOGRAPHY

Abaza, M. (2001) 'Shopping malls, consumer culture and the reshaping of public space in Egypt', *Theory, Culture and Society*, 18, 5: 97–122.

Archer, J. (1997) 'Colonial suburbs in South Asia 1750–1850, and the spaces of modernity', in Roger Silverstone, ed., *Visions of Suburbia*, London and New York: Routledge, pp.26–54.

Archer, J. (2005) *Architecture and Suburbia: From English Villa to American Dream House 1690–2000*, Minneapolis: University of Minnesota Press.

Black, I. (2008) 'Dubai reaches for sky with plan for tallest tower – one kilometre high', *Guardian,* 6 October: 27.

Çelik, Z. (2008) *Empire, Architecture and the City: Ottoman–French Encounters, 1883–1914*, Seattle: University of Washington Press.

Cohen, R. and Kennedy, P. (2007) *Global Sociology*, London: Palgrave Macmillan.

Crawford, David (1990) *British Building Firsts: The First Castle to the First Airport*, Newton Abbot and London: David and Charles.

Foucault, M. (1973) *The Birth of the Clinic*, London: Routledge.

Foucault, M. (1979) *Discipline and Punish: The Birth of the Prison*, New York: Vintage.

Gledhill, R. (2007) 'Thousands of churches face closure in ten years', *Timesonline*, 10 February. www.timesonline.co.uk/tol/comment/faith/article1362709.ece, accessed 5 February 2009.

Hopkins, A.G., ed. (2002) *Globalization in World History*, London: Pimlico.

King, A.D. (1980) *Buildings and Society: Essays on the Social Development of the Built Environment*, London and Boston: Routledge and Kegan Paul.

King, A.D. (1984) *The Bungalow: The Production of a Global Culture*, London: Routledge and Kegan Paul (second edition, with new introductory preface, Oxford University Press 1995).

King, A.D. (1990) *Urbanism, Colonialism and the World-Economy: Cultural and Spatial Foundations of the World Urban System,* London and New York: Routledge.

King, A.D. (2004) *Spaces of Global Cultures: Architecture, Urbanism, Identity*, London and New York: Routledge.

King, A.D. (2006) 'Building, architecture and the new international division of labour', in N. Brenner and R. Keil, eds, *The Global Cities Reader*, London and New York: Routledge, pp.196–202.

Lefebvre, H. (1991) *The Production of Space*, Oxford: Blackwell.

Markus, T.A. (1993) *Buildings and Power: Freedom and Control in the Origin of Modern Building Types*, London and New York: Routledge.

Nasser, N. (2006) 'Metropolitan Borderlands: The Formation of BrAsian Landscapes', in N. Ali, V.S. Kalra and S. Sayid, eds, *A Postcolonial People: South Asians in Britain*, London: Hurst and Co., pp.374–91.

Pieterse, J.N. (2004) *Globalisation and Culture*, Lanham, MD: Rowman and Littlefield.

Robertson, R. (1992) *Globalisation: Social Theory and Global Culture*, London and New Delhi: Sage.

Scarre, C. (1995) *The Penguin Historical Atlas of Ancient Rome*, London: Penguin Books.

Sée, H.E. (1968) *Modern Capitalism*, London: Ayer Publishing, trans. H.B. Vanderblue (first edition 1928).

Upton, D., ed. (1986) *America's Architectural Roots: Ethnic Groups that Built America*, Washington, DC: Preservation Press.

Vale, L. (2008) *Architecture, Power and Identity*, second edition, London and New York: Routledge.

Voigt, W. (1996) 'From the hippodrome to the aerodrome, from the air station to the terminal: European airports 1909–1945', in J. Zukowsky, *Building for Air Travel: Architecture and Design for Commercial Aviation*, New York: Prestel and Art Institute of Chicago, pp.27–50.

Chapter 11: Imperialism and world cities[1]

IMPERIALISM

Examining the relationship of imperialism to world cities depends on how both terms are understood. In its simplest sense, imperialism describes a process by which one state extends its rule, usually by military power, over the territory and population of others, in earlier times, to form a contiguous realm. In modern times, imperialism has more often involved acquiring overseas colonies, the aim being to exploit subjugated populations and extract economic and political advantage. Developing as a term and concept in English especially after 1870, imperialism refers to a phenomenon that originates in the metropole; what happens in the colonies, as a result of imperial control, is colonialism, or neo-colonialism (Loomba 1998). As a corollary, imperial or post-imperial cities are in the metropole, colonial or postcolonial cities in the colony.

More sophisticated interpretations of the term link it to the analysis of capitalist accumulation, the periodisation of capitalism into successive eras and, related to this, the political division of the world into different countries (Weeks 1988). As stated earlier, in the late nineteenth century, world space was dominated by some 16 (mostly European) empires, each with their imperial capital, other major inland and port cities and the marine, land and, eventually, aerial transportation links between them. These disseminated their languages, laws, systems of governance and education, religions, cultures, building and land regulations, architectures and built environments.

WORLD CITIES

While the current interest in world cities as key nodes in the world economy can arguably be traced back to the 1970s, the term itself is much older. In the eighteenth century, the German poet and thinker Goethe used *weldtstadt* to describe the cultural pre-eminence of Paris and Rome (King 1995). In the late nineteenth century, 'world city' was used by the *Illustrated London News* to describe Liverpool as 'the New York of Europe, a world city' (Wilks-Heeg 2003), and in 1915, British planning pioneer Patrick Geddes used the term to refer to 'certain great cities in which a quite disproportionate part of the world's most important business is conducted' (Hall 1984). Expanding substantially on Geddes' interpretation, current use of the term represents the world city as a site for capital accumulation and primarily as a business centre, playing a key role in the inter-linked global economy (Friedmann and Wolff 1982), a site for corporate headquarters, international banks and trading houses, and especially, for the presence of key advanced producer service firms (accountancy, advertising, law, real estate). The identification of major cities in the world as specifically named 'world cities' and their hierarchical ranking according to the presence and quantity of advanced producer service firms in each city, as in the 2008 'Globalisation and World City' roster, has emphasised this economic understanding of the term. Other interpretations add political and cultural criteria, as represented by the presence of international organisations of governance and administration, a minimally large and diverse population, media, communications and publishing activities, museums, theatres, educational facilities, religious sites for pilgrimage and tourism, and the capacity to sponsor global sporting or cultural events. Infrastructural criteria include the existence of a major airport and transport hub. Visual and architectural criteria include the presence of skyscrapers and a distinctive skyline (Wikipedia 2010). In the first phase of research on world city formation (Friedmann and Wolff 1982), some 30 cities were identified and, drawing on world-system language, were located either in 'core' or 'semi-periphery' countries and arranged hierarchically. Given the absence of a single definition, therefore, and especially a universally agreed list of cities, in the remainder of this chapter, unless otherwise indicated, I take the 2008 Globalization and World City (GandWC) roster of cities as a basis for discussing the relationship between world cities and imperialism. In addition to utilising the Greek 'alpha, beta, gamma' to classify different levels of world city status, I shall also refer to different tiers, including fourth and fifth tiers, indicating some level of 'world city' qualities.

IMPERIAL CITIES

Compared to the quantity of published literature on the 'world', 'global' and 'colonial city', that on the 'imperial city' is relatively sparse. By imperial cities, I refer in the first instance to imperial capitals, that is, the imperial metropole and seat of the emperor or empress, although the term can also be applied to other major cities in the imperial realm. One of the few studies on this topic (Driver and Gilbert 1999) focuses on the capitals of some of the large European empires of recent times – London, Paris, Rome (and implicitly, though not discussed, Brussels, Amsterdam, Madrid, Berlin, Lisbon and Vienna), all but one first-tier world cities today (the exception, second-tier Berlin). Also considered in their study are examples of significant 'secondary' imperial cities such as Liverpool, Glasgow, Seville and Marseilles, cities also included in the lower two tiers of the world cities listing. Where the first tier cities were those of imperial decision-making and governance, imperial science and knowledge, imperial culture and symbolism, imperial literature, art and architecture (and also imperial producer services, though this term is of relatively recent use), secondary imperial cities are more those of empire-dependent manufacturing and processing of (especially) 'tropical' commodities such as tobacco (in Britain, Glasgow, Bristol), slaves (Bristol, Liverpool), cotton (Manchester, Glasgow), or in France, phosphates, colonial labour and the site of the 1922 colonial exposition (Marseilles) (Fletcher 1999). Again, all are included in the lower tiers of the world cities list.

The evidence for the level of integration of such cities into the imperial network can be found in many different places, dependent on where we look. At the simplest of levels, imperial network connectivity is manifest culturally, in imperial toponymy: in London, in thoroughfares named for places located throughout the imperial and colonial world – Malabar, Penang, Benares, Lucknow, Kabul, Khyber, Kashmir, Borneo, Gibraltar, Toronto, Rhodesia and many more (King 2004:101); or in Glasgow, Havana, Jamaica, Tobago, Virginia (MacKenzie 1999:224), just as, reciprocally, imperial names designated the streets of colonial cities (King 2004:146 *et seq.*). At a larger scale there are forms of planning, architecture and built environment where colonial port city forms, functions and styles have more in common with the imperial city than they have with those of the colonial inland town; or in the integration of agriculture and industry in a division of labour across the imperial economy, and continuing post-imperial links in banking and elsewhere in the financial sector (King 1990a).

GLOBALISATION AND WORLD CITIES IN HISTORY

Compared to the 1990s, subsequent interpretations of globalisation have done much to correct the initial Eurocentric and ahistorical focus of that process. As discussed elsewhere (King 2004:28) scholars have not only examined globalisation from the viewpoint of countries (and religions, including Islam) outside the West but have also traced earlier, Islamic phases of globalisation, before European hegemony, as well as later ones, including, since 1950, 'postcolonial globalisation' (Hopkins 2002). Despite these theoretical developments, however, the historical origins and later development of what have come to be called world (or global) cities, either individually or in the form of a network or system (Taylor 2004) is still greatly neglected.

The principal aim of this chapter is to argue that not only are the origins of many of today's world or global cities to be found in their imperial and colonial antecedents, but also, to recognise the corollary, that the major European empires – British, French, Spanish, Austro-Hungarian, Portuguese, Dutch, Belgian (and also Ottoman) – energised by capitalism and the adoption of new technologies, have created vast new intercontinental networks which have done much to lay down the foundations for today's globalised world, foundations that are cultural (such as language), institutional (in terms of finance, commerce, law, education, governance), and infrastructural (communications, transport, urban space and function-specific building forms). In the words of empire historian John Darwin, it was 'the ability of Europeans … to draw the commerce of the world into one vast network centred on the port cities of the West … [that] was the main dynamic behind the gradual formation between the 1860s and 1880s of a "world economy" – a single system of trade' (Darwin 2007:237) and eventually 'a single global market' (ibid.:7).

EMPIRES AND STATES

Taken for granted in current research on the world city, many of which are national capitals, is the idea of world space or territory organised as a system of nation-states. The dominance of the nation-state as the principal form of polity in the contemporary world has tended to obscure the importance of historic empires – over 200 of which are conventionally recognised – in the political and spatial organisation of humankind. The fact that three-quarters of these empires were part of the ancient and medieval, rather than modern, worlds does not detract from the importance of modern empires in influencing the state of our contemporary world.

As stated earlier, in Chapter 6, currently, the United Nations recognises some 208 independent nation-states, each with their own national capital. Yet at the end of the eighteenth century, there were only 14 of what today would be accepted as independent nation-states, the increase occurring mainly in the nineteenth and especially late twentieth centuries. In the 30 years between 1959 and 1989, the number of independent states almost doubled, from 84 to 156, following the collapse of different European imperial regimes especially in Asia and Africa. The leap to 208 largely resulted from the dissolution of the USSR. With the world's population now over 50 per cent urban, with vast numbers living in huge cities, we can say that, over the last century, the identities of some populations have been successively determined to different degrees by imperial, national, urban-city, global as well as local identities.

For the purpose of this chapter, the significance of imperialism lies in the impact various empires have had in establishing the infrastructure of present-day globalisation: making use of and modifying existing cities and transport networks, developing institutions and languages, and, often in collaboration with the local population, creating modern cities (Nasr and Volait 2003). While the modern empires are clearly of importance here, a much older, but equally instructive example of the networked infrastructure created by imperialism is that of the Roman Empire (27 BCE to CE 476).

The Roman contribution to the establishment of urban and transportation infrastructure and networks throughout and beyond Europe is unparalleled. Extending from the Mediterranean into Northern Europe, the Middle East and North Africa between 27 BCE and 330 CE, cities were founded from which the new provinces were governed. Fundamental to this new infrastructure were the characteristically straight roads and also the innovatory grid form around which Roman towns were developed. New types of building were introduced, essential for economic and social activity: the forum as a market place, barracks for the soldiers, occasionally a circus or race track for leisure activities; other distinctively Roman innovations included an amphitheatre providing space for gladiatorial displays; in larger towns, baths, theatres and gymnasia helped keep the garrison occupied. In addition to the networked roads linking towns and settlements across both province and empire, greatly encouraging trade and hence enlarging the new cities, vast aqueducts were constructed bringing water to the cities, as at Segovia in Spain or Nimes in France (Scarre 1995).

A major characteristic of imperial space is its reciprocal nature, produced by both centrifugal and centripetal processes. Where people, ideas, language, institutions, building forms and types move outward from the imperial metropole, to be reproduced in often hybridised form in the colony, other ideas and forms are brought back to the metropolitan centre, or get transferred to other nodes in the imperial network. Equally significant is the persistence, over two millennia, of Roman (incorporating Greek) models of urbanism and architecture in the modern world and the architectural elements, language and building typologies which, through different European colonialisms, have been circulated round the world.

Of the European cities included in the GandWC roster, at least 20 of them can be traced to Roman times, if not before. The network of roads which link them together are routes which – in many cases – still determine present-day ground transportation.

IMPERIAL NETWORKS

With the exception of China, which had the highest population, the five largest empires in terms of territory and population in 1900 were those of Britain, Russia, China, France and the USA (Bartholomew 1901:xiv). Theoretically, it would be possible to make the case for the relationship between imperialism and the development of world cities by reference to any modern empire. While the organisation and practices of these various empires clearly differed in many respects, in order to extract the economic surplus from its colonies or provinces, whether grain, metals, timber or labour, imperial governments require a basic urban infrastructure of port cities, docks, inland towns, with accommodation, communications and transport facilities, along with administrative, governance and security personnel and institutions, amongst others. Thus, as part of its modernisation plan from the 1870s, the Ottoman Empire installed the telegraph from their imperial capital of Istanbul throughout its Arab provinces. For military, economic and religious reasons, an extensive railway network was built from Istanbul, their imperial capital (and potential world city), in the north, taking in Beirut and Jerusalem (to become potential world cities) down to Medina in the South. By 1914, this was to extend to Mecca and Jeddah (another potential world city) on the Red Sea (Çelik 2008:29). Along with railway stations, their modernisation programme included hospitals, schools, post offices, barracks, police stations, bridges, schools, and not least, clock towers, providing a (modern) form of time to compete with that coming from the minaret. Following the collapse of the Ottoman Empire, key cities like Beirut and Baghdad were taken over by French and British successors.

The 'first empire' of the French had taken them to North America in the seventeenth century, where they established what were eventually to become what today are the actual or aspiring world cities of Montreal, Quebec, Detroit and Ottawa. In the 'second empire' of the nineteenth and twentieth centuries, the French were to re-develop the Arab cities in their north African colonies of Morocco, Algiers and Tunisia (Wright 1991). Between the 1840s and the early twentieth century, they built a railway along the Mediterranean coast, from Oran and Algiers in the west to Tunis and Bizerte in the east, having annexed Tunisia in the 1860s. In towns and cities along the route they introduced strict grid plans, re-planning city centres, separate from the indigenous city, on which they built a modern urban infrastructure. The square was a key central feature, around which were modern institutions: town hall for a municipal government, post offices, schools, theatres, hospitals. The railway was essential for transferring phosphates, olive oil and other products into the docks and onto the steamships back to France. Ports were re-built and cities re-planned on 'dual city' colonial lines (Çelik 2008). In Morocco, Casablanca formed a major colonial node, and after Moroccan independence, maturing into what is now classified as a world city. Managing the logistics of these extensive new colonies, millions of French men and women migrated to France's North African possessions. Across the world, Saigon (now Ho Chi Minh City) and Hanoi were France's key colonial cities, totally re-modelled as modern cities (Wright 1991), each today classed as 'world cities'.

IMPERIALISM AND RELIGION

The connection between imperialism and religion has been a major force affecting the development of both imperial as well as world cities. Throughout history, emperors and imperial governments – whether Roman, Arab, Spanish or British – have allied with religious institutions, appropriating their values, resources and practices to found cities, and within these, construct spectacular religious buildings – cathedrals, mosques, temples, but also schools, hospitals, madrasas. As a powerful force for social cohesion as well as social conflict, bestowing identity and transforming social practices, religion has also provided mechanisms for the division and ordering of territory, from provinces to parishes. In established or aspiring world cities, the promotion or defence of particular religious identities has, for decades, if not longer, been the defining force in the city's space and politics, for example, in Belfast, Jerusalem, Beirut, Rome, Mumbai, Istanbul, Baghdad and Tehran. Religious conflict or cooperation have been key factors affecting a city's economic and political stability, influencing its claims to function as a node in the world economy. Different religious beliefs and practices have influenced economic transactions, governed the nature of interest rates, affected the accumulation of capital, hours and days of work and the nature of property ownership.

WORLD AND IMPERIAL CITIES

Is there further evidence to support the hypothesis that imperialism was a major factor in establishing many of what today we designate as world cities, not only individually, but also as part of an integrated network? If we take the 2008 GandWC roster as our database, we can see that, of the 40 alpha world cities, 15 of them (mostly in Europe) at one time or another have been imperial capitals; a further 18 have, at various recent points in time, been major colonial cities, populated and administered as part of a larger empire (whether British, French, Dutch, Spanish, Portuguese or Ottoman). The imperial and colonial histories of these 33 cities, all part of one or more larger networks, would doubtless also help to explain why, already over a century ago, most of them were among the world's largest 80 cities (Bartholomew 1901:xiv).

If we widen the net to accommodate beta and gamma categories to make 128 cities in all, some additional 55 colonial cities could be included.[2] That is, roughly two-thirds of 128 cities have some kind of imperial or colonial connection to at least one imperial network. In 1901, for those wishing to travel from the UK around these networks, a table of 126 'Travel Routes All Over the World', indicating port of departure (Southampton, Liverpool, London, Marseilles, Hamburg, New York, San Francisco and others), shipping lines, destination (from Accra to Zanzibar), distance in miles, and duration of journey (in days) was easily available – if not yet on the internet – but in standard respected atlases (Bartholomew 1901:xiv).

In the early days of world city research in the late 1980s, I attempted (using UN and World Bank data sets) to predict the development of what Friedmann (1986:72) called 'basing points for capital' in countries of the 'semi-periphery', surmising they could become world cities by the year 2000. The criteria chosen to identify these 'third' or 'fourth order' world cities, to use Friedmann's classifications at that time, included (a) state policies oriented towards, or not opposed to market oriented growth; (b) a minimum country population size of 15 million providing potential market growth; (c) the largest city in the country to have a minimum size of one million, providing a potential market for consumer goods. In the case of states with large populations (India, China), more than one world city was likely to develop (d) a continuous average growth rate between 1965 and 1985 in the region of 1 per cent. The list compiled related only to the World Bank's 'middle-income' and 'low income' countries and did not include 'industrial market economies' in Europe (King 1990b:51–2). On the basis of the 2008 GandWC roster, 16 out of the 17 predictions proved to be accurate (Shanghai, Tientsin, Jakarta, Kuala Lumpur, Calcutta, Bombay (now Mumbai), Delhi, Karachi, Colombo, Istanbul, Cairo, Casablanca, Lagos, Nairobi, Bogota, Lima). The one exception was Tehran, unsurprisingly, given the unstable political and religio-cultural circumstances which have persisted and which had already been stated in the original listing of 1990. What all these 17 cities, national or regional centres, had in common, however, is that all were either strongly influenced by (especially) Western colonialism, were direct colonial products or, in the case of China, colonial 'free ports' (or in the case of Istanbul, a major imperial city).

Among the many factors which might explain this outcome is less the presence in these cities of advanced producer services at that time (about which, little is known) but rather the underlying infrastructures necessary for those services: international language knowledge, education, availability of local and expatriate skilled manpower, business connections to the metropole, transnational banks and offices, among others.

IMPERIAL TO WORLD CITY

The reciprocal growth between imperial capital and its overseas empire and its maturation into a world city is best illustrated by the historical development of London (see King 1990b, from which this much condensed account is taken). The expansion of British military, naval and trading power in the Caribbean and North America and profits from slavery, sugar and tobacco did much to establish an infrastructure for an overseas trading economy in the late seventeenth century. Merchants in this trade were behind the establishment of Lloyd's Insurance (1687), a Stock Exchange (1670s) and the Bank of England (1694). Simultaneously, trade with the east had been stimulated by the East India Company (founded 1600). Conquests in India and the Caribbean in the mid-eighteenth century and the boom in the Atlantic economy boosted London's role as the largest centre of international trade, demanding extensive new docks 50 years later. Between 1750 and 1910 (the highpoint of British imperial power) London remained the world's largest city. As trade grew, the city was already a world financial centre by 1815, boosted by the Industrial Revolution and with capital flowing into overseas investment. Between 1815 and 1925, over 25 million people emigrated from the British Isles, ten million of them to British possessions, especially Canada, Australia and South Africa. Between 1808 and 1900, the growth in overseas trade attracted dozens of foreign (including colonial) banks, from, among others, Hong Kong, Australia, New Zealand, the Middle East, Canada, Ottoman Empire, France, Switzerland, Germany, Italy, Belgium, Russia, the USA and Japan. The 1861 Census recorded some 29,000 people working in the City, mainly merchants, bankers, stock and commercial brokers, accountants, commercial clerks, the predecessors, in some cases, of workers in advanced producer services firms of today (King 1990b:79). By 1900 London already had a substantial multicultural population. In the words of novelist H.G. Wells, London was 'the richest city in the world, the biggest port, the greatest manufacturing town, the Imperial city – the centre of civilization, the heart of the world' (Wells 1908:73). In the late nineteenth century, Britain's empire had been extended by one-third, with new colonies in Southeast Asia, Southern, Central and West Africa, South America, South Asia and Hong Kong. New buildings were provided for an expanded Foreign Office, Colonial Office, and India Office; institutions for scientific research and education were established in the Imperial College of Science and Technology; a School of Hygiene and Tropical Medicine (1899) and later, a School of Oriental (and subsequently) African Studies catered for the needs of colonial cadres. New centrally located institutions dedicated to the interests of particular colonies – Australia House, India House, Canada House, Africa House – were established in the 1920s. The British Empire Exhibition of 1924 provided the country's first national sport stadium at Wembley.

The transformation of London from imperial to post-imperial, international and, subsequently, world and global city, following the mid-twentieth century demise of empire, is most evident in its cosmopolitan, multicultural population where half the country's ethnic minority population lives in London, where it forms over one-quarter of the city's population and speaks over 300 languages. Along with cosmopolitan educational and cultural sectors – museums, universities, libraries, theatres, research institutes, stadiums, architectural and festive spectacles – a bloated financial services industry, including banking, insurance, real estate, law, accountancy, once providing the infrastructure for maintaining an empire, now, massively expanded, serves the interests of a capitalist world economy.

NOTES

1   From Anthony D. King, 'Imperialism and world cities', from Ben Derudder, Michael Hoyler, Peter J. Taylor, and Frank Witlox, eds, *International Handbook of Globalisation and World Cities*, 2012 © Edward Elgar.
2   Including those developed in the USA after 1776 and being ultimately dependent on the colonial origins of the state.

BIBLIOGRAPHY

Bartholomew, J.G. (c.1901) *Twentieth Century Citizen's Atlas of the World*, London: George Newnes.

Çelik, Zeynep (2008) *Empire, Architecture and the City: Ottoman–French Encounters, 1883–1914*. Seattle: University of Washington Press.

Cohen, Robin and Kennedy, Paul (2007) *Global Sociology*, Basingstoke: Palgrave Macmillan.

Darwin, John (2007) *After Tamerlane: The Rise and Fall of Global Empires 1400–2000*, Oxford: Oxford University Press.

Driver, Felix and Gilbert, David (1999) *Imperial Cities: Landscape, Display and Identity*, Manchester: Manchester University Press.

Fletcher, Y.S. (1999) '"Capital of the colonies": real and imagined boundaries between metropole and empire in 1920s Marseilles', in F. Driver and D. Gilbert, *Imperial Cities: Landscape, Display and Identity*, Manchester: Manchester University Press, pp.136–55.

Friedmann, J. (1986) 'The world city hypothesis', *Development and Change*, 17, 1: 69–84.

Friedmann, J. and Wolff, G. (1982) 'World city formation: an agenda for research and action', *International Journal of Urban and Regional Research*, 6, 3: 309–44.

GandWC (2008) 'The world according to GandWC'. www.lboro.ac.uk/gawc/woeld2008t. html.

Hall, Peter (1984) *The World Cities*, London: Weidenfeld and Nicolson.

Hopkins, A.G., ed. (2002) *Globalization in World History*, London: Pimlico.

King, Anthony D. (1990a) *Urbanism, Colonialism and the World-Economy: Cultural and Spatial Foundations of the World Urban System*, London and New York: Routledge.

King, Anthony D. (1990b) *Global Cities: Post-imperialism and the Internationalization of London*, London and New York: Routledge.

King, A.D. (1995) 'Representing world cities: cultural theory/social practice', in Paul K. Knox and Peter J. Taylor, eds, *World Cities in a World-System*, Cambridge: Cambridge University Press.

King, Anthony D. (2004) *Spaces of Global Cultures: Architecture Urbanism Identity*, London and New York: Routledge.

King, A.D. (2006) 'Building, architecture and the new international division of labour', in Neil Brenner and Roger Keil, eds, *The Global Cities Reader*, London and New York: Routledge, pp.196–202.

Loomba, Anita (1998) *Colonialism/Postcolonialism*, London and New York: Routledge.

MacKenzie, J.M. (1999) 'The second city of the Empire: Glasgow – imperial municipality', in F. Driver and D. Gilbert, *Imperial Cities: Landscape, Display and Identity*, Manchester: Manchester University Press, pp.215–38.

Nasr, Joe and Mercedes Volait (2003) *Urbanism: Imported or Exported? Native Aspirations and Foreign Plans*, Chichester: Wiley-Academic.

Scarre, C. (1995) *The Penguin Historical Atlas of Ancient Rome*, London: Penguin Books.

Taylor, Peter J. (2004) *Global City Network*, London: Routledge.

Weeks, J. (1988) 'Imperialism and world market', in Tom Bottomore, *A Dictionary of Marxist Thought*, Oxford: Blackwell, pp.223–7.

Wells, H.G. (1908) *Tono-Bungay*, London: Odhams Press.

Wilks-Heeg, S. (2003) 'From world city to pariah city? Liverpool and the global economy', in R. Munck, ed., *Reinventing the City? Liverpool in Comparative Perspective*, Liverpool: Liverpool University Press, pp.36–52.

Wright, Gwen (1991) *The Politics of Design in French Colonial Urbanism*, Chicago: Chicago University Press.

Chapter 12: Imperialism and the Grand Hotel: case studies of colonial modernities[1]

NAMES AND NUMBERS

In Murray's *Handbook to Switzerland* for 1904 the final 50 pages display some 200 advertisements for hotels, about a quarter of them called 'Grand Hotel', either *tout court* or otherwise qualified according to location (Grand Hotel Algiers, Grand Hotel Beirut), ethnic patronage (Victoria, d'Angleterre) or other criteria. There are 'Grand Hotels' of one kind or another in Algiers, Andermatt, Arles, Arosa, Bonn, Brussels, Constantine, Constantinople, Frankfurt, Menton, Nantes, Palermo, Poitiers, Rouen, Taormina, Zurich, among many other places.

While this might tell us something about the popularity of this term (English/ French) and the extent to which it had, by the early twentieth century, become completely internationalised, or even the degree to which the 'grand hotel', as a particular *type* of building, had become an essential component of the modern European and, via imperialism, Middle Eastern or North African city, none of these names tell us what a 'grand hotel' actually *is* (or *was*). Is it primarily – with capitals – a proper name? A mere description? A specialised category of building? Or all of these?

'Hotel', of course, is a type of building defined primarily by its function, i.e. for the temporary accommodation of travellers.[2] The adjective 'grand' in 'grand hotel' incorporates two inter-related meanings: large, in terms of building scale and number of rooms, and spectacular, in terms of architectural style, luxurious fittings and overall splendour. The eponymously named 'Grand Hotel' (or the descriptive term or category 'grand hotel') referred in the late nineteenth century to a specialised building form or type, with 100–500 or more bedrooms, innovative technologies, electricity throughout (after 1880), baths and telephones in each room, steam heating, pneumatic lifts, lavish furnishings and frequently adjacent to the railway station (Markus 1993).[3] The grand hotel of this kind originated in Paris in the mid-1850s. Subsequently, nine 'Grand Hotels', named as such, were built in the imperial metropole of England between 1864 and 1905, the majority located along the south coast, the remainder in coastal locations elsewhere. Their access to 'sea air' announced their leisure and pseudomedical functions; their location by the railway, their dependence on industrialised transport; their patronage, the new bourgeoisie spawned by industrial capitalism and the revolution in levels of consumption. Other grand hotels in the imperial capital of London, some with historically prestigious names – Savoy, Grosvenor, Langham – served the aristocracy, new bourgeois business and political classes, foreign tourists and travellers, and the female patrons of the new department stores.

The grand hotel was one of many new building types generated in Europe by the revolutionary changes of capitalist industrialisation. In Berlin, Germany's imperial capital, the five-storey Grand Hotel, with 185 rooms, was built in 1884, situated on the corner of Berlin's most prestigious square, the Alexanderplatz. The more luxurious Kaiserhof, 260 rooms, electricity throughout, baths and telephones in every room, had been completed five years earlier. Along with the Central Hotel (1879–80) these three new facilities had added some 500–600 hotel rooms to the city in the space of ten years, confirming the capital's increasingly 'modern' role as international conference or convention centre.

If we need further proof of this, months after the Grand Hotel was completed, the hotels were to host the leading statesmen (and their retinues) of the Great Powers of Europe, the United States and Ottoman Empire, at the infamous 'Congo Congress' of November 1884, concluding the so-called 'Partition of Africa' which sliced up the African continent between them.[4]

In these years, the spatial expansion of Berlin's built environment was to mirror, on a smaller scale, the overseas territorial expansion of Germany's empire; not in the form of offices, monuments or urban design, as in Europe's other imperial capitals (e.g. London, Brussels, Lisbon, Rome – see Driver and Gilbert 1999) but, in these hotels, in less obvious ways. As Bismarck was bent on expanding Germany's colonial empire – creating export markets, accessing raw materials, finding investment opportunities[5] – we can speculate about the number of *gescheftsleute* gathering in these Berlin hotels to lobby members of the government.

These, of course, are speculations. But it is by this circuitous route that I arrive at the main aim of this chapter – to explore the relationship between European (and especially British) imperialism and the worldwide spread of the grand hotel. How have British imperial policies influenced the building of grand hotels in different parts of the imperial world? What have been the social and spatial consequences? What can these case studies tell us about the factors affecting the development of local social, cultural or behavioural modernities? How do the functions of colonial grand hotels differ from those in the metropole? I shall pursue these and other questions through a series of case studies.

IMPERIALISM AND THE GRAND HOTEL

The half-century which saw the introduction in Europe and subsequent worldwide spread of the 'grand hotel' (1865–1914) was also one in which Europe's 'new imperialism' reached its peak. The largest European overseas empires in terms of territory were those of Britain, France, Germany, Netherlands, Portugal, Spain and Italy (Hobson 1938/1965:23). Though any of these empires would offer opportunities to explore these questions, I confine this chapter to a consideration of British imperialism, the reach of which expanded significantly during this period, especially into East and South Africa, South and Southeast Asia, Upper Burma, and the Hong Kong Territories.

The new luxury hotels of the *fin de siècle* were both part and also symbol of the transformation in the built environment linked to a marked expansion in the world economy, a phrase increasingly in use from the 1870s: the expansion in international and intercontinental travel (including the opening of the Suez Canal); the rapid growth of international trade; high levels of foreign direct investment, the development of an international financial system based on bills of exchange, the emergence of the precursors of modern-day multinational companies, and the massive growth of intercontinental migration, mostly to the colonies and especially from the 1880s, and the growth of the international economy, driven by a British colonial mode of production (Wilks-Heeg 2003:37–8). If these were some of the economic and sociocultural forces behind the diffusion of the grand hotel idea to British colonies worldwide, where were these and how did their functions and design differ from those 'at home'?

I have argued elsewhere (King 1990:138–50) that, between 1800 and 1900, there was established round the world a British colonial urban system, largely consisting of colonial port cities and inland towns which, in many cases, were based on pre-existing indigenous settlements, and encompassing some 60 major urban locations. This system was part of a distinctive international division of labour which, in turn, was part of a larger world economy.

> What is significant about these cities and towns is that their built and spatial
> environments (as well as other phenomena) began to have more in common
> with each other than each had with the economically, politically and culturally
> very different environments of the interior of the countries and continents where
> such ports and towns were located.

> (King 1990:140)

For at least half of these towns and cities, there was, by the first decade of the twentieth century, a grand hotel, in many cases with standards of comfort, technology and services comparable with those of the metropole, and especially when compared with local provision.[6] By the end of the nineteenth century it was possible for upper middle-class tourists, colonial administrators, merchants, writers and others to travel round the empire without leaving the comforts of home. As one observer writes about Cairo, grand hotels were 'outposts of Europe planted on Egyptian soil' (Humphreys 2012:15).[7] Grand hotels offered their clients what they were accustomed to, whether the latest copies of *The Times*, or European doctors and nurses (ibid.). Like McDonald's today, they took the risk out of the strange and unexpected.

Yet the colonial grand hotel was very different from that at home. To begin with, its location was often at some distance from the indigenous settlement. The attraction of hill stations in India, built for the British, was not only the absence of the intolerable heat of the plains but also the relative absence of the indigenous population. Where space in the metropolitan hotel was used to maintain divisions of class, in the colony it was primarily to mark divisions of race. For the British living in the colonies, the grand hotel was primarily a place of refuge, a place to relax, let one's hair down, and especially, be at home with others of a similar race, class and culture. The same was true of the French in Vietnam, for whom the hotel in the highlands was 'a little piece of France', a 'decompression chamber' for people living in the tropics, a space of 'multiple escapes' (Jennings 2003:168).

Writing of colonial hotel culture in India some two decades after Independence, the eminent Indian scholar, journalist and historian K.M. Panikkar states:

> Social life was, of course, exclusive, and from hotels and even from certain parks, unwritten rules excluded Indians…. The Europeans in India, however long they lived there, remained strangers in the country. An unbridgeable chasm existed between them and the people…. They lived in two countries, Anglo-India and India, and the two never met. The one governed the other.
>
> (Panikkar 1965)

Around the *fin de siècle* these large, visually over-powering hotels extended European cultural space further into the Anglo-Indian colonial landscape. For the British coming from the metropole, they functioned largely as platforms, or springboards, into an unfamiliar environment. As the newcomers stepped off the boat into a hot, humid and apparently chaotic cultural environment, the familiar classical architecture was reassuring, helping to maintain the illusion that the visitors were still relatively close to 'Home'. Though part of private rather than public (i.e. government) space, the hotels also acted in some way as 'tools of empire' (Headrick 1981), part of the infrastructure of the colonial state. The environs, whether tropical gardens, interior decor or even each individual solar topee, were props to help residents maintain their racially constructed identities – as white, British, generally male and middle class. Both for coloniser and colonised, the architecture exuded a form of 'soft power', a way of asserting superiority, a constant reminder of who was in charge. For senior government servants and military officers (and increasingly their wives and children), they provided accommodation, services and sociability similar to what they were accustomed to. In the large cities, the new hotels offered, in addition to the Indian fare, their own versions of a European cuisine, games and social rooms, tennis courts, occasionally, a library. While each hotel had its own social life and personnel (Peleggi 2012:140), from menials to managers, together they represented a microcosm of colonial society. They also acted as a welcome alternative to the up-country circuit houses and dak bungalows which for long had provided an 'exclusive' space bubble for Europeans travelling inland.

In all cases, location was critical: how close or distant from the railway station, the 'native city', the army cantonment or the nearest hill station. Not least, following the opening of the Suez Canal in 1869 and the increasingly comfortable steamships that began to come through, these new hotels catered for the growing numbers of tourists for which publishers Karl Baedecker and James Murray provided their now well-established guide books. As Peleggi writes, 'the age of high imperialism furnished the political stability, material infrastructure and ideological superstructure that allowed upper-class Europeans and Americans to tour Asia in safety, comfort and self-assuredness' (2012:124). By 1900, Thomas Cook had offices in Bombay, Calcutta, Colombo, Rangoon, Hong Kong and Yokohama (ibid.).

What the often European-owned hotels represented was the essential *mobility* of colonial life – the displacement of civilian and military personnel between metropole and colony and in the latter, between different stations. For those in civil society, it was an 'exclusive' place which reproduced the institutions, sociability and customary activities they knew. Like the club, the grand hotel offered exclusive spaces for male bonding; billiards, smoking rooms and drinks at the (often men-only) bar; later, the more luxurious hotels provided women with separate rooms for dressing, conversation and writing; for both sexes there were parties and dances. Also like the club, it was also a place for gossip, comparing notes, chance encounters. In locations where racial mixing was possible, it could also be a place to do business with the indigenous elite, resolve political or economic disputes and build social relationships. Where 'European-style' accommodation and bathroom facilities for high-status visitors were unavailable, or where they lacked the necessary status symbols, a hotel was built to provide them. But where, in the metropole, access to the exclusive standards of the grand hotel was mainly a matter of money, in the colonies it was also governed by unwritten rules of race and class. As Hobsbawm writes in *The Age of Empire* (1989:71):

> The sense of superiority which united the western whites, rich, middle-class and poor, did so not only because all of them enjoyed the privileges of the ruler, especially when actually in the colonies. In Dakar or Mombasa the most modest clerk was a master, and accepted as a 'gentleman' by people who would not even have noticed his existence in Paris or London; the white worker was a commander of blacks. But even where ideology insisted on at least potential equality, it was dissolved into domination.

THE GRAND HOTEL IN INDIA

The front cover of the *Indian Year Book* for 1930, published by *The Times of India*, carries an advertisement for Bombay's 'Hotel Majestic':

> Situated in the hub of Bombay, yet exclusive, and hospitable. Noted for its cuisine, faultless service, Cabaret and Dance Orchestra.

The key term here is 'exclusive'. A sense of the 'exclusive' nature of European colonial culture implicit in this advert can be found in the names of other hotels recommended in the Year Book, addressed, as its contents make clear, to Europeans/British in India. All are located in some 40 Indian towns and cities where Europeans (government officials, business people, tourists) were living. Significantly, the most common signifier is 'Grand Hotel', to be found either in India's principal cities (Bombay (now Mumbai), Calcutta (now Kolkata), Allahabad, Ahmedabad, Gwalior) or, equally prominently, in the Himalayan hill stations (Simla, the government's official summer capital, Darjeeling, Mussoorie, and Naini Tal). And if not the 'Grand' there were other prestigious and aristocratically named hotels to appeal to the socially 'exclusive' consciousness of the English traveller – the Cecil, Hotel de Paris, Clarendon, Metropole, West End, Regent, Continental, Great Eastern, Park, Golf Links, Hamilton, Burlington, Royal, Rugby, Savoy, Connaught, Napier, among others (only two of the recommended hotels bore Indian (place) names). As elsewhere in the colonial world, the hotel – grand or more modest – was a site of, and means for establishing, and also maintaining, social, spatial and racial segregation.

It didn't take long before the idea, and more especially, the material reality, of the grand hotel to travel from metropole to colony. The design, size and clientele of each hotel depended largely on its location. And though Calcutta, India's capital, with over one and a half million population in 1900, was colonial India's largest city, it was in Bombay – nearer to the West, the largest port, and main industrial and, especially textile, business centre – where the idea of the grand hotel, or an early version of it, took root in India.

'Watson's Hotel' was a (literal) transcontinental transplant. The building's cast-iron frame, designed and fabricated in England, was shipped to Bombay and then erected with the help of local Indian architects. Five storeys high, with 130 guest rooms around a central atrium, Watson's was built in the early 1860s and opened, to 'Whites Only', in 1863. To make patrons feel more at home, English waitresses were employed in the dining room. Later fitted with electricity, Watson's was long known as India's leading hotel.

Where Watson's was near the waterfront, Calcutta's Grand Hotel was in the city centre. Located, like the (Europeans only) Bengal Club, on the prestigious Chowringhee Road in 1887, it had three storeys and 500 rooms. With its pillared entrance and classical facade, its proximity to legislative offices, banks, and the Chamber of Commerce, gave the Grand the appearance of a government building.Much larger than Watson's was the Taj Mahal Hotel, opened in 1903 and located on a spectacular site facing the Gateway of India. It is said that the Parsi industrialist and philanthropist Jamsetji Tata was prompted to build the Taj Hotel after being refused, as a non-White, entry to Watson's. The Taj, with 350 rooms on six storeys, made extensive use of imported technology. Designed by a firm of Indian architects in the Indo-Saracenic style (invented by the British to project a more user-friendly image to local elites – Metcalf, 1989) and completed by an English engineer, it was the first hotel in India to install a steam elevator, imported from Germany, and electric fans from America. English butlers were employed.

While the conditions giving rise to grand hotels in both metropole and colony were clearly linked, there were also striking differences. In England, the growth of travel had been the result of a rapidly expanding economy, the improvement of roads and vehicles and, from the 1840s, the rapid expansion of the railway. Escaping from smoke-polluted towns and the growing practice of sea-bathing encouraged the development of seaside resorts. By the early 1800s, large purpose-built hotels, on three or four storeys, had already been established in these resorts (as also in America: Berger 2011). These paved the way for the more spectacular 'grand hotels' of the later 1860s, built primarily for consumption and leisure and also absorbing some of the social functions of the earlier clubs and assembly rooms (Markus 1993).Their multi-storey height and increased number of rooms was made possible by developments in cast iron and concrete structural frames, hydraulic lifts, sanitation improvements (water closets, baths, showers), telephones and other advances in communication technology (Markus 1993:165; Pevsner 1976).

In India, however, the development of railways from the 1850s was, initially, a result of the country's dependent status: when introduced, the building of railways was driven by a military logic, the new technology enabling troops to be rushed to places of civil unrest. For the native population, travel was much more restricted, motivated as much by religious as economic factors. Pilgrimage to religious sites was a long-established tradition and, where pilgrims and other travellers rested overnight, it was either in the *dharmsala*, a religious sanctuary or rest house provided as part of religious obligations, or the *serai*, for travellers and caravans, although by the early twentieth century Indian hotels were becoming more common. It was, however, political developments in British India that provided a third site for the development of the grand hotel. In 1911, the colonial government moved India's capital from Calcutta to Delhi. Locational factors are key to understanding where the grand hotel would be built and who would be its residents.

LOCATION, LOCATION, LOCATION: MAKING COLONIAL MODERNITIES – DELHI 1890–1940

As Delhi was not India's capital until 1911, it was a late-comer in making hotel provision for the military, tourists and governing elite. When eventually built, the city's first grand hotel was to reinforce a colonial urban geography determined by India's first War of Independence of 1857. Maidens Hotel, opened by the two English Maiden brothers in 1894, was situated among the sprawling colonial bungalows in the shady and bucolic Civil Station, next to the equally spacious military Cantonment, seven miles from the over-crowded, insanitary and crumbling city of Old Delhi. Apparently prompted by the impending Coronation Durbar, the hotel was refurbished and reopened in 1903. This tripartite pattern, of old city,

Cantonment and Civil Station, was to provide the setting for other grand hotels in India (such as Clarke's or the Hotel de Paris in Benares). Hosagrahar (2006) shows how, in the later nineteenth century, some of the old city's more educated residents gradually adopted western habits and moved into bungalows alongside the British. For members of this Indian urban elite, the Civil Station's European residents became models of modernity which they wished to emulate.

Widely considered 'the best hotel in Delhi', Maidens catered primarily for officers of the British Raj. Its architecture reproduced the dominant tropical classicism of Lutyens' New Delhi – balustrades, white, and on a grand scale with high-ceilinged rooms. However, despite the limited entry of the Indian elite into the neighbourhood, a 1908 coded advert leaves a strong impression that the hotel's 'exclusive' English identity really meant social and racial exclusion. Under 'Maidens Metropolitan Hotel' it reads 'An Experienced Englishman (the proprietor) controls this hotel.' With a nod towards indigenous facilities (or the lack of them), the hotel's 'specialities' are listed as 'Cleanliness ... Wholesome food' and the fact that the hotel occupied 'the best situation in Delhi' (doubtless because it was seven miles from the native city and directly '(o)pposite the club') , which, like all such colonial clubs in India, was for exclusive European use.

Maidens Hotel retained its exclusive reputation for some years. Architect Edwin Lutyens stayed there, supervising New Delhi's development. The extent to which the values of what were once known as colonial oppressors have been absorbed by the present owners is evident in the hotel's online marketing:

> Maidens Hotel oozes colonial charm ... classical rooms and large suites, spacious with high ceilings and unique when compared to the box-like rooms of modern hotels ... all colonial charm and architecture, set amidst eight acres of lush gardens.

NEW DELHI AND THE GRAND IMPERIAL HOTEL

India's new capital provided the opportunity for the city's 'first luxurious grand hotel'. The suggestion came from the Viceroy in 1936, the name, the Imperial Hotel, from the Viceroy's wife. With 233 rooms and located on the city's central boulevard (today, Janpath), the hotel's architecture was 'a mix of Victorian, old colonial and Art Deco', as hybrid as the elitist Westernised culture it cultivated. Weekly dances were held in the ballroom and, given its patronage, it is unsurprising that it specialised in Western cuisine (including alcohol). As Peleggi suggests (2012:135) the restaurant is 'a foundational institution of European modernity' and the consumption of alcohol, a key marker of identity. As for 'exclusivity', social status was privileged over race. According to a contemporary account in 2012, the Imperial, 'the most luxurious hotel in Delhi', was 'the place where an anglicized elite like civil servants, army men and Indian princes socialised'. Patrons invested status in the building just as the building lent status to the patrons. Here, in 1946, Nehru, Gandhi, and Jinha met with Viceroy Mountbatten to discuss the partition of

India and creation of Pakistan. Today, as at Maidens, the hotel's colonial past has been commodified: the extensive display of colonial memorabilia includes late eighteenth century art works by Thomas and William Daniells (1749–1840 and 1769–1837), the first European artists to bring back to Britain contemporary idealised representations of India.

As the new city developed after 1911, other, less prestigious, hotels were built in New Delhi, each catering primarily for either an indigenous or European clientele and situated in the appropriate area of the city. Separate provision for members of each culture was sufficiently taken for granted for (tourist) guides at the time to list those hotels 'under European management' and others, 'under Indian management' (King 1976:259).

Grand hotels such as the Imperial imperceptibly became a stage for trying out new values, behaviours and social practices. Amongst the indigenous elite, different styles of behaviour were increasingly adopted for different situations. One, suited to the 'traditional' environment, involved the wearing of loose-fitting, traditional dress, sitting cross-legged on the floor, eating with the fingers, consuming traditional Indian food. The other, appropriate for the 'modern' Western or European environment of New Delhi's hotels, involved the wearing of tight-fitting European dress, sitting on chairs, at a table, eating with specialised cutlery, consuming unaccustomed forms of food and participating in new types of behaviour. Simultaneously, members of the European community adopted local foods and absorbed into their vocabulary a rich array of Indian terms (King 1976).

PENANG, SINGAPORE, HONG KONG: THE GRAND HOTEL IN FAR AND SOUTH EAST ASIA

Safeguarding the sea links between the metropole and India was for long Britain's main motivation for extending its colonial empire, especially in Southeast Asia (Porter 1975). Penang had been acquired by treaty with the local sultan in 1786, safeguarding the route to China and acting as Britain's first commercial entrepot in the region. For similar reasons, the British took Singapore in 1819 and also acquired Malacca from the Dutch by treaty (ibid.). Occupying Malaya was justified by the need to keep the sea route free from pirates. In 1867 the Colonial Office in London took over from the India Office what had by then become the British Straits Settlement (Penang, Malacca and Singapore). The strategy was to make treaties with the different Malay states, as in India, with an official 'British Resident' in each place. However, by the late 1880s, the status of 'protected state' soon became real occupation and real government (Porter 1975:197). Hostility between the French and British was behind the British occupation of Upper Burma, which, in 1885, was incorporated into British India.

With the opening of the Suez Canal and the arrival of steamships, travel to East Asia took on a degree of luxury. Penang became a major emporium for merchants, missionaries and wealthy tourists, especially from America. The building of big hotels, therefore, was to follow the flag. Here, the legendary

Sarkies brothers, economic refugees from Armenia, played a major role in developing the hotel trade.

Originally from Isfahan, the four entrepreneurs were instrumental in bringing the notion of the 'grand hotel' to 'Far' and South East Asia. Between 1884 and the late 1920s, they built and managed nine major hotels in the most prominent cities in the region (possibly the first hotel chain); the Eastern, in Georgetown, Penang (1884), and also the Oriental (1885), were later combined as the Eastern and Oriental in 1885. This was equipped to the highest standards of London's grand hotels with 100 rooms, 40 with adjoining bathrooms, hot and cold water and individual telephones in each room. The most famous, the Raffles Hotel of Singapore (1887), noted particularly for its acceptance of guests from all races, had electricity throughout. The Strand, in Yangon, the Burmese capital, on the other hand, was 'exclusively white' and, like most of these hotels, its patrons mainly male. A second hotel in Singapore, the Sea View, originally built in 1906, was reopened in 1923, and the Crag Hotel on Penang Hill, in 1929. A cousin managed the Hotel Oranje in the Dutch colonial town of Surabaya, opened in 1911.

From the 1870s to 1931, when the last brother died and the business collapsed, the Sarkies were to have a major influence on colonial grand hotel culture in South East Asia. The extent of cultural change they helped introduce is suggested by a Sarkies boast that one of their hotels had 'the largest ballroom in Asia'. As members of a diasporic community, they were ethnically, culturally and politically neutral figures between the colonial British and the local population. They were also astute operators in the ethnically mixed environment of the region. With extensive business experience, their success doubtless benefited from their close family connections.

Towards the end of the century, major colonial industries such as tin mines, tea and rubber plantations attracted increasing numbers of Europeans to the region. The new hotels provided much needed social life, including music and ballroom dancing. Yet as hotel guests were predominantly male, there was a serious shortage of dancing partners, partially resolved in Malaya by the appearance of young Chinese and Eurasian women enrolled by the hotels as 'taxi-girls', partners-for-a fee, half of which was taken by the hotel. The 'promiscuous sociability' promoted by some hotels meant that they became 'well established in the public imagination as ideal locations for adulterous rendezvous' (Peleggi 2012:141), with leisure sites catering for different social strata.

Other major hotels were established in the region. British exports of opium from India to China had led to the so-called 'opium wars', resulting in a decisive defeat of China. The ensuing Treaty of Nanking in 1842 obliged China to hand over Hong Kong, to become a major trading base in the region (Porter 1975). Here, the Astor House Hotel, supposedly the first Western hotel in China, was opened in 1856, the prestigious 'Astor' adopted from the New York hotel of the same name. Sold to an English buyer in 1861, the hotel had a 12-table billiard room and, in 1882, was the first hotel in China to have electricity, piped water and opium on room service. In the late 1880s, it was described as 'a landmark of the white man … for foreigners, a centre of social activity'. It was not, however, open to the Chinese. Not till 1928 was the first truly grand hotel opened in Hong Kong. The Peninsula, with 200 rooms, was located directly opposite the quays where passengers from the West disembarked. It was also the last stop on the trans-Siberian railway bringing passengers from Europe.

The architecture of many of these hotels is by now familiar – European colonial classicism writ large, with white or cream facades, Doric columns and capitals, pediments, smooth rusticated masonry, high ceilings, devoid (at least from the exterior) of any reference to local culture except for the tropical vegetation. It was an international style *avant la lettre* (Peleggi 2012) which, in helping to blend together and represent a variety of different ethnicities, played a major role in constructing the essentially colonial notion of 'the tropics'.

Rangoon (now Yangon) was the chief market for English goods intended for the Burmese capital and upper Siam (Gill 1900). The Strand Hotel, Yangon, on three storeys and built in 1895, recalled one of London's main thoroughfares. It was 'one of the most luxurious hotels in the British Empire'. Its 'long portico and classical pediment' had welcomed such prominent documentors of colonial culture as Rudyard Kipling and Somerset Maugham. Burmese were not admitted till 1945.

From the late 1880s imperial expansion took grand hotels round the world. A map of 'The British Empire in 1914' in *The Anchor Atlas of World History* (1978) displays a semi-circular arc designating 'the core of British rule'. The arc begins at Singapore and runs round Colombo, Calcutta, the Persian Gulf, the Suez Canal, and takes in Egypt, Sudan, Uganda, Kenya, Rhodesia (Zimbabwe) down to Cape Town, more or less ringing the whole of the Indian Ocean. In his classic study, *Imperialism* (1936), J.A. Hobson pointed out that while one-third of the British Empire with some 420 million people had been acquired since 1870, the movement

> did not attain its full impetus till the middle of the eighties … the vast increase in territory and the method of wholesale partition which assigned to us great tracts of African land may be dated from about 1884. Within fifteen years some three and three quarter millions of square miles were added to the British Empire.
>
> (Hobson 1938:18–19)

Before the Sarkies, other entrepreneurs had been active in the East. When it opened in 1875 the Grand Oriental Hotel in Colombo, Ceylon (Sri Lanka) boasted of 154 luxury and semi-luxury rooms. Like Maidens in Delhi, conscious of its racial identity, the hotel's adverts assured prospective customers that it was 'managed by experienced Europeans', claiming it was 'the only fully European owned and fully equipped hotel in the East'. We can assume that, like the others, the clientele was predominantly male, white and western.

Tracing the arc round Calcutta, with the Grand (1887) and the Taj Mahal (1903), brings us to Africa and probably the most notorious grand hotel in the colonial world.

SHEPHEARD'S HOTEL, EGYPT: LANDMARK TO FUNERAL PYRE

The extraordinary planting of grand hotels in Egypt in the late nineteenth century 'age of capital' was the outcome of many developments: overland trips to India, ever-increasing tourist numbers, discoveries of ancient Egypt, Thomas Cook's steamship journeys up and down the Nile, seasonal seekers of warmer climates, and more. Humphreys' (2012) account suggests that the new grand hotels provided for a wealthy, English-speaking social elite; the aristocracy and high bourgeoisie.

Egypt came under British control in 1882 after the collapse of the country's banking and financial system and following the debacle over the financing of the Suez Canal. The British occupied the country and took control of its finances. A formal 'Protectorate' status was established in 1914 (Porter 1975:92).

Shepheard's Hotel opened in 1850 and was first known – reflecting their patronage – as the British Hotel. Renamed by its owner in 1860, entrepreneur Samuel Shepheard, its growing reputation is evident in its four major renovations before 1909. The refits of the hotel reflected changes in the city itself as Egypt's ruler, prompted by a visit to Haussmann's remodelled Paris, decided to create a whole new city planned along European lines and in celebration of the opening of the Suez Canal. The ever-expanding flow of travellers meant that many other grand hotels were to follow, built either in Cairo or on the Nile, their English names reflecting the origin of many of their (British and American) residents: Grand Continental (1880), Mena House (1886), Bristol (1894), Savoy (1898), Semiramis (1898), Continental (1898), Eden Palace (1899), Cataract, Aswan (1899), Windsor (1902), National (1905), Winter Palace, Aswan (1907), Majestic (1914) and others. By 1900, the hotel trade was dominated by the English, Greeks, Italians and Swiss. In Humphreys' words, hotels became

> bridgeheads for African explorations, neutral territories for conducting covert diplomacy, headquarters for armies, providing home comforts for writers, painters and archaeologists in the field and social entertainment for an international elite … It was through the hotels that the West – adventurers, travellers, tourists – experienced the Orient.

> (2011:15)

The history of the grand hotel in Egypt is also tied up with the fact that in the 70 years between 1882 and 1952, the finances and government of Egypt were in British hands. Constructing the first Aswan dam between 1898 and 1902 was one business deal that helped give the British contractor, John Aird, a seat in the (British) House of Lords.

Prior to the twentieth century these 'outposts of Europe' offered restaurants, bars, a weekly dance, balls and fetes that became a mainstay of social life (ibid.:15). They provided a social link between tourists doing the season and long-term residents, for whom they brought new faces from London and Paris. The international clientele included the rich, aristocracy, and occasional royalty.

Architecturally, Shepheard's was simplified classical. With 340 bedrooms and 240 bathrooms on four storeys it was the first Middle Eastern hotel to have electricity. Its modest exterior contrasted with the interior: the entrance hall, in a striking pharaonic style, with huge lotus-topped columns and artists' paintings of Upper Egyptian monuments. The grand staircase was guarded by two bronze, semi-nude women in pharaonic headdress, lighting up the stairs. Everywhere was luxury, excess, extravagance: plush Persian rugs, stained glass and multi-coloured lamps. One observer suggested it resembled Chartres Cathedral converted into a harem (Humphreys 2012:82, 84).

The most important socio-spatial feature of this, and other hotels, was the verandah, or outside terrace, two metres from the ground, where guests, sitting on rattan chairs could see and be seen, watching the world go by.

Apart from servants and street traders there was little contact between hotel residents and the local populace. Writing about the most popular guide-books to Egypt, Humphreys states that, in their comments on the local inhabitants, they are 'paternalistic' and 'condescending', at worse, by today's standards, 'casually but deeply racist' (2012:20). In later years, the hotel became notorious for the vast contrasts in wealth it represented and riots in 1919 protested against British rule. With the corrupt and lascivious King Farouk frequently passing his time at Shepheard's Hotel and with anti-British sentiment in the country at its highest, the hotel was considered to be 'the epitome of imperialism and foreign influence in Egypt'(ibid.:96). If we want to know what the social meaning of Shepheard's Hotel was, the answer came on 26 January 1952. Anti-British rioters set fire to European-owned businesses across the city. Shepheard's Hotel, once famed for its opulence and grandeur and the most visible symbol of Egypt's colonial past, was reduced to cinders (ibid.:97). The Egyptian revolution had begun.

I suggested earlier that the building of colonial grand hotels led to a process of urban and architectural homogeneity. In that they originated under many different conditions and therefore appeared in a variety of forms they also, as I shall show, brought urban heterogeneity.

Less notorious than Shepheard's is the Grand Hotel, Khartoum, built in the Sudan in 1906. This two-storey building, with an open gallery on both floors, was evidently a result of General Kitchener's unique re-planning of the city following the crucial battle of Omdurman in 1898. After yet another imperial war in Africa and the eventual defeat of the Mahdi revolt, Kitchener (the British commander) declared an 'Anglo–Egyptian settlement or condominium' over the Sudan. In the new city of Khartoum which he laid out, he based the plan on the pattern of the Union Jack (the British national flag) 'in a symbolic statement of British dominance' (Home 1997:41). Photographs show that the gallery railings were made to match.

EPILOGUE

Some of the world's most spectacular grand hotels are in Canada, in 1900 an independent 'dominion' of the empire. Built between 1862 and 1909 during the global grand hotel boom and often designed to look like spectacular European castles, they sprang up along the path of the Canadian Pacific Railway as it blazed its way across the continent. With perhaps the sole exception of the city hall, there are few better examples of buildings being designed, sited and displayed to give their city a distinctive and recognisable identity. The first, the Queen's (later, the Royal York), in Toronto (1862) boasted of its status as 'the tallest building in the British Empire'. The Windsor Hotel, Montreal (1875) was supposedly built to symbolise the city's rapidly growing wealth and prestige. Canada's colonial French identity was projected in two enormous chateau-style buildings, the spectacular Chateau Frontenac in Quebec City (1893) and the emblematic 12-storey Chateau Laurier, built by the Grand Trunk Railway in 1912. My focus here, however, is on the Empress Hotel in Victoria , and its essentially British imperial connection, clearly evident in its toponomy.

Victoria (Britain's Queen and Empress of India), is the name of the capital city of British (sic) Columbia, situated on Vancouver Island, and named for the British naval officer who 'discovered' it. Here, at the terminus of the steamship line, the Empress Hotel with its 477 rooms, eight storeys, and blatantly British 'Victorian' decor, was built in 1908 (about the same time as the Coronation Durbar in Delhi). Only by recognising the historical colonial (and now postcolonial) cultural framework can we recognise, and understand the meaning of, the Empress Hotel's most well-known feature, used to market the hotel worldwide. This is the 'Bengal Lounge', where the decorative theme is that of colonial Anglo-India. A huge trophy tiger-skin fills the space over the chimney breast. On the walls are reproductions of the Daniells brothers' eighteenth-century Indian landscape paintings (as in the Imperial Hotel, New Delhi), prints of British Raj Indian soldiers in coloured tunics. Darjeeling tea and Indian curries are served. Everywhere is the continuing power of an Anglo-centric colonial imagery. What message do these images convey to Canada's First Nation peoples? Indeed, as colonial grand hotels around the world are conserved and promoted as part of local 'heritage' while the buildings of indigenous peoples are ignored or left to decay, what sort of cultural and political questions do they raise? (Peleggi 2005).

CONCLUSION

I have endeavoured to show how the history of the colonial grand hotel is not only different from the history of that in the metropole but also one that raises very different issues. In his comparative study of the colonial hotel in Singapore and Ceylon, Peleggi (2012:141) represents them as either 'comfort zones' or 'contact zones' where different social, ethnic and national groups interacted and where race produced 'antagonism and exclusion' as well as 'interaction and intimacy'. Where much of the scholarship on colonial architecture and urbanism has emphasised processes of social segregation, Peleggi suggests that the idea of the contact zone focuses attention on co-presence and interaction between colonisers and colonised 'often within radically asymmetric relations of power' (ibid.:146).

What this also highlights is that, in particular colonies, hotel spaces have constructed what Craggs (2012:223) calls 'distinctive narratives of segregation'. Writing about early 1960s Rhodesia, she describes how the notorious colour bar operated differently in different places. The capital's grand hotels were 'places where racial boundaries were constructed … safe spaces where multi-racism could be gestured towards … sites in which the politics of multi-racial partnerships could be performed and contested' (ibid.).

A relatively late arrival in the colonial city, the grand hotel was to provide a politically important space in which innumerable social, cultural, political and behavioural changes took place, from the ideological to the behavioural, the culinary to the cerebral. While it was a place which made race explicit, it also enabled it to be ignored. Architecturally, like the tall building in aspiring global cities today, it was a sign of urban modernity. It also became a *fin de siècle* symbol in which the *zeitgeist* was to find its truest local expression.

NOTES

1   © Anthony D. King
2   Built as the Assembly Rooms in 1769, what today is the Royal Clarence Hotel, Exeter, was then re-named 'The Hotel' in 1770 by its French manager. It is credited with being the first hotel in England to carry that term. In 1774 'the first so called "Grand Hotel" in the world' opened in London's Covent Garden and seems to have had the monopoly of that name till the mid-1850s.
3   A grand hotel, having the necessary degree of luxury, can either be named as such (Grand Hotel) or otherwise (e.g. Victoria Hotel). Images of all the grand hotels discussed are accessible on the internet.
4   I am indebted to Adam Bisno for confirming this account. The actual meeting between the Great Powers' representatives took place in the Reichskanzlerpalais (Graichen and Grunder 2005:93).
5   So identified was German imperialism with the consumption of plantation products – tea, coffee, cocoa – that they became collectively known as 'Kolonialwaren', a term still occasionally visible on grocery store windows in Germany.
6   There were grand hotels named as such in Aden, Australia, the Bahamas, Bechuanaland, Botswana, British East Africa (Kenya), British Guiana, Burma, Canada, Ceylon, Hong Kong (1928), Egypt, Fiji Islands, India, Ireland, Jamaica, Malta, New Zealand, Nigeria, Northern Rhodesia, Sarawak, Singapore, Uganda, amongst others.
7   Best illustrated by the appropriately named Grand Hotel de l'Europe, built by a Frenchman in Singapore in 1865 and renamed, after a face-lift, the Europe Hotel in 1918. Here, a whole continent and its cultural values were symbolically superimposed upon another. The Europe Hotel was particularly popular with the Singapore Cricket Club, and had dinner dances every Tuesday evening. Visiting guests included the Duke of York, the Prince of Wales and Prince William Hohenzollern of Germany.

BIBLIOGRAPHY

Berger, M. (2011) *Hotel Dreams: Technology, Luxury and Urban Ambition in America 1829– 1929*, Baltimore: Johns Hopkins University Press.

Craggs, R. (2012) 'Towards a political geography of hotels: Southern Rhodesia 1958–62', *Political Geography*, 31: 215–24.

Driver, F. and Gilbert, D., eds (1999) *Imperial Cities: Landscape, Display and Identity*, Manchester: Manchester University Press.

Gill, G. (c.1900) *The British Colonies, Dependencies and Protectorates*, London: George Gill and Sons.

Graichen, G. and Grunder, H. (2005) *Deutsche Kolonien: Traum und Trauma*, Berlin: Ulstein.

Headrick, D.R. (1981) *The Tools of Empire: Technology and European Imperialism in the Nineteenth Century*, Oxford: Oxford University Press.

Hobsbawm, E.J. (1989) *The Age of Empire 1875–1914*, New York: Vintage Books.

Hobson, J.A. (1938; first published, 1902) *Imperialism: A Study*, Ann Arbor: University of Michigan Press.

Home, R. (1997) *Of Planting and Planning: The Making of British Colonial Cities*, London: Spon.

Humphreys, A. (2012) *The Grand Hotels of Egypt in the Golden Era of Travel*, Cairo: American University of Cairo.

Hosagrahar, J. (2006) *Indigenous Modernities: Negotiating Architecture and Urbanism*, London and New York: Routledge.

Jennings, E.T. (2003) 'From Indo-China to IndoChic: The Lang Bian Dalat Palace Hotel', *Modern Asian Studies*, 37, 1: 159–94.

Kinder, H. and Hilgeman,V. (1978) *The Anchor Atlas of World History*, vol II, New York and London: Doubleday.

King, A.D. (1976) *Colonial Urban Development: Culture, Social Power, Environment*, London and Boston: Routledge and Kegan Paul.

King, A.D. (1990) *Urbanism, Colonialism and the World-Economy: Cultural and Spatial Foundations of the World Urban System*, London and New York: Routledge.

Markus, T. (1993) *Buildings and Power: Freedom and Control in the Origin of Modern Building Types*, London and New York: Routledge.

Metcalf, T.R. (1989) *An Imperial Vision: Indian Architecture and Britain's Raj*, Berkeley: University of California Press.

Murray, J. (1904) *Handbook for Switzerland*, nineteenth edition, London: Edward Stanford.

Panikkar, K.M. (1965) *Asia and Western Dominance*, London: Allen and Unwin.

Peleggi, M. (2005) 'Consuming colonial nostalgia: the monumentalisation of historic hotels in urban Southeast Asia', *Asia Pacific Viewpoint*, 46, 3: 255–66.

Peleggi, M. (2012) 'Comfort zones as contact zones: the social and material life of colonial hotels, British Colombo and Singapore 1870–1930', *Journal of Social History*, 46, 1: 124–53.

Pevsner, N. (1976) *A History of Building Types*, London: Thames and Hudson.

Porter, B. (1975) *The Lion's Share: A Short History of British Imperialism, 1850–1970*. London and New York: Longman.

Times of India (1930) *Indian Year Book, 1930*, Bombay: Times of India.

Wilks-Heeg, S. (2003) 'From world city to pariah city? Liverpool and the global economy 1850–2000', in R. Munck, ed., *Reinventing the City? Liverpool in Comparative Perspective*, Liverpool: Liverpool University Press.

Chapter 13: Globalisation and homogenisation: the state of play[1]

INTRODUCTION

A central theme in the debate on globalisation is that contemporary social, economic, political, cultural, technological and other forces subsumed under that term are, according to one viewpoint, leading towards a homogenisation of all aspects of social life worldwide. These also include the built and spatial environments in which such social life occurs and by which it is also influenced. Others reject this view. They claim, on one hand, that heterogenisation in these realms is much more likely to be taking place, not least in the form of active resistance to processes of homogenisation. Yet others suggest that both processes develop in society simultaneously, though not necessarily in parallel. My aim in this chapter, therefore, is to examine recent literature pertaining to this topic. This includes those authors that support the contention (that globalisation is encouraging the homogenisation of representations) and also those who contest it.

First, however, we need a clarification of terms. By globalisation, I refer to what Held has called 'the speeding up in world-wide connectedness in all aspects of social life' (Held *et al.* 1999:2) and by homogenisation of representations, I refer especially to the idea that what we see in cities – the urban landscape – is becoming increasingly visually similar, particularly as a result of the similar ideologies of modernity being brought to bear upon it. In referring to the effects of globalisation on the built and spatial environment, I also include its effects on architecture, urban design and on the built environment in its widest and most general sense. This, in turn, we recognise as part of a larger process of the globalisation of, for instance, the economy, culture, knowledge, politics and language.

Finally, if our particular concern is the supposed 'homogenisation of (architectural) representations' we also need to acknowledge that architectural firms (who produce most of the designs) are by no means autonomous. They depend on clients, the public, media, builders, politicians, civil servants and fund managers, among others. Most obviously – and here I refer especially to so-called 'global architects' whom I discuss below – their expanding activities round the world are linked to the expansion of transnational companies (McNeill 2009).

My argument takes the form of addressing some basic questions relevant to these issues, the first of which aims to locate our problem within a larger historical perspective.

1. SINCE WHEN, BY WHOM, AND WHY HAS THE 'HOMOGENEITY OF REPRESENTATIONS' COME TO BE SEEN AS A 'PROBLEM'?

Numerous statements affirming the apparent homogenising effects on cities of what, since the mid-1980s, has been called globalisation (or processes which we would today accept as part of that process) can be found, many of them certainly earlier than those cited here. For example, in *A Geography of Urban Places* (1970) Murphy writes, 'With the creation of a global commercial network, the spread of industrialisation and the technological revolution in transport and transferabilities, cities everywhere are becoming more like one another' (Murphy 1970:32). In 1973, David Harvey writes, 'What is remarkable is not that urbanism is so different but that it is so similar in all metropolitan centres of the world in spite of significant differences in social policy, cultural tradition, administrative and political arrangements … and so on' (Harvey 1973:278). Fast forward three decades to 2007 and we read

> A growing volume of literature documents the spread of spatial concepts and urban forms: garden cities, green belts, new towns and, more recently, waterfronts, megamalls, and new urbanist 'villages', have found their way into every city in the world, creating high levels of physical homogeneity.
>
> (Watson 2007:68)

Others speak of 'urban convergence' between cities of the north and south.

What we see here is that while each quotation offers explanations for what is supposedly causing homogenisation (industrialisation, imported transport technologies, the spread of spatial concepts), the statements are imprecise. What, exactly, is meant by 'urbanism', 'garden cities', 'new towns' or 'new urbanist "villages"'? Do these authors imply that these particular urban phenomena are identical wherever they exist? What other transformations in economic and social life, values and lifestyle have brought about these physical and spatial changes?

2. WHAT DO WE MEAN BY THE 'HOMOGENISATION OF REPRESENTATIONS'?

The charge that 'globalisation means homogenisation' is one that is more frequently made in relation to the media and popular culture, such as films, advertising or dress codes. When made in relation to people's visual perception of the urban landscape, it usually refers to their observation of one or more features in the city, e.g. the similarity of skylines or the proliferation of similar building types worldwide (shopping malls, high-rise towers, multistorey car-parks, mosques or primary schools). What people see, and note, is that which is different from what was there before, what for them was familiar. Seeing is a selective act of 'cultural appraisal'. We recognise what we already know and overlook what is unfamiliar. Other common features frequently remarked on might include types of urban design (waterside re-developments, gated communities, heritage landscapes); particular architectural styles (neo-vernacularism, postmodernism); similar materials (glass, concrete) and technologies (suspended roofs, curtain walls); ideologies and urban policies (preservation, squatter upgrading), signature architecture and 'branding'; and especially logos of multinational chains (McDonald's, Starbucks), to name some of the most obvious. At a different (and perhaps more abstract) scale, perceptions of homogenisation might also, as Soja (2009) suggests, refer to the overall spatial structure of the city itself: the business district, inner and outer suburbs, 'edge cities'. The global circulation of all these phenomena – from building types to styles, materials and ideas – forms the subject matter of Guggenheim and Söderström's book on the influence of global mobilities on the architecture and urban form of cities worldwide.

These features are all phenomena that are added to the urban landscape. The alternative charge is that of familiar ('traditional') forms disappearing. Both may transform the urban landscape but they result from the differential exercise of power by different authority figures in the city. We need to distinguish between these different phenomena and identify the particular economic, social and political forces behind them. Some (multinational logos, luxury shopping malls or the gentrification of old historic districts) may signal a national or local governmental shift to neo-liberal urban policies, including the opening up of the urban economy to foreign inward investment; others (squatter settlement upgrading, public transport initiatives) could be the outcome of radical protest from urban social movements. Upgrading squatter settlements not only provides essential shelter, creates employment, and increases consumption, but also, in generating banks of voters, helps to change the political process.

In discussing whether globalisation leads to the increasing homogenisation of the built environment, Hans Ibelings' book, *Supermodernism: Architecture in the Age of Globalization* (1998), is one attempt to make the charge more specific. He suggests it was the 'big hotels' and 'glass box' office buildings of the 1950s and 1960s which sparked off the global 'architectural homogenisation' thesis.[2] Ibelings maintains that 'uniformity and standardisation' also manifests itself in 'singular structures like conference halls, theatres, exhibition complexes, churches and stadiums'. Yet difficult as it is to believe, he does not address the enormous social, economic, religious and cultural changes behind the appearance of these building types and what they mean for the growth of civil society, employment opportunities or any other aspects of social development; for Ibelings, 'worldwide standardisation' [*sic*] is to be (simplistically) explained in terms of 'economics, similar architectural principles as well as construction systems' (1998:42). In the context of Ibelings' comments, therefore, we need to ask:

3. HOW IS THE QUALITY OF 'SIMILARITY' AND 'HOMOGENISATION' IDENTIFIED AND WHO IS MAKING THE JUDGEMENT?

Who is the critic and from where is the critique being made (geographically, socially, and not least, politically)? Which reference groups does the critic defer to, or distance her/himself from applying their own criteria of judgement? What are the power relationships between different institutions commissioning these projects and the general public?

Ibelings, an 'outsider' and 'non-local', does not acknowledge his own position, not only as a member of the globe-trotting elite but also as an architect and critic whose gaze (unlike that of an often architecturally indifferent public) is invariably drawn to architectural objects. He ignores the agency of the state, or institution, or patron, or public, to resist what he describes.

It is now conventional wisdom that when ideas about architectural styles, building types and forms are transplanted from one place in the world to another, they are invested by the local population with different cultural, social and ideological meanings (and often given different uses). Transplanted objects and ideas are invariably located in different cultural, spatial and historical settings. Historical studies of building types reproduced in different cultural sites, such as the villa or bungalow (King 2004), invariably reveal transformations in use, form and meanings. The innovative idea of the 'garden city' housing estate, used in early twentieth-century Britain to provide social housing for the working class, was transferred to British colonies overseas where it was used to maintain strict racial segregation between white and non-white subjects (Home 1997).

4. WHAT DO WE MEAN BY HOMOGENISATION AND WHAT MEANINGS CAN IT HAVE?

Homogenisation, the idea of some or all things becoming or being made the same, can be understood from various viewpoints. To imitate or copy, in a conscious act of mimesis, can be a form of flattery, of admiration for that which is copied. As mimicry, it can also be mockery – what is copied is deliberately distorted, made fun of or made 'almost the same but not quite' (Bhabha 1992:89). The point of mimicry is to acknowledge the presence of others and yet simultaneously assert one's own presence and identity.

Imitation can also be used to create an equivalence – whether between buildings, cities, countries or cultures – if only in ironic fashion. Advertisements for luxury villa developments in Beijing, for example, are marketed as being 'Just like Long Island in New York, Just like Beverly Hills in California, Just like Richmond in Vancouver' (King 2004:118). Images of Beijing's new commercial centre, the Sun Dong An Plaza, are published alongside those of London's Canary Wharf, New York's Manhattan and Tokyo's Ginza development, implying that they are of equivalent architectural or aesthetic standard (King and Kusno 2000:45).

When 'homogenisation' is used in referring to the urban landscape, in most cases it can be assumed that criticism is implied. Homogenisation is *ipso facto* 'bad'. Yet homogenisation in the sense of making things similar by eliminating difference, in the sense of reducing social conflict and creating harmony, would, for most observers, be seen as desirable. Urban landscapes manifesting massive difference in scale between the size and costs of buildings, between the gross provision of luxury housing for the rich and the dismal squatter conditions of the poor, present obvious opportunities for more homogeneous development.

The subtle differences between the concepts of copying, mimesis, mimicry and imitation discussed above by no means exhaust the rich vocabulary prompted by a consideration of the blunt concept of 'homogenisation'. This provides a veritable buzz of analogous or cognate terms, each of which creates possibilities for differentiating between different parts of what some describe (with negative assumptions) as our increasingly 'homogeneous' urban and architectural environment: we can speak, for example, about affinity, analogy, approximation, cloning, comparison, emulation, facsimile, replica, reproduction, resemblance, simulacrum, verisimilitude (Roget and Roget 1967), each with subtly different meanings. Some of the distinctions can be used to fill in the conceptual space between what Soja implicitly suggests there exists between the binary concepts of homogeneity and heterogeneity (Soja 2009). Poets or novelists often know better than many social scientists not just what and how we see, but especially how we articulate what we see. Visual perception depends on our own sensibilities and the richness or poverty of our vocabulary to express it.

5. THE HOMOGENISATION OF REPRESENTATIONS. WHAT CAN WE LEARN FROM A HISTORICAL PERSPECTIVE?

The fact that similar types of buildings, used for the same purpose and frequently bearing a similar name, appearance and spatial form, can be found in different places in the world is well known. The oldest examples are probably buildings of worship – the temples, churches, mosques, synagogues, shrines, and also religiously related schools, madrasas, hospitals, monasteries – resulting from the spread of the major world religions. The phenomenon may result from population migrations, and also include the diffusion of technologies and the establishment and spread of regional and later global empires (see below) which continued the process. As trade routes were expanded, migrating populations simultaneously transferred beliefs, values, institutions, practices, and the complementary architectural forms in which they were accommodated, around the world. In all cases, such architectural forms have played a key symbolic as well as socially functional role in establishing the presence of diasporic world religions.

Today, secular shifts away from religion in some parts of the world transform both the form and use of what were once religious buildings. In Britain, for example, urban churches have been turned into apartments, gyms, circus and climbing schools, community centres but also, with the changing ethnic and religious demographics of the population, into mosques, gurdwaras and temples. In Rio de Janeiro, and other Brazilian cities, the rapid growth of Pentecostalism has transformed empty cinemas into places of worship.

Modern European empires have adopted – and, equally important, also adapted – the forms and styles of ancient ones (especially from Greece and Rome) in extending their political reach – in Asia, Africa, the Americas and also elsewhere. Architects in contemporary cultures, such as China and India, have, in adopting modified versions of Postmodernism and later styles, appropriated the neo-Classical styles of their European predecessors, modifying them in the process. Probably the most visually and structurally similar building form, used for palaces, parliaments and post offices in colonial cities round the world is the Classical columned portico of the Greek temple, popularised by the Palladian villa (King 2004:ch.7). In all these cases, however, the political and social meaning invested in the design has been that of those who have used it.

From medieval times, technologies of warfare and gunpowder have ensured a comparability (and similarity) of defensive installations, with forts and castles, transplanted by Spain and Portugal from Europe to South America and the Caribbean. Transportation technologies have largely determined the representational architecture of docks, railroad stations, airports, and automobile parks. Nineteenth- and twentieth-century developments in building materials – iron, concrete, steel, glass, plastics – have been combined with Modern Movement ideology, originally from Germany's Bauhaus (Baumeister 2007; Ray 2010), to bring a specific form of representational homogeneity to cities all over the world, from Brasilia to Chandigarh, Addis Ababa to Jakarta (Holston 1989; Prakash 2002; Fuller 2006; Kusno 2000), long before the recent present. Yet as Baumeister (2007) and Ray (2010) point out, the principles behind Bauhaus practices have been adapted, in each case, to local political and geographical conditions and prevailing ideologies. Modernist architecture has been used to sustain regimes of democratic socialism (Germany), colonial oppression (Italy), and postcolonial nationalism (India).

In all of these cases where apparently similar architectural and spatial forms have been transplanted around the world, bringing with them, especially for the 'outside' observer, an apparent visual homogeneity between the places where they exist, nowhere can it be said that the process has erased, or submerged, the distinctive identities of the populations which have occupied these places. There are, of course, some worldwide commonalities which must be acknowledged, for example, the sense of religious belonging among adherents of particular world religions, of sharing a language in common among a postcolonial population, or of experiencing an ethnic identity. Yet as sociologist Roland Robertson (1992) has written, globalisation has usually 'exacerbated' a sense of individual and ethnic identity, not erased it.

If we ask what makes the present 'global situation' distinctive and different from the past, it is the recent spectacular speeding up in communication, the compression of space and time (Harvey 1989), generated by the rapid growth of jet air travel from the 1970s and the instantaneous projection of images through the internet, television, as well as film and photography; for those born since 1980, this has mostly happened during their lifetime. For this particular cohort, an impression has been conveyed that the global circulation of urban and architectural forms is somehow a recent phenomenon.

6. THE GREATEST FORCE IN 'HOMOGENISING' THE BUILT ENVIRONMENT: IMPERIALISM OR GLOBALISATION?

As earlier citations suggest, the processes of what, since the late 1980s, we have called 'globalisation', were there long before the word entered our vocabulary. Imperialism and colonialism as forerunners of the present phase of globalisation are addressed in historian John Darwin's book, *After Tamerlane: The Global History of Empire* (2007). Darwin argues that empires are the rule, not the exception, in world history, referring not simply to the European empires of the nineteenth and twentieth centuries, but also earlier ones in Asia (Qing Chinese, Korean, Mughal, etc.), Central and South America (Inca, Aztec) and elsewhere. It is these and especially later empires which laid the foundations of contemporary globalisation.

In a similar vein, in *Globalisation in World History* (2002), Anthony Hopkins argues that globalisation has a much longer history than is often acknowledged. Not only does he emphasise the non-Western phases and experiences of globalisation (including those of Islam), he also draws attention to its earlier historical forms, which he terms the archaic (prior to 1600), proto (from the eighteenth century), modern (from the nineteenth, and including the imperial phase) and postcolonial globalisation (after 1950 or 1970). As Said (1993) shows in regard to language, literature and the arts, and many other scholars have shown in relation to the architecture, space, urban design and planning of cities, different forms of colonialism have had a massive, and often continuing influence on innumerable cultures and territories, not least in creating the structural similarity of 'dual cities' in Asia, Africa and the Middle East. These histories are part of an extensive literature on this topic (AlSayyad 1991; Çelik 2008; Fuller 2006; King 1976, 1990; Scriver and Prakash 2007).

What Salvatore (2009:21) calls 'the three big Islamic empires of early modernity, Ottoman, Safavid and Mughal' informed by specific religious beliefs, brought different forms of civilisational modernity to conquered territory than those brought by the later empires of Europe. This is a theme recently explored in Çelik's comparative study of the urban and architectural modernisations in the French colonies of the Maghrib and Ottoman Arab provinces in the Middle East (Çelik 2008).

Imperialism brings to its territories both similarities as well as differences. First is the spatial mark of conquest, of political and military power: the imposition of barracks, parade grounds, armouries, prisons and the implementation of institutional authority expressed in buildings and spaces of social control. But then each empire is characterised by its own cultural (and often religious) values such that, to a certain degree, French colonial urbanism in Algeria may have features in common with that in Vietnam just as British planning laws in Southern Africa have something in common with those in the West Indies (Home 1997). On the other hand, not only are the indigenous cultures and landscapes of colonised territories all very different, but the cultures and practices of imperial powers are also dissimilar.

Of most importance, the political and cultural influences of imperialism were not just instances of one-way traffic; they have, in turn, been resisted, accommodated, adapted and transformed over time by many local agents (Chattopadhyay 2005; Hosagrahar 2005; Nasr and Volait 1999; Yeoh 1996). The outcome has been a vast range of urban landscapes of hybridity, diversity and innovation (AlSayyad 2000; Pieterse 2004).

How have these historical colonial cities impacted the contemporary everyday lives of the postcolonial societies where they exist? This is a massive question which would need to be addressed at the level of each individual city. The remnants of the 'dual city' certainly continue to divide the rich and poor in many states, with the initial colonial structure of the city still determining the shape of its contemporary development, influencing the nature and type of social and political relationships and contributing to the maintenance of social hierarchies. This phenomenon of imperialism, however, is only part of a larger question:

7. HOW ARE QUESTIONS OF HOMOGENISATION AND HETEROGENISATION AFFECTED BY DIFFERENT SOCIAL, POLITICAL AND ECONOMIC FORMATIONS?

As representations, buildings, architectural styles, spatial forms belong to specific modes of production, systems of meaning and modes of expression. As such, they are part of the city's visual culture.

These images, however, are epiphenomenal; that is to say they are secondary symptoms of larger economic, social or political formations, forms produced by different distributions of power and divisions of labour. We need to understand what social institutions, what functions the buildings accommodate and the spaces contain or display (Markus 1993). If there really is 'architectural homogenisation' in the world's cities, what are the economic, social, political and cultural forces behind this?

Throughout history, changes have taken place in the political and social formations that have produced different forms of building, planning and architecture, different skylines and urban cadastres, giving cities and their inhabitants distinctive identities.

In medieval Europe, for example, the principal forces (and patrons) were the church, monarchs, ducal courts, religious foundations and guilds of wealthy towns. In the nineteenth and early twentieth centuries, patronage lay with imperial, colonial and national governments, banks, national and international corporations, and the military and industrial knowledge complex.

And as suggested earlier, changes in the forms of architecture and urban space have as much to do with the disappearance of particular types of patron and user as much as the appearance of others.

Moreover, particular modes of production and ideologies, some global in scope, such as socialism, fascism and capitalist consumerism, with different forms of patronage, have challenged the role of the nation-state as the major influence on architectural identity (Smith 1990). Yet as a force in forming the space of modern cities, the nation-state cannot be so easily dismissed. Most recently, neoliberal governments, privatising public services and handing public space to multinational corporations, are accused of eliminating cultural differences everywhere, introducing similar consumer innovations: suburban shopping malls, gated communities, multiplex cinemas, franchised food outlets and theme parks. How do these processes take place in the contemporary world?

8. THE 'CORPORATE CITY': THE EPICENTRE OF CONTEMPORARY HOMOGENISATION?

According to some critics, it is the 'corporate city' that preserves and promotes the hegemonic and homogenising discourses of globalisation and consumerism (Daskalaki *et al.* 2008:53). Utilising glass-faced, anonymous office blocks, capitalism's corporate forces 'convert places that could encourage difference and interaction into "non-places" of homogenisation and indifference' (ibid.). Environments which previously encouraged cultural diversity and encounter have been replaced by those encouraging alienation and passive consumption. These critics cite the Swiss Re building and its surroundings in the City of London and the public space of Berlin's Potsdammer Platz, as having been designed to have 'maximum visual impact' on their surroundings.

According to Arif Dirlik, global architectural firms 'seem to derive their aesthetic legitimation … from their ability to represent global capitalism, and the clientele it is in the process of creating' (Dirlik 2007:38, referring to China). The local is commodified and made over. In the case of China, the political power responsible for these developments is the (undemocratic) national government.

Daskalaki *et al.* (2008) describe the resistance developed to the architectural culture and spaces of the corporate city. Started in the Paris suburbs in 1988, '*parkour*' or 'free-running' is a literal form of 'embodied protest'. Activists use their bodies to resist the dominance of the faceless environment by 'breaking the lines of the city', challenging the given structures of space by running and leaping through the 'forbidden' spaces of the city. Their activities and philosophy act as a metaphor for active participation between the actual and possible structures of the world. Similar resistant practices include skate-boarding, the pervasive activities of graffiti artists or, earlier, the Situationist movement and its performances in Paris.

9. HOW POSSIBLE IS IT TO SPEAK OF 'GLOBAL ARCHITECTURE' OR THE 'ARCHITECTURE OF GLOBAL CAPITALISM'?

The terms 'global architecture' or 'the architecture of global capitalism' have, in recent years, rapidly gained currency. Both terms suggest that there exists a unitary, 'homogeneous' concept which also refers to a material reality. Yet while the term may legitimately function as a metaphor, logically, the idea of a literal 'global architecture' is just not feasible. This would either imply an architecture which could be found in every corner of the globe, which is impossible, or alternatively, an architecture which, geographically, had developed from roots originating in every place on the globe, which is equally nonsensical.

As everything has to have a place of origin, and also the appropriate economic and political conditions in which to develop, what today is referred to as 'global architecture', as a form, practice and style, is derived from an adaptation in terms of materials and design, of twentieth-century notions of German, and subsequently Euro-American, Bauhaus design and its imitators (so-called Modernism), though today stripped of its original social commitment to egalitarianism (McNeill 2009:126). Its history is to be traced partially in Europe but predominantly in the cities of the USA, where it was dependent on its corporate sponsors and immense economic resources; subsequently, it has been adopted by the emerging Asian economies. Though always adapted, indigenised, and given meaning by its location (Baumeister 2007), in each instance it becomes 'local' even though it is connected to a larger historical tradition (see also Holston 1989).

Referring to China and specifically to Beijing, Ren (2007) suggests that (in China) 'global architecture' refers to a capital-intensive form of design, produced by international architectural firms operating in cities worldwide and is identifiable by the fact that it eschews or refuses any reference to traditional local practice; it might even be defined as architecture that is beyond local economic and technological capacities. 'Global architecture', in this sense, is defined primarily by its non-local nature. (This is similar to forms of imperial architecture of centuries ago.)

In a similar context, other scholars have referred to specific 'global types' of building or urban design: the high-rise tower, the standalone, bourgeois suburban house or villa (Dovey 2008) or the gated community (Genis 2007) which today can be found in an increasing number of cities worldwide. Yet while they have some features in common, none of these phenomena can be described as totally alike. As for the idea of a 'global skyline', this is a concept that, if not lexically expressed as such until quite recently, has, from the late nineteenth century and then accelerating in recent years, become central to the competitive practice of constructing 'the tallest building in the world' (King 2004). This phenomenon exists only in virtual reality and the realms of imagination.

10. DO 'GLOBAL ARCHITECTS' CONTRIBUTE TO 'ARCHITECTURAL HOMOGENISATION?

Many ideas about cultural homogenisation result from the diffusion worldwide of both social and urban theory, not least concepts about the 'world' or 'global city' (Sassen 2001) and what are seen as the minimum spatial and symbolic requirements needed to achieve this status. What are the implications of this for both the built as well as the living environment? In terms of the built environment, this 'global city theory' is interpreted to mean not only what needs adding to the city (high-rise office towers, signature buildings, convention centres, 'world class' hotels, luxury apartments, flyovers, and not least, a 'modern' skyline) but also what requires removing from it, most notably, squatter settlements.

'Signature' buildings, and what has come to be called 'starchitecture', however, and the 'branding' of the city with the designs of 'global architects' (also part of the 'global city' agenda) requires commitment on the part of local, city (and national) sponsors to the value system of where this practice originates. The resultant collection of signature 'trophies' can reduce cities which were previously identified by their own architectural vernacular to imitative clones of each other.

In this context, as a contribution to 'global knowledge', the invention and proliferation worldwide of a particular notion of the 'global city' has had a disastrous effect. From the start, the definition of the term has focused almost solely on economic criteria, paying little, if any, attention to the historical, cultural or religious context in which the world or global city developed in the West (King 2006). This has resulted in attention being focused especially on economic institutions in the city and also to its superficial physical and spatial attributes. As McNeill has suggested, 'Globalisation as a process of capitalist development has advanced quickest in the domain of symbols' (McNeill 2009:96), most of them becoming known through the widespread circulation of 'promotional' architectural magazines and journals. As the global clamour greeting yet one more 'iconic' building is displaced by that of another, the idea of the 'icon', now part of every global architect's vocabulary, has transformed the spectacular into the ordinary.

Adam (2008) suggests that, as the majority of transnational companies are American, so are the global architectural firms which serve their interests. 'North American cash has brought North American architecture.' According to Adam, of the 50 major architectural firms with global business, 22 are from the US, 15 the UK, and others from Australia and Ireland. Eighty percent are Anglophone. Their work sets the framework for global competition and 'clients are sold a uniform global brand' (Adam 2008).

These architectural megapractices, with AEDAS, for example, employing 800 creative team members spread around six countries, or SOM with another 800 producing standard architectural designs that often have little reference to local cultures, have been responsible for creating the spread of 'a commercial brand of postmodernism' (McNeill 2009) which has been used to brand particular buildings and cities. The linking of some of these firms (and brands, such as Foster +

Partners) to venture capital groups, and the tendency to sign up more deals in a specific geographical area to gain economies of scale and time (ibid.:31), has contributed to a reduction in diversity and, for outside observers, created an impression of homogenisation.

Particularly associated with the notion of 'global architecture' is the rise of the phenomenon of the 'starchitect' from the 1990s, whose signature building marks him (or occasionally, her) as a celebrity. The assumption that a spectacular building can transform the economic fortunes of a city – the so-called 'Bilbao effect', following the building of Frank Gehry's 'iconic' museum in that city – has created a demand, in some cases, for exactly the same design to be used in other cities. Designs become stereotyped, 'trophies' to be collected by particular cities. According to McNeill, what is not recognised is that many other factors, coincidental to the building of Gehry's museum, were also responsible for the improvement of Bilbao's economic fortunes (McNeill 2009:81). In many cases, the new concentration of wealth caused by the maldistribution of income worldwide, with the gains in economic growth going predominantly to rich countries, has been behind the commissioning of work from 'starchitects'.

In adopting the 'celebrity architect' in an attempt to transform the fortunes of declining cities, what is also overlooked is the specific cultural context, central to the functioning of American capitalism in which this concept developed, namely the privileging of the individual at the expense of the social. This is not a set of values currently widespread outside the USA, but the practice may indeed encourage such values to develop in the public sphere. 'Visual homogenisation' may also be encouraged by the rapidly increasing number of global architectural competitions and prizes involving committees travelling around the world, using a given set of aesthetic criteria to evaluate buildings which often have little or no connection to the local. The outcome can often be a case of 'the monotony of the exceptional'.

11. GLOBALISATION OR DELOCALISATION?

The decision of firms to 'go global' requires a delocalisation of both representational architecture and the symbolic nature of its design and also of the company name. Over a century ago, photography mogul George Eastman sought a company name that was short, easily written and remembered, and pronounceable in most world languages. The name he came up with was 'Kodak'. Employing a similar logic, today's corporations and architectural firms consciously disconnect themselves from their local or national architectural and geographical origins or from the names of their founders, and replace names with 'placeless' acronyms which are perceived as 'globally mobile' (McNeill 2009:28) – AEDAS, KPF, SOM, HOK, IKEA, and more recently, AVIVA (previously Norwich Union, 'the world's fifth largest insurance company'). To cite one of the company's representatives, 'As a global company we need a name that will be recognised anywhere' (Hughes 2009).

'Placeless' names, like 'placeless' architectural styles, may delocalise in one place, yet in contemporary China, as I discuss below, they attempt to confer a spurious 'global' identity on some architectural project elsewhere. The essence and assumed logic of this is in the simultaneous creation of both difference and similarity: *temporal* difference, in relation to distinguishing itself from what was there before; *geocultural* difference, in relation to what continues to exist within the relevant cultural and spatial region of the nation-state. Similarity, on the other hand, is constructed in relation to the architecture of other cities, irrespective of location, but which are part of the reference group to which the particular building patron, or occupant institution, wishes to belong. As detailed earlier in the chapter, this simultaneous establishment of both similarity and difference attempts to claim the necessary attribute of equivalence. In other words, the process of 'being' or 'becoming global' is no different from the familiar old story of 'being' or 'becoming modern'. The act, and the outcome that results, is entirely relational, that is, we are 'global' or 'modern' but only in comparison to someone or somewhere else.

12. WHERE IS HOMOGENISATION IN CITIES?

If homogenisation of representations means bringing similarity to, and perhaps between (especially) 'Global South' cities worldwide then in one sense this might be acceptable. Policies contributing to neo-liberal globalisation grossly exacerbate uneven urban development, not only between rich countries and poor countries but also between rich and poor populations in cities worldwide. Outsourcing employment from rich to poor countries depends on these gross disparities. The one accepted conclusion about 'global cities' that three decades of research have shown us concerns the massive economic, social and spatial polarisation between the rich and poor, both locationally in terms of their place in the city and materially, in their differential access to space, shelter and services (water, electricity, schools, markets, etc.) Homogenisation in this case is in the similarities of contrasts in the city, with iconic spectacles, luxury condos, new shopping malls for the wealthy on one hand, and gross overcrowding, homelessness and squatter settlements for the poor on the other.

13. WHAT ARE THE IMPACTS OF HOMOGENISATION ON THE PUBLIC SPHERE? A VIEW FROM BEIJING

As I suggested at the start of this chapter, one argument supporting the 'architectural homogenisation' thesis concerns not just what is added to the city but also what is taken away, including the disappearance or neglect of culturally different lifestyles and the spaces and built environments that support them. In the long term, it is suggested that this has led to the loss of cultural identity and, with this, a social and psychic shift to more 'modern' subjectivities and identities.

The misconceptions of such generalisations are best brought out by specific case studies which provide some insight into contemporary processes of identity construction. According to Xuefei Ren's empirical studies of transnational architectural production in China (2007), the new 'transnational architecture' introduced by prominent international architects (Rem Koolhaas, Norman Foster, Herzog/de Meuron, Paul Andreu and others) in recent years into Beijing has been subject to different interpretations in the public sphere. Dependent on the commissioning agent concerned, the results are invested with different meanings. For the local developers, avant-garde designs become a branding tool in order that they can market their products more successfully. For city officials and administrators, avant-garde design policies have been used to advance their political careers. For the Communist authoritarian state itself, the ultra-modern, very deliberate 'non-Chinese' modernist design functions to symbolise the arrival of 'modern China' on the world stage. In a neat contradictory inversion, therefore, 'being global' (whatever this means) is used to promote and enhance a nationalistic agenda. As 'space is consumed globally by a worldwide audience of spectators watching images circulating in global television networks' (as with the Olympic Games) 'means that it is constantly subject to multiple, and often contradictory interpretations, whether by local and translocal actors'. (Ren 2007:xi–xii). To be seen as 'modern', foreign and futuristic, Chinese architects have adopted a style of the 'severest minimalism', i.e. without any decoration or 'featuring' whatsoever. For a younger generation of Chinese professionals, keen to display their rising status and anti-traditional stance, expressly non-Chinese cultural symbols are the key (Ren 2007:121–40).

Similar interpretations have been offered in earlier times. Over the last 50 years, in different historical and geographical circumstances (Brasilia, Jakarta, Chandigarh, Tripoli) reformist (as well as colonial) governments and political leaders have used so-called Modernist or International Style architecture in various ways (Holston 1989; Kusno 2000; Prakesh 2002; Fuller 2006; Ray 2010). In all cases, however, what needs to be recognised is that architectural style, in itself, has no intrinsic meaning except in relation to the discourses that accompany it.

Breidenbach and Zukrigl (1999) have suggested that societies are becoming different in more uniform ways. This could well be an accurate observation if made in relation to the increasing adoption worldwide of 'heritage' policies. What are seen by local officials as historic and culturally significant vernacular buildings, or even entire urban enclaves embodying collective social memories, are refurbished or even rebuilt with the specific objective of marking them off from other places. Yet as all histories are different, are the differences manifest in similar ways?

CONCLUSION

If it is accepted that there is an increasing degree of 'homogenisation of representations' in the architecture and urban spaces of cities worldwide (and I have argued that this cannot be taken for granted) and if action has to be taken to modify this, it must lie in the field of politics: for governments, institutions, and publics to resist the persistent pressure from (especially) non-local corporate power; for architectural schools to rethink curricula and put the needs of society and values of economic and social equity at the centre of the curriculum, accepting that architecture is not just an art or technical object, but also a social object. Continuing present trends, encouraging high-energy, unsustainable buildings and glass-walled skyscrapers on air-cooled beaches, is a road to disaster.

NOTES

1   From Anthony D. King, 'Globalisation and homogenisation: the state of play', in Modjitaba Sadria, ed., *Homogenisation of Representations*, 2012 © Aga Khan Award for Architecture.
2   The following paragraphs are taken from my 2004 book, *Spaces of Global Cultures: Architecture Urbanism Identity*, New York and London: Routledge, p.41.

BIBLIOGRAPHY

Adam, R. (2008) 'Global and local architecture and urbanism since the end of the Cold War'. Online; accessed 20 January 2009.

AlSayyad, N., ed. (1991) *Forms of Dominance: On the Architecture and Urbanism of the Colonial Enterprise*, Aldershot: Avebury.

AlSayyad, N. (2000) *Hybrid Urbanism: On the Identity Discourse and the Built Environment*, Westport: Praegar.

Baumeister, R. (2007) 'The worldwide proliferation of Bauhaus and its cultural legacy' in R. Baumeister and S. Lee, eds, *The Domestic and Foreign in Architecture*, Rotterdam: 010 Publishers, pp.156–78.

Baumeister, R. and Lee, S., eds (2007) *The Domestic and Foreign in Architecture*, Rotterdam: 010 Publishers.

Bhabha, H. (1992) *The Location of Culture*, London and New York: Routledge.

Breidenbach, J. and Zukrigl, I. (1999) 'The dynamics of cultural globalisation: the myths of cultural globalisation.' www.instat/studies/collab/breidenb, accessed 30 November 2015.

Celik, Z. (2008) *Empire, Architecture and the City: French–Ottoman Encounters, 1830–1914*, Seattle and London: University of Washington Press.

Chattopadhyay, S. (2005) *Representing Calcutta: Modernity, Modernism, and the Colonial Uncanny*, London: Routledge.

Darwin, J. (2007) *After Tamerlane: The Global History of Empire*, London: Allen Lane.

Daskalaki, M., Stara, A. and Imas, M. (2008) 'The "parkour organisation": inhabitating corporate spaces', *Culture and Organisation*, 14, 1: 49–64.

Dirlik, A. (2007) 'The architecture of global modernity, colonialism and places', in R. Baumeister and S. Lee, eds, *The Domestic and Foreign in Architecture*, Rotterdam: 010 Publishers, pp.37–46.

Dovey, K. (2008) *Framing Places: Mediating Power in Built Form*, London and New York: Routledge.

Fuller, M. (2006) *Moderns Abroad: Architecture, Cities and Italian Imperialism*, London and New York: Routledge.

Genis, S. (2007) 'Producing elite localities: the rise of gated communities in Istanbul', *Urban Studies,* 44, 4: 77–198.

Guggenheim, M. and Söderström, O., eds (2010) *Re-Shaping Cities: How Global Mobility Transforms Architecture and Urban Form.* London and New York: Routledge.

Harvey, D. (1973) *Social Justice and the City,* London: Arnold.

Harvey, D. (1989) *The Condition of Postmodernity,* Oxford and Cambridge, MA: Blackwell.

Held, D., McGrew, A., Goldblatt, D. and Perraton, J. (1999) *Global Transformations: Politics, Economics and Culture,* Cambridge: Polity.

Holston, J. (1989) *The Modernist City: An Anthropological Critique of Brasilia,* Chicago: University of Chicago Press.

Home, R. (1997) *Of Planting and Planning: The Making of British Colonial Cities,* London and New York: Routledge.

Hopkins, A.G., ed. (2002) *Globalisation in World History,* London: Pimlico.

Hosagahar, J. (2005) *Indigenous Modernities: Negotiating Architecture and Urbanism,* London and New York: Routledge.

Hughes, O. (2009) 'Bleaching out a brand', *Guardian,* 22 January 2009.

Ibelings, H. (1998) *Supermodernism: Architecture in the Age of Globalization,* Amsterdam: NAI Publishers.

King, A.D. (1976) *Colonial Urban Development,* London and Boston: Routledge and Kegan Paul.

King, A.D. (1990) *Global Cities: Postimperialism and the Internationalisation of London,* London and New York: Routledge.

King, A.D. (2004) *Spaces of Global Cultures: Architecture Urbanism Identity,* London and New York: Routledge.

King, A.D. (2006) 'World cities: global? Postcolonial? Postimperial? Some cultural comments'. In N. Brenner and R. Keil, eds, *Global Cities Reader,* London and New York: Routledge, pp.319–24.

King, A.D. and Kusno, A. (2000) 'On Bei(ji)ng in the world: globalisation, postmodernism, and the making of transnational space in China', in A. Dirlik and X. Zhang, eds, *Postmodernism and China,* Durham, NC: Duke University Press, pp.41–67.

Kusno, A. (2000) *Beyond the Postcolonial: Architecture, Urban Space and Political Cultures in Indonesia,* London and New York: Routledge.

Markus, T.A. (1993) *Buildings and Power: Freedom and Control in the Origin of Modern Building Types,* London and New York: Routledge.

McNeill, D. (2009) *The Global Architect: Firms, Fame and Urban Form,* New York and London: Routledge.

Murphy, R. (1970) 'Historical and comparative studies', in P.G. Putnam, F.J. Taylor, P.G. Kettle, *A Geography of Urban Places: Selected Readings.* Toronto: Methuen, pp.25–32.

Nasr, J. and Volait, M., eds (1999) *Urbanism: Imported or Exported? Native Aspirations and Foreign Plans,* Chichester: Wiley-Academic.

Pieterse, J.N. (2004) *Globalization and Culture,* Lanham, MD: Rowman and Littlefield.

Prakash, V. (2002) *Chandigarh's le Corbusier: The Struggle for Modernity in Postcolonial India,* Seattle: University of Washington Press.

Ray, K.R. (2010) *Bauhaus Dream-house: Modernity and Globalization,* London and New York: Routledge.

Ren, X. (2007) *Building Globalization: Transnational Architecture Production in Urban China.* Chicago: University of Chicago Press.

Robertson, R. (1992) *Globalisation: Social Theory and Global Culture,* London, Newbury Park and New Delhi: Sage.

Roget and Roget (1967) *Roget's Thesaurus*, Harmondsworth: Penguin Books.

Said, E. (1993) *Culture and Imperialism*, London: Vintage.

Salvatore, A. (2009) 'From civilisations to multiple modernities: the issue of the public sphere', in Sadria, M., ed., *Multiple Modernities in Muslim Societies*, London: Aga Khan Award for Architecture, pp.19–26.

Sassen, Saskia (2001) *The Global City: New York, London, Tokyo*. Princeton: Princeton University Press.

Scriver, P. and Prakash, V. (2007) *Colonial Modernities: Building, Dwelling and Planning in British India and Ceylon*, London and New York: Routledge.

Smith, A.D. (1990) 'Towards a global culture', in Featherstone, M., ed., *Global Culture: Nationalism, Globalisation and Modernity*, London: Sage, pp.171–92.

Soja, E. (2009) 'Homogeneity and heterogeneity?' Knowledge Construction Workshop: Homogeneity of Representations. Aga Khan Award for Architecture.

Watson, V. (2007) 'Engaging with difference', in N. Murray *et al.*, *Desire Lines: Memory and Identity in the Post-apartheid City Space*, London: Routledge, pp.67–80.

Yeoh, B. (1996) *Contesting Space: Power Relations and the Urban Built Environment in Colonial Singapore*, Oxford: Oxford University Press.

Defining contemporary and historical cities

Chapter 14: Imperial cities[1]

EMPIRES, NATIONS AND CITIES

An empire is a form of polity where one state extends its dominion, usually by military power, over the territories and populations of others, generally ethnically and culturally different. In this context, imperial city can refer both to the capital and seat of the emperor and also to other major cities in the empire. Central to the concept of the imperial city is the reciprocal and interdependent relationship between imperial expansion and contraction and spatial and built environmental developments in the capital city.

As indicated in Chapter 11, from a long-term historical perspective, the dominance of the nation-state as a form of polity is relatively recent. As recently as the late nineteenth century, world space had been dominated by some 16 empires, each with their imperial capitals and other important cities. That the six official languages of the United Nations organisation are the languages of what were historically once the world's largest empires (British, Russian, Spanish, Arabic, Qing Chinese, French) is sufficient comment on the continuing importance of previous empires and their principal cities in disseminating their languages, forms of law and governance, religions and cultures.

From the most ancient to the most modern, over 80 different empires have been recognised over the last two millennia, their regimes and ideologies physically demarcated both in space and stone. For example, in the second century BC, Qin Shi Huang, first Chinese emperor and founder of the Qing dynasty, united the majority of the Han Chinese under a government based in what is now the modern city of Xi'an, from here introducing a unified legal code, a common currency and a written language. From this central imperial capital the spatial extent of the emperor's rule was marked by the first stages of China's Great Wall, later extended under the Ming and other dynasties. Subsequently, in the tenth century, China's imperial capital was moved to Peking (modern Beijing), where the Imperial Palace was situated at the heart of multiple layers of walls and gates, enclosing the Forbidden City, simultaneously projecting but also concealing imperial power.

Simply expressed, national capital cities exist by commanding a surplus from the resources and territory of the nation-state and providing services in return. By the same logic, imperial capitals grow richer, larger and stronger by appropriating the resources and territories of an expanding empire. In this way, imperial cities have, throughout history, and especially in the nineteenth century, frequently become the largest, in terms of population, and often the richest of all cities in the world. In some cases, long after the empire itself has disappeared, the accumulated resources, institutions, infrastructure and transportation networks as well as cultural attributes of the earlier imperial regime have continued to exist in the one-time imperial city. These may include institutions of government and law, banks, universities, museums, libraries, military installations, docks, roads, and in the modern era rail and airline transport routes, as well as the offices, symbols and practices of empire, including languages, attitudes and beliefs. To different degrees, therefore, this is true of the imperial regimes and cities of Rome, Istanbul, Peking, Cairo, Venice, London, Madrid, Lisbon, Amsterdam, Moscow, Vienna, amongst others. In this way, many (though not all) one-time imperial cities of the late nineteenth century have, at the close of the twentieth, mutated into what have, since the 1990s, increasingly been termed world or global cities.

Economically, imperial cities have been able to appropriate resources, whether grain, precious metals, labour, looted treasures and scientific knowledge from the far corners of the empire. Slave labour has built massive pyramids, as at Luxor (Egypt) or Teotihuacan (Mexico); in more modern ones, such as that of Britain, slavery built up vast plantation economies in the Caribbean, generating capital for industrialisation and urban development in the metropole. In the imperial cities of Delhi and Agra in the Moghul Empire (1526–1857), spectacular palaces, public works and exotic gardens have been funded from the proceeds of imperial conquest. In the brief but singularly violent history of the Belgian Empire (1901–62), profits from rubber extraction in what was the Congo Free State were used to build and equip the spectacular Musée du Congo in imperial Brussels (later, the Royal Museum for Central Africa) and other monuments. The Second French Colonial Empire (1830–1960) extended its domain into North and West Africa, the Middle East, Southeast Asia and Océana. Paris added to its existing imperial features, including Napoleon's tomb in the Invalides and the spectacular Arc de Triomphe. Following post-war decolonisation, the museum established for the 1931 international colonial exhibition in Paris was transformed into the Musée National des Arts d'Afrique et d'Océanie.

Whether defined by the cultural diversity of its inhabitants or the extent of its trade, the imperial city is, by default, the forerunner of today's international multicultural city. Imperial trade, imperial wars and imperial armies not only added wealth, knowledge and economic and political power to the city, but generated much of its symbolic capital: the monumental arches, ceremonial ways, obelisks, equestrian statues, war memorials, and thoroughfares named for faraway places. The imperial city's arenas and stadiums are sites for spectacular parades, exhibitions, sporting contests or demonstrations of political power.

Imperial cities are either designed from scratch and purpose-built or, as national capitals, acquire imperial features as the empire expands over time. Most large European imperial cities fit into the second type. India, while providing historical examples of both, also offers, in New Delhi, a uniquely modern version of the first type. In the early twentieth century, the imperial government, anxious to escape the growing nationalist movement in Kolkata, moved the capital of the British Raj to a less volatile, more geographically central location. Beaux Arts principles informed spectacular processional ways, endless vistas, the Viceroy's palace, a vast iconic statue of the king-emperor. Accommodation for the imperial bureaucracy was laid out according to a rigid socio-spatial hierarchy.

Of all ancient imperial cities, however, it is Rome and other imperial Roman cities that best illustrate the structural characteristics and political processes which distinguish imperial from other types of cities.

IMPERIAL ROME

As an imperial city and centre of a vast multi-ethnic, multicultural empire spreading from the Mediterranean shores into Northern Europe, the Middle East and North Africa, Rome and the Roman empire provide an example of the centrifugal and centripetal movements that distinguished imperial capitals and the main cities in its provinces. As the empire expanded, cities were founded from which the new provinces were governed. Though influenced by local geographical and cultural conditions, the cities of the empire, located on land and seaborne trading routes, were to become part of a new urban network. They spread the Latin language and culture of the metropole to the colony, but also brought back local knowledge and culture. Carefully planned, Roman cities were generally walled, and in most cases laid out on a grid, a spatial device for colonising new lands and peoples that was to have immense significance, not only for the Romans but also for later empires, such as that of Spain in South and Central America. As Roman rule expanded through Italy, the Eastern Mediterranean and into Gaul and Spain, cities were established where the conquering armies were garrisoned and Roman rule extended. In Pompeii or Trier, where the grid plan dates from the first century, the forum or market place was the centre of public life, with baths, a gymnasium, temples dedicated to different deities, occasionally a circus or race track, and a basilica or audience hall. Imposing gateways often marked the entrance.

Founded after the invasion of Britain in CE 43, London was located at an important river crossing. With a forum, basilica and temples, London, as the capital of a new province, was also the site of a governor's palace. Ephesus, now in Turkey, was the capital of the province of Asia. A busy port, exporting goods back to the imperial capital, in the second century CE it had extensive cultural facilities, including a magnificent library with storage facilities for up to 12,000 scrolls. There was also a girls' gymnasium, theatre, baths, stadium, and temples to the goddess Artemis, a destination point for pilgrims.

Rome itself was built up especially in the first two centuries CE. At the end of the first it had a population of some one million people; under Augustus, emperor for 40 years (27 BCE to CE 14), it became the greatest city in the western world. Augustus drew on the extensive wealth coming into Italy from the colonies and spent immense sums on the city. Grain was shipped to Rome from its province of Egypt; olive oil, for lamps, cooking and food, came from the Roman settlement in Carthage, North Africa. With his friends and lieutenants, Augustus added some of the city's most spectacular buildings, including the original Pantheon, the Baths of Agrippa and the Horologium, an enormous sundial, with an Egyptian obelisk used as a pointer. The Rome of Augustus was a Golden Age for Latin, the legacy measured not only in buildings but also literature and architectural treatises, including the *Ten Books on Architecture* by Vitruvius, of immense significance for architects in the European Renaissance. The Colosseum, the largest amphitheatre in the Roman world, was dedicated in CE 80. The conquests of Emperor Trajan (98–117) were commemorated in the huge column named after him, erected in the Roman Forum.

Along with the grid plan, the Romans brought peace, trade and governance, street layouts, classical temples, municipal baths, huge aqueducts which brought water into cities. Newly built roads helped to link the provinces together.

The significance of the Roman Empire for the development of imperial cities is not limited to their founding. With interest in the architecture of the ancient world revived by the Renaissance, the Roman Empire bequeathed to modern Europe and its colonies, including North and South America, innumerable models of architecture and urban design. Roman models (incorporating the Greek) were spread by European colonialisms all over the world.

IMPERIAL LONDON

As discussed in Chapter 11, in the modern era the reciprocal nature of the imperial city's growth and its overseas empire is well illustrated by the symbiotic development of London and the colonial port cities of the British Empire. Beginning with the conquest of Ireland and the earliest settlements in North America in the late sixteenth century, the subsequent expansion of British military, naval and trading power in the Caribbean, North America, South Asia, Australasia and Africa, was to have a major impact on the physical growth and economic prosperity of London. Trade with the East was stimulated by the East India Company (founded 1600), with its impressive headquarters opened near the Bank of England two centuries later. Reflecting this seaborne empire was a completely new set of docks constructed between 1799 and 1828, their names, West India, East India, London, linking their distant and local destinations. Collectively, they held over 1,400 merchant vessels. The centrifugal flow of capital was accompanied by the centrifugal flow of people. As millions emigrated from the British Isles, ten million to British possessions round the world, taking institutions and cultural attributes with them, their places in the labour market, in some cases, were filled by the inflow of labour from the oldest colony, Ireland. By the early years of the twentieth century, there was a small cosmopolitan population in London, not only from Europe but also from the Middle East, India, China and Africa.

With other major ports in Britain (Glasgow, Liverpool, Bristol), London was part of a much larger imperial trading system that linked all the major port cities of the empire together. While some of these had developed from indigenous settlements existing prior to colonial contact, many developed especially in the nineteenth and twentieth centuries to become the major cities of the empire. In India, Kolkata was long known as the 'second city of the empire' (a title also claimed by Liverpool and Glasgow). With Mumbai and Madras (now Chennai), it had been built up from the seventeenth century. Elsewhere, other cities were part of the network: Singapore, Hong Kong, Cape Town, Durban, East London, Kingston, Sydney, Melbourne, Perth, Canada, Montreal, Halifax. These cities were not only the sites of trade which, in most cases, consisted of raw materials shipped to the metropole for processing, in return for industrial products sent back to the colony, but also, as in the Roman Empire, they were the places where new hybrid cultures developed. And as new industrially made products were introduced by the imperial power, indigenous craft production was forced into decline.

Colonial port cities, as well as others inland, also hosted the institutions and buildings of government, administration, education, technology, and the imperial architecture in which they were built, often combining significantly with those institutions built by indigenous elites (Chopra 2010; Glover 2008). From the mid-nineteenth century in India, much of the colonial administration and engineering works were housed by the Public Works Department, a vast administrative and technical bureaucracy. PWD personnel established a network of civil and military stations all over the country, along with barracks, institutional buildings, offices, canals, roads and railways, linked to the major cities, and enabling the imperial government to maintain control over the country. During the frequent famines in India, brought on by climate failure and the colonial government's policy of replacing subsistence farming by cash crops, such public works were used to help alleviate poverty, but never enough to prevent untold millions of deaths from famine.

As with the Roman Empire, new ideas about town and city planning, developed in the metropole in response to the urban chaos of industrialisation, were exported – and adapted – to the empire's rapidly growing cities (Home 2013). Ideologies about health, race and culture had contributed to the founding of 'dual cities', the native town and the European settlement. The new 'science' of town planning was applied principally to the latter. Noting the rapidly growing cities and consumer markets, metropolitan corporate as well as indigenous interests were quick to establish shops, businesses and factories. Along with the capital and businesses went the urban typologies of the metropole, often drawing for their architecture on Roman models, but also, along with local agency, generating innovative hybrid forms.

IMPERIAL WORLD CITIES: FORMATION AND DECLINE

As stated earlier, the term 'imperial city' may refer not only to the imperial capital but also to major cities whose economy and politics are largely dependent on its role and function within the empire. Frequently port cities, these form 'key nodes' in the global economy; as 'world cities' their fortunes rise and fall in time with imperial fortunes. Where considerable attention and research have been given to examining world cities *in formation*, much less effort has been given to examining world cities *in decline*. Such is the case of the British city of Liverpool. Drawing extensively on a meticulous study by Stuart Wilks-Heeg (2002), the following brief account first traces the main economic and political factors accounting for the formation of Liverpool as a key imperial 'world city', and subsequently for its equally rapid decline.

Towards the end of his essay Wilks-Heeg refers to the way in which, in the early twentieth century, 'Liverpool's standing in the world economy came to be reflected in the built environment' (p.42). However, this precise but modest statement hardly prepares the reader who actually visits the city for the sight of its quite spectacular architecture and impressive urban development, especially along Liverpool's waterfront. Here were built the new headquarters for three of the city's principal commercial concerns: the Mersey Docks and Harbour Board building (1907), the Royal Liver building (1911) and the Cunard building (1914). In terms of design and scale these early twentieth-century buildings would certainly match whatever was being built in contemporary New York or Chicago at that time. As an indication of the city's self-image, the buildings speak volumes. In an early manifestation of the use of a gigantic tower as an essential icon of the world city (King 2004:15) the Liver building – almost 100 metres high and the tallest storied building in Europe when completed – is incomparable. The growth of the cities' office section (stock exchange, banks, insurance, commerce) meant that the city was especially 'noted for its collection of tall buildings', four and five storeys high.

As can be judged from contemporary comments, clearly distinguishing Liverpool from other British cities of the time, the impression of Liverpool as a 'world class city' had obviously been in circulation for some years:

> London and New York stand in the same rank as Liverpool, as commercial cities, but in some respects, as a place of commerce, it surpasses even the great capitals of the Old and the New World.
>
> (Thomas Bains, *Liverpool in 1859*)

> Liverpool is the New York of Europe, a world city rather than merely British provincial
>
> (*Illustrated London News,* 15 May 1886)

> Liverpool is the heart of the world, above all the potent symbol of the Empire of which it is one of the greatest glories.
>
> (Thomas Power O'Connor, MP for Liverpool Scotland Ward, 1924)

'GATEWAY TO EMPIRE'

Apart from confirming the early use of the 'world city' term (see Chapter 4), these powerful statements open up a fascinating historical case study. The key to the city's success was its central role in the colonial economic system. By the 1780s, Liverpool had become the European capital of the transatlantic slave trade, having captured nearly half of the whole European trade, and well over half of the British; around 1811, the slave trade was probably generating some 40 per cent of Liverpool's wealth. Following the abolition of the slave trade in 1808, Liverpool built its wealth on the Lancashire cotton industry and by 1850 was handling 85 per cent of Britain's total annual import of cotton bales, along with increasing volumes of sugar, grain and tobacco; its trading links took in North and South America, the West Indies, Africa and the Far East. In 1857, more shipping was registered in Liverpool than in London. The city's business houses expanded the market for African palm oil, built docks and developed the banana trade with the Canaries. The African connection led to the founding of the Liverpool School of Tropical Medicine (1899), dealing with the medical (i.e. malaria) needs of the British community in West Africa. Similar needs for professional manpower led to the opening of Liverpool University in 1902. In addition to its imports and exports, Liverpool was also the main steamship port of migration from the British Isles, transporting 86 per cent of the five and a half million emigrants leaving between 1860 and 1900. Ancillary growth in the form of banking, futures and insurance markets also occurred. Liverpool became the principal port for steamship travel between Britain and the United States, the home of the new super-liners, the *Lusitania* and the *Mauritania*. For the more affluent about to cross the Atlantic, the Adelphi, opened in 1914 and with 'a telephone in every bedroom', was Liverpool's 'grand hotel'.

CITY IN DECLINE

In the early twentieth century, Liverpool's wealth was linked directly to the country's manufacturing strength, but it was the importance of empire as the principal market for manufactured goods that was to determine its future. Industrial decline after 1914 was to be followed by commercial and shipping decline. Britain's share of world trade in manufacturing fell from 33 per cent in 1890 to 9 per cent in 1995. Where much of the city's wealth had been built on trade with Africa, North America and the 'white dominions' (Australia, New Zealand, Canada) the combination of local competition and the coming of the European Community were to break these links. Gandhi's boycott dried up the Indian market. After 1945, transatlantic passenger lines shrank as air travel increased. As trade with Europe grew it shrank with the countries of the Commonwealth; what had been colonies became independent and set their own agenda. Liverpool was left 'on the wrong side of the country' as east coast ports flourished. The city's population halved. Global restructuring shifted production to low-income countries. Only in recent years has Liverpool's economy been put on the road to recovery, helped by tourism, 'heritage' and the global beat of the flourishing cultural industries.

NOTE

1 From Anthony D. King, 'Imperial cities', in E. McCann, Rob Kitchin and Nigel Thrift, eds, *International Encyclopedia of Human Geography*, 2009 © Anthony D. King.

BIBLIOGRAPHY

Atkinson, D., Cosgrove, D. and Notaro, A. (1999) 'Empire in modern Rome: shaping and remembering an imperial city, 1870–1911', in F. Driver and D. Gilbert, eds, *Imperial Cities: Landscape, Display and Identity*, Manchester: Manchester University Press, pp.40–63.

Celik, Z. (2008) *Empire, Architecture and the City: French–Ottoman Encounters, 1830–1914*, Seattle: University of Washington Press.

Chase-Dunn, C.K. (1985) 'The system of world cities, AD 800–1975', in M. Timberlake, ed., *Urbanization in the World-Economy*, New York and London: Academic Press, pp.269–92.

Chopra, P. (2010) *A Joint Enterprise: Indian Elites and the Making of British Bombay*, Minneapolis: University of Minnesota Press.

Driver, F. and Gilbert, D., eds, (1999) 'Imperial cities: overlapping territories, intertwined histories', in F. Driver and D. Gilbert, eds, *Imperial Cities: Landscape, Display and Identity*, Manchester: Manchester University Press.

Fuller, M. (2006) *Moderns Abroad: Architecture, Cities and Italian Imperialism*, London and New York: Routledge.

Glover, W. (2008) *Making Lahore Modern:Constructing and Imagining a Colonial City*, Minneapolis: University of Minnesota Press.

Hall, P. (1993) 'The changing role of capital cities: six types of capital city', in P. Taylor, J. Lengelle and C. Andrew, eds, *Capital Cities: International Perspectives*. Ottawa: Carleton University Press, pp.69–84.

Hochschild, A. (1998) *King Leopold's Ghost: A Story of Greed, Terror and Heroism in Central Africa*, New York: Houghton Mifflin.

Home, R. (2013) *Of Planting and Planning: The Making of British Colonial Cities*, London: Spon.

Hopkins, K., ed. (2001) *Globalization in World History*, London: Pimlico.

King, A.D. (1990) *Global Cities: Postimperialism and the Internationalization of London*, London and New York: Routledge.

King, A.D. (2004) *Spaces of Global Cultures: Architecture, Urbanism, Identity*, London and New York: Routledge.

Metcalf, T. (1989) *An Imperial Vision: Indian Architecture and Britain's Raj*, Berkeley: University of California Press.

Said, E. (1993) *Culture and Imperialism*, London: Vintage.

Scarr, C. (1995) *The Penguin Historical Atlas of Ancient Rome*, Penguin Books: London.

Skinner, G.W. (1977) *The City in Late Imperial China*, Stanford: Stanford University Press.

Smith, T. (1999) '"A grand work of noble conception": the Victoria Memorial and Imperial London', F. Driver and D. Gilbert, eds, *Imperial Cities: Landscape, Display and Identity*, Manchester: Manchester University Press, pp.21–39.

Steinhardt, N.R.S. (1999) *Chinese Imperial City Planning*, Honolulu: University of Hawai'i Press.

Wilks-Heeg, S. (2002) 'From world city to pariah city? Liverpool and the global economy, 1950–2000', in R. Munck, ed., *Reinventing the City? Liverpool in Comparative Perspective*, Liverpool: Liverpool University Press, pp.36–52.

Wright, G. (1991) *The Politics of Design in French Colonial Urbanism*, Chicago: University of Chicago Press.

Chapter 15: Global cities[1]

INTRODUCTION

'Global city' is a term especially adopted from the 1980s to refer to the key command centres of the global urban system and, especially, the global economy. Initially applied to the three major financial centres of New York, London and Tokyo at the top of the global urban hierarchy, the term has subsequently become interchangeable with that of 'world cities', key nodes in the global urban network categorised by their function as financial centres, and hosting transnational corporation headquarters, international institutions, a growing business services sector, major transportation node, significant (though often declining) manufacturing industry and forming a major centre of population. Such world and global cities are also ranked according to their spatial and economic reach, from those at a global and multinational level, through national, subnational or regional levels. The number of such cities worldwide, defined according to quantitative indices of, especially, different business services such as banking, accountancy, advertising, dependent on the defining source, varied from 30 to 80 in the early twenty-first century. On the basis of any city acquiring more of the defining characteristics, other major cities worldwide are seen as becoming more or less competent to be qualified as global cities. Geographically, such cities are especially clustered in the three world regions of the Americas, Europe, with some connections to the Middle East and South Africa, and Asia and Oceania. More cultural conceptualisations of the term giving greater importance to the political and cultural significance of religion, ethnic complexity, issues of global citizenship, the presence of global cultures in the arts, sciences, media and architecture are discussed below. Historically, many of the world's present-day global cities have previously had the territorial reach and communications infrastructure associated with imperial cities.

HISTORY OF THE TERM

While Goethe already applied the term 'weltstadt' in 1787 to Rome, and later to Paris, to refer to the cultural eminence of these two cities, the more recent usage dates from the end of the nineteenth century following the extensive period of capitalist industrial urbanisation in Europe and North America. As stated in the previous chapter, such was the commercial and economic power of the imperial port of Liverpool that it was described in 1886 as a 'world city', 'the New York of Europe'. In 1915, Scottish sociologist and town planner Patrick Geddes used 'world city' to refer to specific large cities where, in the words of geographer Peter Hall, 'a disproportionate part of the world's most important business is conducted'. This concept was developed in 1966 by Hall, for whom world cities were 'the major centers of political power, the seats of the most powerful governments, international authorities, and of trade'. An early use of the term 'global city' reflecting a particularly economic interpretation of globalisation is the 1977 account by business administration scholar David Heenan, published in the *Harvard Business Review*. In 'Global Cities of Tomorrow', the author discusses the 'evolution of model corporate cities to develop global and regional leadership'. Focusing on Coral Gables, Paris and Honolulu, as they 'strive for globalization' in Latin America, Europe and Asia, Heenan directs his article to chief executive officers 'evaluating sites for corporate headquarters or regional offices as well as to urban planners … eager to attract corporate tenants to their cities'. This economic and business conceptualisation of the global city was to be developed within the frame of a Marxist urban political economy to interpret the extensive restructuring of urban space in Western cities in the 1970s and 1980s. For sociologist R.B. Cohen, global cities were the 'international centers for business decision-making and corporate strategy formulation.... Cities for the coordination and control of the New International Division of Labor'. The concept was developed on a much larger and more sophisticated scale by sociologist Saskia Sassen, whose influential book, *The Global City: New York, London, Tokyo* (1991, 2001), distinguished global cities especially by their role in providing advanced producer services in the world economy, making new economic products in finance, law and accountancy, for example, and where the firms and organisations they hosted exercised 'global control capability'. The sub-title of my own book, *Global Cities: Postimperialism and the Internationalization of London* (1990) puts emphasis on the main argument.

Other interpretations, however, have used the term to represent much broader historical and cultural objectives and ones of a less economistic, and sometimes idealistic nature. In the first book to use the phrase, *The Global City: Freedom, Power and Necessity in the Age of World Revolution* (1969), historian T.H. Von Laue proposed that, since the end of the nineteenth century, 'a common global history (has begun) growing out of the Metropolis', a word he uses metaphorically to describe the 'global community'. It is, however, the 'Western metropolis' which is the 'self-confident creator of the Global Confluence', the phrase used by Von Laue to describe what has subsequently become known as globalisation. In some way related to these more speculative if not messianic conceptions, are the ideas of religion scholar Ninian Smart (1981), for whom the interpenetration of cultures in the global city, promoting the comparative study of religion, has become 'a major ingredient in the formation of a peaceful global city', the location of which, in contrast to Von Laue's account, is not stated.

SOCIETY, SPACE AND THE BUILT ENVIRONMENT

Social and economic polarisation in the population is the most common social feature said to characterise global cities. This has resulted from the excessive wealth generated by the dominance of the financial services industries in such cities and the globalisation of salaries at the top of the social hierarchy, the growth of low-paid service employment at the bottom, generally undertaken by migrant (and frequently illegal) labour, and the disappearance of well-paid industrial employment in the middle. The extent and nature of such polarisation, however, clearly depends on political decisions regarding the social policies and welfare services available in each state in which the global city exists. Substantial foreign direct investment in global cities also adds to inequities between urban and non-urban populations.

The reality of global cities as well as the discourses circulating about them has had a significant impact on their architecture, urban space and built environment. As such cities have emerged in the Global South, increasingly linked up, technologically and economically, in the global urban system with others in the North, competition between them to capture significant, but globally limited, capital investment as well as income from tourism, has prompted the administrations of many such cities to engage in the construction of spectacular megaprojects. This is especially the case in those cities of the Pacific Rim such as Shanghai, Hong Kong or Seoul, a world region seen as having the greatest economic growth potential. Of these megaprojects, constructing 'the tallest building in the world' is the most prominent, not least because the world's hundred tallest buildings are almost all in global cities (even though all global cities do not have such tall buildings). Other megaprojects combine such symbolic objectives with more functional ones, providing so-called 'world class' high-tech, high-quality commercial and residential space aimed at attracting multinational executives, firms and capital. In existing and aspiring global cities elsewhere, 'signature buildings' designed by internationally prominent architects (Sir Norman Foster, Jan Nouvel, Rem Koolhaas, Kenzo Tange, Frank Gehry, Kohn Pederson Fox, Richard Rogers and others) are used to distinguish one global city from another, where each is competing for a larger slice of global tourism or foreign direct investment. Such visual icons (such as Sydney Opera House) aim at establishing, through televisual and other media, the city's name and image on the global as well as the local imagination. Other spectacular events, such as the Olympic Games, Formula One Racing, the World Cup Soccer Final, Commonwealth Games, perform a similar function. In virtually all cases, the provision of such megaprojects or events is at the spatial and financial cost of alternative expenditure on affordable housing, educational, recreational or medical services for low-paid service as well as skilled workers on whose labour the city depends.

CONTEMPORARY GLOBAL CITIES

The economic and presentist focus of much research on the formation of contemporary global cities has tended to downplay the importance of the long-term historical processes of globalisation emphasised in accounts by Hopkins (2001), King (1990) and Robertson (1990; 1992). Hopkins has suggested that different phases of globalisation have occurred in different historical eras, which he refers to as the archaic, early modern and, from the eighteenth century, imperial and, from the second half of the twentieth century, postcolonial globalisation. Regimes of Islamic as well as Western globalisation have also been recognised. The historical significance of imperialism, both formal and informal, in establishing the economic, political and cultural foundations of many global cities is often and grossly understated in the literature, as also is the phenomenon of postcolonial migration, from colonies to the metropole (or other postcolonial states). This has been a key factor in determining the distinctive ethnic, religious, cultural and racial profiles of the multicultural population of many global cities as well as the forms of their public culture (e.g. Paris, London, Hong Kong, New York, Toronto, Rio de Janeiro). The development, from the later decades of the twentieth century, of particular postcolonial cultures and forms of oppositional knowledge aimed at dislodging dominant Eurocentric knowledge paradigms, has resulted from the presence of postcolonial intellectuals and students established in institutes of learning in major global cities in Australia, the United States, Canada and the UK. The transfer of cultural institutions, especially though not only language, during long periods of colonial control and settlement, between the USA and Britain, France and North Africa, the UK and India, or the Philippines and East Asia, has made for extensive labour mobility at all levels between global cities in these countries. In the early twenty-first century, postcolonial language skills in English combined with information technology and high levels of education have enabled the transfer of call centre employment in customer services, medical transcription, risk analysis and related work, from the USA and Britain to the incipient global cities of India such as New Delhi and Mumbai, and making a significant impact on building and urban development in the process. Information technology networking has also extended the natural economic advantages of global cities resulting from population agglomeration.

The magnet of the contemporary global city, whether in the East or West, South or North, for migrants, refugees and stateless persons, has also brought to the foreground issues of global human rights and the necessity of the idea of global, rather than merely national, citizenship. Contemporary as well as historical global cities have also been the sites for the production of different global cultures in science, the arts, politics and religion. As the primary media centres in the world where news is both made and disseminated, such cities are also the natural sites of global protest and terrorism.

NOTE

1   From Anthony D. King, 'Global cities', in Roland Robertson and Jan Aart Scholte, eds, *Encyclopedia of Globalisation* 2007 © Routledge.

BIBLIOGRAPHY

Brenner, N. and Keil, R., eds (2006) *The Global Cities Reader*, New York and London: Routledge.

Bennison, A. K. (2001) 'Muslim universalism and western globalization', in A.G. Hopkins, ed., *Globalization in World History,* London: Pimlico, pp.74–97.

Cohen, R.B. (1981) 'The new international division of labor, multinational corporations and urban hierarchy', in M. Dear and A.J. Scott, eds, *Urbanization and Urban Planning in Capitalist Society*, London and New York: Methuen, pp.287–318.

Driver, F. and Gilbert, D., eds (1999) *Imperial Cities: Landscape, Display and Identity*, Manchester: Manchester University Press.

Friedmann, J. and Wolff, G. (1982) 'World cities in formation: an agenda for research and action', *International Journal for Urban and Regional Research*, 6, 3: 309–44.

Graham, S., ed. (2004) *Cities, War, and Terrorism: Towards an Urban Geopolitics*, Oxford: Blackwell.

Hall, P. (1984) *The World Cities*, third edition, London: Weidenfeld and Nicolson.

Heenan, D.A. (1977) 'Global cities of tomorrow', *Harvard Business Review*, 55, 3: 79–92.

Hopkins, A.G. (2001) 'Introduction: an agenda for historians', in A.G. Hopkins, ed., *Globalization in World History*, London: Pimlico, pp.1–10.

Isin, E.(2013) *Democracy, Citizenship and the Global City*, London and New York: Routledge.

King, A.D. (1990) *Global Cities: Postimperialism and the Internationalization of London*, London and New York: Routledge.

King, A.D. (2004) *Spaces of Global Cultures: Architecture, Urbanism, Identity*, London and New York: Routledge.

King, A.D. (2012) 'Imperialism and world cities', in B. Derudder, M. Hoyler, P.J. Taylor and F. Wilcox, eds, *International Handbook of Globalization and World Cities*, Cheltenham: Edward Elgar, pp.31–9.

Knox, P. and Taylor, P.J., eds, (1995) *World Cities in a World-System*, Cambridge: Cambridge University Press.

Robertson, R. (1990) 'Mapping the global condition', in M. Featherstone, ed., *Global Cultures: Nationalism, Globalization and Modernity*, London, Newbury Park, CA and New Delhi: Sage, pp.15–30.

Robertson, R. (1992) *Globalisation: Social Theory and Global Culture*, London, Newbury Park and New Delhi: Sage.

Sassen, S. (1991; 2001) *The Global City: New York, London, Tokyo*, Princeton: Princeton University Press.

Smart, N. (1981) *Beyond Ideology: Religion and the Future of Western Civilization*, London: Collins.

Von Laue, T.H. (1969) *The Global City: Freedom, Power and Necessity in the Age of World Revolution*, New York: Lippincott.

Wilks-Heeg, S. (2003) 'From world city to pariah city? Liverpool and the global economy, 1850–2000', in R. Munck, ed., *Reinventing the City?Liverpool in Comparative Perspective*, Liverpool: Liverpool University Press, pp.36–52.

Name and place index

Subject index